TREE BIOLOGY NOTEBOOK

To Steve,
Take Time
for Trees

Tree Biology
NOTEBOOK

An Introduction to the
Science and Ecology of Trees

Richard C. Murray

STL Publishing · Silver Spring, Maryland

All photos taken by Richard and Sharon Murray unless otherwise noted.
Original poetry by Richard C. Murray.

TITLE PAGE: *Ginkgo biloba*
PAGE 1: *Sequoia sempervirens*

ISBN 978–0–615–21109–1

Dedicated with love to my wife Sharon.
An artist and academic, she helped make this book a reality.

The Notebook

Collection of information
for reference and for study.
Bits of something unknown or unclear,
but important enough to gather.
The purpose is to connect,
the note is the link.
When added together
they make subjects familiar.
Listing parts, outlining processes,
is just a piece of the story.
The discussions, the connections
or understandings, as you wish,
it's the relationships of the systems,
steady movement, never still,
that's how nature works.
From a layering of interests,
crossing paths,
explore new questions,
seek out where answers lie.

Contents

Part III: Associations & Evolution

Part IV: Projects

Color section starts after page 138

Introduction

The *Tree Biology Notebook* is a collection of notes that defines, describes and discusses fundamental aspects of trees and tree ecology. It began as a desire to consolidate and expand on information from various seminars and over thirty-five years experience as an arborist in Maryland and New England. It took on a life of its own as my interest grew through referencing other published material and by examination of trees themselves. Observing trees opened a personal window that has enriched my life and given purpose to my work. It's not merely learning the parts and processes that's important, but understanding the relationship of trees to nature. I have tried to emphasize a holistic perspective to the ecology of trees throughout the topics examined.

The notebook is intended for the continuing education student, especially those who have the desire to participate in issues concerning global ecology. The topics presented are directed towards the nonscientist, but will still add to the knowledge of those with a more scientific background. This is not a traditional book in that it's not a narrative. Rather, it is reference oriented with a collection of subjects. After an initial review of the text, one should return to specific sections to study in greater depth. Please note that instead of

Author in woodyard. Cloverly, Maryland.

a glossary, definitions and descriptions are interspersed throughout the discussions. Refer to the index as a guide to locate terms. Keywords (listed in Appendix A) represent themes that are carried throughout the chapters.

The writing was accomplished during winter breaks from my tree business over the course of several seasons. Some sections are covered in greater detail than others. This book is meant as an introduction rather than a final say on the topics examined. The goals are to provide usable information and to help make connections between trees and other living systems.

There are many tree issues in the world today, but before we can understand the problems, we must first understand the tree. Trees are difficult to study as they are large, partially underground and outside in the elements. It is important that we view them as dynamic, successful organisms and appreciate their contribution to the health of our planet.

The *Tree Biology Notebook* is best used in conjunction with walking among trees in their own environment and through physical examination of their parts. Not everyone needs to run a chain saw, but we can gather samples from an outing in the woods or a walk around the neighborhood. Visual cues help clarify and instill concepts. Be outdoors, follow the seasonal changes and keep a notebook. Objective observation is key to understanding natural events. The emphasis of active participation allows us to see for ourselves into the world of trees.

Acknowledgments

The scientific concepts and principles outlined in this book are not my own, but come from the pool of scientific knowledge. References are given in the bibliography, which also provides a source of suggested reading. The discussions attempt to offer an objective perspective of the subjects.

I was introduced, through publications, to the work of Dr. Alex L. Shigo in the late 1970s. In 1989, I attended his seminar on tree biology in Boone, North Carolina. Notes from this seminar and subsequent ones form the basis of this notebook. Dr. Shigo's research, among other things, investigated patterns of discoloration and decay in living trees through interactions between trees and associated organisms. He emphasized energy management as a fundamental theme of the tree system. The introduction of the compartmentalization concept by Dr. Shigo, with help from other researchers, has greatly advanced the understanding of tree biology. Dr. Shigo recently passed away. For me he was a challenging educator and, more importantly, a generous friend.

Alex Shigo with Sharon and Richard Murray, Washington National Zoo, February 1998.

Dr. Charles W. Owens, retired chemistry professor, participated in some of Dr. Shigo's seminars. He introduced chemistry basics for biology students in a manner that was not intimidating. It's this user-friendly approach that I have tried to incorporate. Several scientists and professionals were kind enough to review portions of a draft of this notebook. Dr. Kevin Smith, research scientist, explained scientific concepts without compromising scientific integrity. Dr. Virginia Lerch, professional educator, contributed helpful insights for the text. Jack Phillips, arborist consultant, provided organizational input. Ms. Sandy Flowers, master gardner, shared her experience of the public perspective. Ms. Jo Moore, biological illustrator, provided thoughts on sequencing text topics. Professor Edward Barrows, field biologist, reviewed current information regarding nomenclature. Ms. Mary Pat Rowan, landscape architect, discussed ideas associated with urban ecology and encouraged me in this endeavor. Pogo Sherwood, arborist and entrepreneur, participated in tree adventures and autopsy projects with me. I thank Judy Shigo Smith, of Shigo and Trees, Associates, for permission to use photos from her father's collection. My thanks to all who have helped me along the way, especially to my sister (and business manager) Kathleen Murray.

PART I

Trees & Ecology

The Tree

The tree, the magnificent living entity,
the ancient sentinel of forest life.
Witness to two hundred million
years of fire and ice.
History keeper, enduring and brave,
yet unsympathetic and indifferent to change.
Seemingly stoic, but nay so,
for the life in us, and that surrounding,
is of the tree's paternity.
Deep set in our cultural soul,
yet still a stranger, neighbor unknown.

FIG. 1.1 Trees capturing sunlight.

1   Trees and Energy

Trees are woody, perennial, compartmented, shedding plants. They're a magnificent biological system, capable of dynamic actions. Trees regulate their mass by growing new parts and by shedding. Static parts are externally cast off or encased in the tree core.

Trees are made up of many compartments. Cells, the primary compartment, have thick walls made of cellulose and lignin. These substances give trees their woody characteristics and allow for their large stature. When injured, trees can't restore or replace cells in the same spatial position, or rid themselves of infection as animals do through the process of healing. Trees actively defend themselves by forming protective boundaries to wall off injuries and infections through the process of compartmentalization.

The major distinction between plants and animals is that plants are a generating system and animals are a regenerating system. To survive, trees must grow new parts in new spatial positions.

The subjective issues in defining a tree involve distinguishing height and form among trees, shrubs and vines. A tree is often said to have a single trunk with a height over three to six meters tall (10 to 20 feet). Many trees, however, have multiple trunks or are less than three to six meters. A shrub, also a woody perennial plant, has parallel features to a tree except for being less tall, with a spreading growth habit and multiple stems that originate at or near ground level. A woody vine is a perennial plant requiring outside support to grow vertically.

Many of the unique features attributed to trees center around their amazing mechanical structure and longevity. They're the largest, tallest and oldest living organisms on earth, with a survival record that rivals any other organism. They make their own food by harnessing energy from sunlight and transferring it, through photosynthesis, to carbon-based molecules (fig. 1.1 & plate 1). These energy-containing substances, produced by trees and other plants, ultimately yield food for most living things on earth. There are no metabolic dead ends between the plant and animal communities. Trapping and transferring energy may be the most significant thing trees do.

Trees use energy very efficiently and have little waste. By-products are regulated and eliminated in several ways. Oxygen and carbon dioxide gases are released into the atmosphere through photosynthesis and respiration. Exudates (organic carbon materials) are released into the soil. They're critically important to soil organisms and the overall ecology of the soil. Secondary metabolites are altered to form protective compounds. The resulting phenol- and terpene-based materials are stored in cells throughout the tree. It's difficult to consider any of these by-products as waste.

A feature unique to trees is that the living parts control the dead parts. Wood and bark have living cells integrated among dead and dying cells. Another interesting feature contributing to the long-term success of trees is that they have a low nitrogen-to-carbon ratio compared to other organisms. This evolutionary characteristic serves as an important protection feature because nitrogen is a limiting and contentious factor for growth in all organisms.

Trees are a major part of the worldwide environmental system. They connect with each other and diversified communities of other organisms in ways that insure mutual survival. In addition to providing protective habitats and food to associates, trees serve as large air filters by helping to clean and exchange air. The removal of carbon dioxide and contribution of oxygen occurs in seasonal cycles that benefit all organisms. Climactic conditions are influenced by trees through transpiration of water for rain, shade for cooling surface areas, and by wind breaks. Their root network helps to stabilize soil and minimize erosion, and also protects waterways. Trees have played an important role in human ecology. The vital connection to trees extends beyond fuel, shelter and food materials. There is a majesty associated with their stature and beauty.

Trees survive by virtue of a strong capacity for defense. In a sense it's the tree's theme. Defense is about energy and energy management. Trees have evolved successful biological and mechanical methods for survival. Healthy trees react immediately and effectively when injured. Trees have developed long-standing associations for survival with many other organisms. They comply with the second law of thermodynamics, which asserts that living systems must have a continued supply of energy to survive. Energy is needed to maintain order in any system. For a tree, a low energy reserve is equivalent to a lower defense ability.

ENERGY is the capacity to do work. Although the concept is elusive, it can be thought of as the force that moves matter. Matter is any substance that occupies space. Energy in trees is stored in living cells, their dynamic mass. Static mass refers to dead cells. All living cells are connected in a network referred to as the SYMPLAST. The network of nonliving parts and spaces is the APOPLAST. As a tree ages, a layer of dynamic mass grows over the core of static mass. A young tree is 100% dynamic mass, whereas an old tree can be as much as 90 percent static mass.

Trees regulate their mass-to-energy ratio by shedding and altering living parts into a static state. The amount of energy required to maintain the parts and processes changes as the ratio of static parts to dynamic parts changes though growth and with age. The MASS-ENERGY RATIO is an important but hard to quantify concept that implies trees (living systems) will not survive when growth (mass) begins to exceed energy available to maintain order.

Potential energy is stored energy, similar to a savings account. Kinetic energy, derived from potential energy, is energy in use, and is analogous to spending money. Trees use energy in several ways:

METABOLISM, food breakdown to maintain physiological processes;
GROWTH, making new parts;
REPRODUCTION, continuation of the species;
DEFENSE, dynamic protective actions for survival;
EXUDATES, biological release of carbon based compounds.

Growth increases the maintenance (metabolic requirements); the two can't be separated. Any time the size of a system increases, energy is first removed. Everything in nature has a cost. The energy debt needs to be repaid and energy reserves must then be increased to a level greater than the amount present when the stimulation of growth started. For trees, bigger and faster are not necessarily better. No system can grow beyond its means and remain healthy.

Trees die in three ways:

· Depletion, they run out of energy;
· Disfunction, a part or process no longer works;
· Disruption, mechanical injury or failure.

Trees die as a result of starvation, but they don't necessarily starve to death. Before this occurs, pathogens can infect the still living but poorly defended tree. Most trees die when energy reserves are so low the defense system doesn't function effectively.

PHENOLOGY is the timing of natural processes. Trees have five phenological periods:

1. The onset of growth.
2. Preformed parts open and develop (buds, leaves, flowers; see fig. 1.2 & plate 4)
3. Photosynthesis manufactures food.
4. The growth of new parts (wood, bark) and storage.
5. Partial dormancy.

FIG. 1.2 Preformed buds of Beech (*Fagus sylvatica*) open to begin the growing season. Protective layers of silky hair held through the winter by calyx covers.

An allegoric scenario is to wake up, get dressed, eat, work and rest. Phenological patterns are controlled by geographic region, climate, species of tree and genetics. The energy reserves are at their lowest point during period 2, with gradual rebuilding during periods 3 and 4. During periods 5 and 1, stored energy levels are stable, but must last through to the next cycle. Both healthy and weak trees follow these same patterns, although unhealthy trees are more vulnerable to problems.

THE THREE-TREE CONCEPT addresses tree relationships on both an individual and community level.

    Tree 1: The young tree, mostly branches, and the branches on larger
             trees.
    Tree 2: The maturing, well developed tree.
    Tree 3: The community of connected trees.

Survival factors differ between these groups. For example, pathogens are harmful to the individual, but the group requires them to eliminate weak or defective members.

2

Tree Ecology

TREE ECOLOGY is the study of trees in relationship to their environment. Biology investigates the science of life. It views life as a orderly system of parts and process with the capacity to repeat. Energy is the most basic requirement and its management is the overriding theme.

The anatomical and physiological elements of life are connected in ways that insure survival. Success, however, is not a given, as many combinations of living and nonliving factors influence the outcome. Ecology is about biological and environmental connections. Although the topic is broad, with complexities beyond the scope of this text, awareness of it on an introductory level offers a holistic perspective of trees and associated issues.

Trees are prominent members of the global BIOSPHERE, the zone of life. They affect and are affected by the cycles and physical forces of the earth. From humble beginnings 300 million years ago, they have become venerable celebrities of the biotic world. Trees, as a group, have adapted and evolved despite climatic and geologic changes over the ages. Their dominance of the terrestrial world was achieved not only by adaptation, but by influencing regional climate and soil conditions, as well as other plant and animal life.

Although trees no longer occupy all land areas as they literally did over past geologic periods, they're still an essential part of the current global environment. Trees capture solar energy and convert it into a usable form. They filter air, stabilize soil and provide habitat for wildlife. The capacity of trees to trap carbon and release oxygen is highly significant in this era of fossil fuel consumption. The products and services provided by trees have been a fundamental aspect of human ecology.

Trees are part of a greater community of many diverse organisms interacting with each other and influenced by their physical environment (fig. 2.1 & plate 2). These combined biotic and abiotic factors form an ECOSYSTEM. Within the system, interdependent relationships and processes power the flow of energy, chemical compounds and mineral elements.

Trees and other plants are referred to as producers in the primary level of the food web, termed a TROPHIC LEVEL. The second level consists of primary consumers (herbivores) and secondary consumers (carnivores and parasites).

FIG. 2.1 Juniper (*Juniperus virginiana*) saplings resulting from birds roosting in Oak stand.

The third level consists of the decomposers; that is, fungi, bacteria, and small animals that break down organic material.

Only a small percentage of chemical energy in food is captured and converted into BIOMASS (living material). It's thought that about ten percent is converted by consumers and one percent by producers though photosynthesis. The majority of energy is displaced as heat. Most biomass in an ecosystem is ultimately used (decomposed) by fungi and bacteria. Biomass refers to organic matter and is measured based on the dry weight of living organisms per unit area.

A single species occupying the same HABITAT, the area where organisms live, is referred to as a POPULATION. A specialized part of a habitat adapted to, or altered by, a population is a NICHE. Populations of plants, animals and other organisms associated with each other, within a given area, form a COMMUNITY. Dominant populations often define a community and influence, through support or suppression, the success of affiliated members.

Physical and biological factors (geographic features, climatic variations, occurrence of disturbances) determine the combinations of populations, numbers of individuals and succession populations in a community over time and space. The relationships within communities between populations and individuals are primarily competitive, as resources and space are limited. In the struggle for survival, they either outperform or interfere with each other to succeed. Relationships can also involve MUTUALISM, where survival potential is enhanced by close associations between species. Relationships ultimately require pathogens, particularly fungi and bacteria, to reduce weak and dying individuals, break down dead organic material, and aid in the cyclic distribution of elemental resources.

The progression of inevitable change in an ecosystem is known as a SUCCESSION. The rate of change occurs in stages. Certain trees and organisms are characteristic to the stages of succession. Early pioneer species, such as Pine (*Pinus*) and Birch (*Betula*), grow rapidly in open conditions. Later succession stages become more difficult to interpret, because populations integrate and are widely affected by nature. These succession species, such as Oak (*Quercus*) and Hickory (*Carya*), tend to be more tolerant of shade and live longer than pioneers. In the climax stage, succession theoretically peaks and a community is self-sustained. It's characterized by mature populations of old-growth trees in forest communities (fig. 2.2 & plate 3).

Reversals or fluctuations in the direction of successions is also part of the process of change. Peripheral areas are prone to gradual transition from the influence of neighboring communities. Natural disturbances provide a more dramatic form of change. They're an important part of successions through

FIG. 2.2 A row of conifers nurtured by a rotting log in the continuation of the forest community. Temperate rain forest, Olympic Peninsula, Washington.

the creation of opportunities for diversity. Although disturbances occur somewhat suddenly and randomly, nature depends on them. Fires, floods, landslides, weather events and pest cycles are examples. Humans are a dominant ecological force in that their activities are causing changes to ecosystems worldwide.

BIOMES are large communities of organisms that occupy distinct regions governed by climate and geography. Terrestrial biomes play a key role in global ecology through their biological activities. Vegetation types define distinctive regions. Factors such as altitude, latitude, weather patterns and soil conditions influence the vegetative patterns. In addition, distinct animals, microorganisms and geographic features (mountains, streams, lakes) also help characterize regions. Member communities blend as range limits for species give way to other species, but the general habitat, topography and environment remains constant within regions. Examples of forest biomes in North America are eastern deciduous, temperate mixed, west coast conifer, subtropical broadleaf and northern boreal (taiga). Nonforest biomes include desert, scrub, grassland and arctic tundra.

EVOLUTION is the process by which species arise and change over time. It's tied to ecology through the diversity of organisms and their adaptation to changing environments. SPECIATION is specialized change occurring gradually over long periods time and by geographic or reproductive isolation. Geographic separation or environmental challenges can induce periods of more abrupt change (in geologic time). Within a general area, separate habitats, pollinating insects or flowering cycles can cause closely related species to become reproductively isolated. Rare in nature, hybrid (interbreed) crosses can occur through disturbances or cultivation.

Adaptation combines physical and biological adjustments that result in a buildup of characteristics conducive for survival. Tree survival strategies are fixed through reproductive success. Although the theme is similar among species, there are countless variations. For instance, cross-pollination between individuals of a given species offers insurance for genetic diversity, whereas self-pollination offers advantages to isolated species.

Taxonomy classifies organisms based on genetic characteristics, evolutionary relationships and morphological distinctness. The genetic makeup, GENO-TYPE, is associated with heredity and variation of dominant and recessive traits. PHENOTYPE refers to the physical aspects resulting from genetics and the environment. An ECOTYPE is a distinct phenotype determined by the environment and adapted through natural selection. Red Maple (*Acer rubrum*), for example, has a large range, but the phenological cycles for bud break and shedding differ between Maine and Georgia.

Morphological features are anatomical characteristics related to form and internal structure: large versus small leaves, or wood with ring-porous versus diffuse-porous vessels. Specific characteristics and survival strategies, ingrained in the far-distant past, specialize in ways that utilize the environment and build biological relationships with other organisms to accomplish the reproductive goal. Tree ecology is about the cumulative effects of interactions between trees and their environments over time.

Trees are the most prominent part of a forest. As a biological system of overlapping parts and processes, a forest, in a sense, is a composite organism. For three hundred million years, forests have been a major force in shaping and maintaining the earth's biosphere. Forest systems worldwide are being rapidly reduced and altered through exploitation, fragmentation and pollution. Questions, with no clear or easy answers, come to mind when considering the contemporary role of forests and the community of life they encompass in relationship to global and human ecology.

1. Are escalating human pressures outpacing the tolerance limits of forest systems?

2. What percentage of parts can be removed from a forest and still allow it to be a viable system?
3. Are small remaining areas of old-growth forest ecologically important and sustainable?
4. Is the harvest rate of tropical and boreal forest trees yielding long-term environmental problems?
5. What role will trees play in association with human population growth and urbanization trends?

These are but a few of the many questions concerning forest and global environmental issues.

Human ecology is complex, but nature is more so and ultimately indifferent to the long-term outcome, at least from a human perspective. Relative newcomers (in geologic time), people have historically shaped their environment (fig. 2.3 & plate 14). Currently, with unprecedented population increases and technological advancements, the intensity and scale of environmental change is testing the limits of biological systems around the planet. Conflicts pit man against man with oblivious disregard for environmental consequences. The destruction of natural resources with the associated pollution and loss of biodiversity is disconcerting and, as time passes, existing problems worsen and new ones emerge. Any feasible solution will be a long-term project and will require concessions.

🌲

Ecological systems have always been dependent on photosynthetic organisms. Virtually every living thing provides food to some other organism. Interactions between organisms cycle essential elements but energy must be continually added; it's captured by green plants. Nature is a system of systems with multilayered connections where all living components are contingent on energy and a suitable habitat. Stable ecological systems are relatively self-regulating. Biotic equilibrium (not balance) in nature requires the preservation of biodiversity.

A biological fix may offer part of the solution. The earth is basically a greenhouse in space. Its protective stratosphere was stable enough 450 million years ago to support life in water and on land. Global atmospheric changes occurring now are associated with the rising levels of greenhouse gases. The buildup of these gases traps heat, which escalates climate change.

Human activities have reduced biodiversity and, coupled with atmospheric and climate changes, are accelerating the rate of extinctions world wide. Extinctions, if the current course of affairs continues, could encompass three-quarters of the world's species by the end of this century. Only a handful of mass

FIG. 2.3 American Elm, *Ulmus americana*.

extinctions have occurred over the span of geologic time and each appears to have been related to an environmental catastrophe.

Without oversimplifying the seriousness and complexities of environmental and ecological problems, trees may be part of the solution. Their ability for photosynthesis facilitates the exchange of gases and stores carbon, slowing the momentum of environmental change. All ecological systems on earth are connected. Stabilizing biological habitats will require maintaining forests. Tree biology becomes relevant as it makes visible the connected web of life within the intrinsic parameters of nature. These studies may prove eminently valuable to the future.

3   Forest and City Trees

Forest trees have adapted to site conditions over long periods of time as generational successions produced stable populations. Numerous combinations of organisms are associated with tree communities and the well being of the greater forest system. As ecological systems evolve together, environmental conditions influence the process of adaptation for all members.

City trees involve individuals that have been removed from that system, yet they still retain the genetic codes of their ancestors. When comparing forest and city trees, the role of adaptation to the environment becomes apparent, although the hereditary influence is ever present and little changed.

Trees evolved while living in groups, but forest ecology has been greatly affected by the presence of man. Industry, agriculture and urban development have reduced the quality and quantity of forests and disrupted their natural associations. When forested areas are removed for roads, subdivisions, or other reasons, some trees may be left. Although the remaining trees are native and adapted to the local climate, their growing environment has changed. Many of the associated trees, understory plants and microorganisms that are necessary for healthy survival have been reduced or eliminated. Trees become more exposed to environmental extremes and to different vegetative competitors and pathogens. The soil conditions are altered. Beneficial microbes and fertile constituents are often reduced. Trees, especially mature ones, that suddenly find themselves in conditions different from those to which they were adapted, are predisposed to stress problems.

Few of the many trees that sprout in the forest make it to maturity. Forest conditions influence growth, although growth rate isn't necessarily a measure of tree health. Growth strategies for trees vary, but the two general patterns are to grow tall rapidly, or to grow slow and stay small.

A combination of factors influence tree growth, such as the availability of light, space and soil moisture. The influence and competition between tree species and individual trees also affects growth. Pioneer species in an open setting, such as Pine (*Pinus*) or Birch (*Betula*), compete for space. They grow quickly, require sun, and their roots are often facultative for mycorrhizae when young.

Young trees in a dense forest setting must acclimate to low light conditions. Natural understory species such as Hornbeam (*Carpinus*) or Dogwood (*Cor-*

FIG. 3.1 Growth pattern in a forest setting.

nus) are shade tolerant and don't grow large, whereas other forest species such as Beech (*Fagus*) or Hemlock (*Tsuga*) can survive in a large or dwarf state. Dwarfs establish position until an opportunity for growth, such as openings in the forest canopy from blowdowns or dominant trees dying, occurs. Dwarf trees operate on a low energy budget. They delay reproduction and, because of their size, receive few wounds. The oldest forest trees are often those that started as dwarfs.

Rapid, tall growth is the predominent pattern of forest trees (fig. 3.1). It's characterized by upright (excurrent) growth of a single dominant trunk and few lower branches. In the forest canopy, maturing trees develop codominant stems. Treetops become spread out and rounded. The codominant branching, pattern allows trees to obtain more light over a greater growing surface and to suppress competition below. This architectural change is a sign of maturity in a forest.

Forest canopy height reflects forest maturity, the character of the terrain, and the influence of disturbances. Before the Europeans arrived, New England forests crowned-off at a height of 50 to 60 meters. The temperate rain forest along the west coast was about 90 meters. Now, fragmented remnants of those forests crown-off at about one-third of their original height, a substantial loss of biomass over a short period of time.

Forest trees receive light from one direction, downward. They seldom have large lower limbs. Twigs and branches tend to die at the end of the growing season. Compounds containing nitrogen and other essential substances (simple sugars, amino acids) are partially recycled. The reason branches die is influenced by the lack of available light, but energy management is the prime reason. Branches die because they no longer produce enough energy for themselves or the tree. Shade is a secondary factor. Dwarf trees prove this point; they live in low light but have long-lived branches.

Trees in a nonforest setting encompass an eclectic variety of species, environmental circumstances and purposes. Examples range from the managed trees of plantations, nurseries, and orchards to the self-propagated trees along the edges of fields, streams and roadways. The tree itself is the common denominator, because it still retains the genetic codes established in the forest.

Looked at broadly, city trees can be divided into three categories: remnants of the original forest (as discussed), self-propagated (volunteers), and introduced trees (cultivated). Volunteer trees establish themselves by happenstance though seeding or clone sprouting. They're aided by birds, other animals and by human activities. Trees can be from native, naturalized or exotic species. Depending on circumstances, volunteers can be excellent trees or an invasive nuisance.

Cultivated trees are those introduced and cared for by people. These may be derived from seeds, transplants of naturally occurring trees, or cultivars (selected tree varieties propagated by asexual processes and only known in cultivation). Culturing trees is about selective characteristic development; that is, form, flower, fruit, fall color, and so forth. Cultivars are predominently used in orchards, ornamental gardens and city landscapes.

City trees tend to retain lower limbs and develop a spreading (decurrent) form (fig. 3.2). Conditions with open space and strong light stimulate them to grow and mature rapidly. Compared to forest trees, they establish a codominant branching pattern and flowering parts early. Codominant growth and reproductive activity are signs of maturity in trees.

Large size doesn't necessary mean old age, nor is it a measure of health (ability to resist stress). Biological functions demand energy, and the demand increases exponentially with growth. Architectural development (associated with a spreading form and large size) increases the potential for structural defects; for example, included bark in branch crotches and overweight lateral limbs.

FIG. 3.2 Open growth
pattern in a nonforest
setting.

Public safety is an issue with city trees. Other factors also predispose trees
in an urban setting to health and structural problems, such as confined root
spaces, harsh soil conditions and exposure to disturbances. Both city and forest trees face substantial challenges to survival, and relatively few of either
achieve long lives.

🌳

Diversity of and within species is the norm for biological systems. Subtle
changes strengthen species against pathogens, competitors and environmental
challenges. Genetic variability benefits the group, but not always the individual. A forest is a biologically diverse system that operates and evolves in ways
that insure survival of its member groups.

Based on the number of individuals and species, trees are minority members in a forest, but based on collective size and volume, they're the majority. The forest community relies on the stages of development, decline and
death of its members for healthy survival. Older trees, for example, tend to die
back from their crown and end roots. This provides food for microorganisms
and habitat for wildlife, as well as opportunity for younger trees to occupy the

space. Studying trees as they exist in nature gives insight for managing those in nonforest environments.

The demographics of biodiversity are greatly reduced among nonforest trees. Declining old trees pose safety concerns in urban areas, and rotting forest material doesn't always meet with modern aesthetic values. Coppice tree stands, treed public parks, backyard trees and woodlots aren't forest, but are ecologically important. Space is an essential requirement for trees. They prefer to live in broad, undisturbed areas rather than in narrow strips. Leaving dead and dying trees is beneficial when it's safe. Leaf layers are also beneficial and should be part of the landscape. Volunteer trees have great survival potential and add diversity in age and species to urban areas. Ideal situations and perfect solutions to problems are rare, but compromise is constructive and offers promise concerning forest and city tree issues.

4   Trees and Wildlife

Many birds, mammals and other animals live closely with trees and use them for food, shelter and nesting (fig. 4.1). Animals use trees for reasons that support survival. Occasionally their activities damage trees (fig. 4.2). Wounds are caused by feeding, pecking and marking territory.

Certain birds and wildlife rely on large, mature trees. Deep hollows and wide crotches make ideal, well-protected nesting sites. Aging trees provide a diverse and spread-out source of seeds, fruit, insects and fungi for food. The preservation of mature tree stands with dying and dead trees helps wildlife.

Forests are made up of populations of individual tree species connected to each other and to other communities of diverse organisms in time-tested ways that ensure long-term survival for all members. Diversity in tree species and aging stages is only a part of the survival requirements. Space is needed to support trees and diverse wildlife populations. The loss of specific habitats (niches) can lead to the loss of individual species and break essential connections between remaining members.

Forestry and urban landscape practices can be altered in ways to benefit trees, wildlife and people without substantial compromises from private interests. Ecologically conscious changes in management methods can yield tangible environmental benefits. Economical and attractive alternatives for urban landscapes, for example, include choosing plants that curb the use of water, chemicals and gas-powered tools, and produce minimal yard waste.

Conservation can begin by introducing native and companion plants that are better suited to local conditions. Preserving tree stands with native understory vegetation, and planting trees in clusters separate from lawns and flowerbeds, are practical ideas. Trees and lawns are natural adversaries, and lawn-care procedures in general don't benefit trees. Reconsidering the concept of weeds, with a tolerance for diversity, is ecologically sensible. With landscapes, perfection is an impractical notion. The 80–80 rule of thumb for success is more in keeping with nature: when 80 percent of a landscape is healthy and attractive 80 percent of the time, then it's successful.

FIG. 4.1 Bird nest in decayed tree trunk.

FIG. 4.2 Beaver-felled Beech tree.

FIG. 4.3 Spider
dwelling in Pine tree.

The relationships between trees and wildlife are complex, competitive, and
constantly changing, but essential for the health of forests and wooded areas.
The territories of birds and other animals vary from year to year based on availability of food and suitable reproductive sites. The numbers and success of
offspring are dependent on these factors. Many birds will aggressively drive
out competitors, regardless of size, to defend their space. Squirrels will relo-
cate from an unsanitary nest, or if they fear a local predator. Later in the season, after young birds have fledged, insects occupy abandoned nests. Predatory
Baldface hornets build paper-like nests that are suspended from the ends of
limbs. Spiders are another tree-dwelling predator (fig. 4.3).

Woodpeckers live, breed and feed in trees. Many are migratory, as are many
other bird species associated with temperate forest trees. Yellow-bellied sapsuckers peck an orderly sequence of shallow holes in trees during the spring
(fig. 4.4). Sometimes these areas are just above preexisting wounds. They feed
on sap and insects, especially ants, drawn to the wound holes. The males often
arrive before the females to lay claim to a territory. For unknown reasons they
tend to choose exotic trees to mark.

FIG. 4.4 Sapsucker injuries to Hickory (*Carya* spp.) seen on a 20 cm diameter sample (approximately 65 years old). The concentric injuries occurred at about 28 years. Later injuries can also be seen.

Carpenter ants are a favorite food of woodpeckers. The ants occupy only altered wood or preexisting cavities (see fig. 22.1). Large birds will peck through decaying or sound wood to get at them. The holes they make are large, but differ in shape from nesting holes. Bird holes expose surrounding wood to pathogens.

Certain deciduous trees transport sugars in vessels for a relatively short period of time in the spring (see chap. 14). External sap flow is a natural tree response to wounds, such as those introduced by sapsuckers, at this time of the year. Yeast infections often cause sugary sap to ferment. The spring nectar is attractive to birds and small animals. Sooty-mold will colonize wet bark and cause black staining (see fig. 21.5). Sapsucker wounds trigger a defense response from trees to form a reaction and barrier zone (see chap. 9). Internal streaking above and below the wound can occur within the reaction zone. A ring shake separation (circular crack) may eventually form and spread along the barrier zone.

Squirrels feed on bark and sap in the early spring. They bite off twig tips and bark from the upper, sunny side of branch stems. Branch wounds frequently go on to develop canker infections. Borer insects often access stressed trees near canker lesions. With the formation of leaves, the consistency of sap changes and its external flow ceases. Squirrels adjust their diet according to seasonal availability of resources, which includes flower parts and seeds. Squirrels, birds, bees and other insects, through feeding activities, provide trees an essential pollination service.

Domestic animals can affect trees and wildlife in small and large ways. City dogs harm young trees and shrubs with their waste. Concentrated waste of domestic and agricultural animals pollutes and alters ecological systems (i.e., soils, wetlands and waterways). Runoff from chemical products used on urban landscapes and farmlands are also sources of pollution that affect wildlife and forests.

As natural habitats shrink, wildlife is attracted to urban areas. People provide sources for food and shelter either directly or indirectly. For example, feeding songbirds increases the population of squirrels and other rodents, which in turn increases the number of predators such as hawks and foxes. Urban landscapes are attractive to deer. They also graze park and woodlands, feeding on tree saplings and other understory vegetation. High numbers can alter the characteristics of natural areas.

5

Abiotic Influences

Abiotic (nonliving) factors of the environment influence living and ecological systems (fig. 5.1). Factors include climate extremes, water issues, geographic features, soil conditions, and pollution. Although abiotic factors are noninfectious, they predispose trees to stress and disease. For example, if a heavy wind blows the top off a tree, it reduces the tree's biological potential and structural integrity, and exposes the tree to infection. The biological and structural condition of trees reflect the level of exposure over time to abiotic influences and their ability to resist or compensate for them.

Abiotic influences affect trees in several broad, overlapping ways and fall under three general categories: secondary stress, toxic exposure and physical injury. Secondary stress occurs when substances and conditions essential for life are at extremes (too little or too much). Factors include water, mineral elements, temperature, and soil pH. Toxicity is the exposure or buildup of poisonous substances such as salts, herbicides, petroleum products, and water and air pollutants. Physical injuries cover many events ranging from weather extremes to human activities. Trees also injure themselves in numerous ways: overweighted limbs break, defective branch junctions split, girdling roots constrict, or falling branches and trees cause abrasions.

Weather is a dominant environmental force controlling tree and plant life (fig. 5.2). Weather-related tree injuries occur from wind, ice, lightning, flooding, drought, heat and cold. Trees have adapted over millennia to climatic conditions. Weather events occasionally exceed structural or biological limits of trees, as with heavy storms or during extended dry or cold spells. Except for catastrophic events, most trees survive harsh weather, although some survivors are left with substantial defects. Challenging weather events, in a sense, benefit tree communities by thinning out weak or defective members. Adversity strengthens species in this way.

The quality of soil, water and air are important environmental factors influencing tree life. If the condition of these factors deteriorates, trees and their associates are predisposed to stress. Fire and flooding are examples of natural events that periodically cause soil, water and air problems. Influences from human activities cause, or indirectly contribute, to tree problems. Chemical pollution occurs from many sources; for example, toxins that leak from industrial sites or from vehicles onto roadways.

FIG. 5.1 At top, Eastern Hemlock (*Tsuga canadensis*) established on boulder. Below, Spruce (*Picea* spp.) on exposed rocky ledge compared to Spruce growing with other conifers in a forest setting. Note differences in site conditions.

FIG. 5.2 Weather conditions challenge survival. Birch withstand harsh conditions although heavy ice loads can cause damage.

Trees and their habitats in urban areas are affected by construction activities that compact soil. Plant roots and soil microorganisms are easily damaged. Overwatering lawns and landscapes, as it changes soil conditions, can also be harmful to trees and soil microbes. Overharvesting woodlots is another example. Remaining trees, understory vegetation and soil are often damaged and left exposed.

The purpose of this discussion is not to criticize the activities of people but to introduce awareness that many factors influence living systems. When looking at the big picture, little things matter.

Lightning damages and kills thousands of trees each year. Lightning is a violent discharge of static electricity neutralizing atmospheric electrical charges with the ground. Its flow follows the path of least resistance. The upward movement of water vapor, droplets and ice crystals create static electricity. Built-up electrical charges separate in large storm clouds at different strata and temperature levels. Cloud-to-ground lightning strikes occur between cloud leaders (fingers of negative charges) pushing downward and connecting with positive charges of ground streamers flowing up from tall topographical features that serve as conductors. As the paths of opposite charges connect, several discharges occur producing a powerful electrical charge, intense heat and an associated shock wave heard as thunder. The discharges last only a fraction of a second, and the combined flash lasts about a half second.

The variability in lightning strike force affects trees in different ways (fig.

5.3). The damage is from disruptions to vital tree areas, generated heat, and the shock wave moving through wood. Even a shallow or narrow strike separates bark and exposes the cambial zone. Water movement is reduced. The tree defense response produces a barrier zone. The greater the percentage, in circumference, of stem damage, the greater the chances for tree decline or death.

Root damage also occurs but is difficult to diagnose. Crown wilting may be associated with physical or heat damage to roots, stems or branches. Steel bolts in trees can cause the lightning path to be directed inward. Lightning may, in extreme cases, split or blow trees apart. Survivors must contend with the resulting injuries and are predisposed to health problems and infections. Little can be done to effectively help trees struck by lightning. The few proactive measures include scribing separated bark sections, watering root zone areas, pruning dying limbs, and monitoring for decline.

Flooding damages trees by interfering with absorption. The processes of respiration, photosynthesis and transpiration are diminished. Oxygen is critical for the process of respiration. Flood water occupies porous soil space and suffocates absorbing roots. This in turn minimizes oxygen and essential elements from moving into trees. Flooded trees not only suffer from starvation and suffocation, but also decline, paradoxically, from lack of water (dehydration).

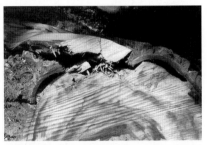

FIG. 5.3 Some trees survive lightning strikes (*left*); others don't (*right*). Left Tuliptree (*Liriodendron tulipifera*) lost crown section and developed trunk decay. Note bark/wood separation on close-up of right Tuliptree.

Flood conditions change soil ecology. Important aerobic organisms benefi-cial to trees and the soil rhizosphere are harmed, as is the soil structure from leaching and silting. Stressed trees and soil attract opportunistic insect and disease agents. Anaerobic bacteria increase in saturated soil, as do other poten-tial tree pathogens that cause root rot, such as *Phytophthora* spp.

The loss of support, as woody roots die, is a serious and potentially fatal problem for trees. Wet soil, in itself, offers diminished support. Swaying motions from the wind cause trees in soft soil to uproot more easily. A domino effect can occur should one tree fall on another.

Certain tree species that naturally evolved in wet conditions are bet-ter suited than others for coping with flooding. Tolerance is often better in broadleaf trees than conifers, with the exception of Bald Cypress (*Taxodium distichum*), Northern Tamarack (*Larix laricina*) and Dawn Redwood (*Meta-sequoia glyptostroboides*; see fig. 8.3 & plate 3). Mid-aged trees fair better than young or old trees. Flooding is usually better tolerated during the dormant season when temperatures are colder. The timing of flood conditions is worse for trees during the active growth period and at low-energy periods, such as the onset of growth when leaves are forming, or the transition phase when leaves fall.

Frequent, shallow watering in heavy or compacted soils is unhealthy for trees. Lush lawns, heavily fertilized and irrigated, foster stressed and unstable trees.

6   Predisposition

PREDISPOSITION means to be inclined towards something in advance. Events influence susceptibility for a condition. With trees, many events and agents accumulate over time that predispose a host to stress and pathogens. The blame for a tree's decline or death is often assigned to a visible insect or fungus. They're easy to see and, for this reason, the concept of a single pathogen for a single disease is widely accepted. Small events occurring over time aren't noticed or remembered. Abiotic stress, for example, isn't usually tangible or able to be isolated. The predisposition concept for disease, of multiple factors over time, is less recognizable or easily proven.

The survival of living systems is contingent on energy. Organisms require a continued supply to function and remain healthy. The depletion of energy reserves in trees equates to a decrease in defense. Low defense and the factors associated with it predispose trees to health problems and pathogens.

Pathogens are always present, but most are opportunistic and only infect a host when it's in a weak or defenseless state. If pathogens could infect or kill at will, trees wouldn't exist. Few insects or fungi, even when wounds occur, are able to establish themselves in the tissue of healthy trees.

Trees are dynamic, responsive organisms with multiple built-in protection features. They defend and protect their biological and mechanical systems through compartmentalization. It's an effective method for survival after injuries and infections but has limitations. The process demands energy and the infected areas, once compartmented, no longer store energy reserves. The process of new growth after wounds and infections is essential for survival but also uses a high amount of energy. When compartmentalization is more rapid than the ability of a tree to generate new wood, both processes stall. Unhealthy trees attract insect pathogens and fungi that cause rot and cankers. The subsequent infections and decay develop rapidly.

Trees receive numerous wounds throughout their lives from natural events such as self-wounding, animal wounds, defoliation cycles, fires, droughts, storms, and periods of extreme heat or cold. In nature, a dynamic oscillation exists between living systems that helps to compensate for natural events. Trees and forests are subjected to human population pressures, as is the environment in general. The rate of environmental change has challenged the capacity of nature to compensate. Examples such as overly aggressive forestry and

FIG. 6.1 Uprooting Red Oak (*Quercus rubra*) with fruit bodies of *Armillaria mellea*. Note past construction and landscape activities.

land-management practices predispose trees, the land, and wildlife to problems. Outbreaks of beetle and bud-worm insects are symptomatic. Leftover stumps and remaining trees of poor quality provide food to large populations of pathogens, such as *Armillaria* spp. (root rot), with few to no natural controls. Construction and landscaping activities in urban areas can easily injure trees and damage soil, making them more susceptible to stress and disease (fig. 6.1). The net result is that trees and environmental systems are predisposed to problems.

Predisposition for success in nature has occurred ever so gradually through evolution. The combination of qualities influencing successful survival in trees includes genetic tendencies for disease resistance and effective compartmentalization. These and other characteristics benefit trees in urban centers and other nonforest settings. Strong genetic traits, however, aren't enough without a suitable habitat. Ample space and biological diversity are also necessary for the healthy survival of trees in any setting. Predisposition for a positive outcome involves protecting tree and wildlife habitats.

7   Survival Theme

Trees have many safeguards for survival but those safeguards don't always work. In nature, survival is more an exception than a rule.

SURVIVAL is the ability to stay alive under conditions that have the potential to kill or stop a system, to compete effectively with other organisms for space and an energy source, to respond rapidly and effectively when injured, and to live long enough to complete a life cycle and reproduce. General survival factors include energy, genetics, space, water, essential elements, temperature, time, and the concentration of these factors. Trees have a long and impressive record of survival. They are resilient and, within limits, can adapt to change and adversity (see chap. 32).

Trees are a natural living system, and within this system there's little waste. Trees grow only enough to effectively compete for space and an energy source (sunlight, fig. 7.1). They regulate their growth rate and mass. The concept of a surplus doesn't exist, but the condition of a deficit does.

Trees and other organisms must live within their means. A living system that exceeds (or underachieves) its limits to remain in a orderly state (healthy) won't survive. The energy required for growth comes out of storage reserves. When new parts (tissues) are made, they must be paid for up front and then maintained. Size and rate of growth are competitive risks. The two basic growth strategies for trees are to grow big quickly or stay small by growing slowly. Each strategy involves survival benefits and risks.

The general physiological and anatomical themes between tree species are similar. Special traits are the cumulative result of evolutionary adjustments that benefit survival and allow for the continuation of a given species. With trees, as with many other organisms, natural selection favors the group through the success and variations of individuals. Trees evolved under group forest conditions over millions of years. Genetic change occurs ever so gradually. The phenotypic differences we see today, for example, between self-propagated city and forest trees are largely the result of environmental factors rather than biological change (see chaps. 2 & 3).

Tree survival is dependent on many other organisms, including the pathogens. These relationships have evolved together. Trees provide their associates with a suitable habitat and, in return, receive numerous survival benefits

FIG. 7.1 Trees compete for space and light.

linked to fundamental processes such as absorption, reproduction, protection and decomposition.

Success is defined by how well a species as a group adapts and competes in its environment. Nature's perspective is one of indifference; there are no good or bad, attractive or ugly, clean or dirty, valuable or trash trees. All tree species alive on the earth today are evolutionary success stories.

8   Rhizosphere

The RHIZOSPHERE is the absorbing root-soil interface. This narrow zone (approximately one millimeter wide) is the less obvious, business end of the tree. The rhizosphere is a delineated band surrounding the epidermis of non-woody roots, including root hairs and mycorrhizae boundary cells, as well as extending hyphae strands. It's small in human terms, but large and teeming with life on a microscopic scale.

The rhizosphere is a coral reef off the coast of an island (the tree) in the vast ocean (the soil). It's a rich source of food and shelter for a high population of diverse life forms, but it's also fragile and easily damaged. The elusive RHIZO-PLANE is the absorptive boundary through which water and elements enter a tree and organic compounds exit. Microorganisms and tree cells merge in this jelly-like microscopic mix, making the exact boundary indiscernible.

The rhizosphere and surrounding soil supports a constantly changing array of organisms. These inhabitants are locked in a continual interactive struggle for water, food and space. A partial profile of the drama includes viruses infecting fungi and bacteria, bacteria attacking other bacteria, fungi working against other fungi, protozoa eating bacteria, and nematodes spearing roots and in turn being trapped and eaten by earthworms. Examples of the many other diverse rhizosphere organisms include members of actinomycetes, protists (slime molds and protozoans), nematodes (roundworms) and arthropods (including centipedes, millipedes and mites).

Many relationships are predatory or parasitic, not only among themselves but also to the tree. Although rhizosphere organisms are not altruistic, many share mutually beneficial relationships. Mycorrhizal fungi are biologically smart. They form a partnership with trees and don't need to compete for food with other rhizosphere organisms. Another advantage of beneficial associations usually includes mutual protection. The cumulative effect of an active and diverse community of rhizosphere organisms is healthy soil and plants, and a healthier environment. Small organisms in small places do big things.

❦

Conditions in the rhizosphere are quite delicate and exacting. It doesn't take much to disrupt them. When change happens faster than adaptation, living systems are threatened. Problems in the rhizosphere lead to problems in trees. The two systems are interdependent. Sick trees with decline symptoms are often an indication of trouble in the rhizosphere.

FIG. 8.1 Dead trees and decaying leaves are major sources of carbon for rhizo-sphere organisms.

The upper layer of soil, where the bulk of absorbing roots grow, is teeming with life. The soil, in a sense, is alive. Soils depleted of fertile components won't adequately support soil organisms. It's a form of starvation that affects trees. Absorption and the interconnected processes of respiration and photosynthesis are diminished. Energy, the most essential requirement for all living systems, becomes progressively deficient in unhealthy trees.

A low energy reserve equates to lowered capacity for defense. Long before we become aware of a tree's deficiencies, opportunistic pathogens recognize and take advantage of weaknesses. The pathogens become the focus of blame and are often considered a sudden threat. The point is that trees are predisposed to problems associated with the quality of the rhizosphere. Problems are cumulative and complex and usually there's nothing sudden about them. The dependence between trees and other organisms is a fundamental aspect of tree biology. The following discussion attempts to outline major points within this topic.

Food in the rhizosphere comes from other living organisms, decaying organic matter, and tree exudates. EXUDATES are organic carbon compounds, including carbohydrates, released by trees. They contain secreted hydrogen protons, organic acids, vitamins, and other substances. Five to forty percent of the dry-matter production of organic carbon from photosynthesis may be released. Exudates increase when trees decline. Trees evolved over millions of years in group forest situations. Cultivated trees retain the genetic codes of their ancestors, which still influence the way they live and die.

The SELF-THINNING RULE OF ECOLOGY implies that for continued growth, some trees must die. The resource potential on any given growing site is capable of sustaining only a limited amount of living mass. Natural selection benefits an elite minority of trees. The successful survivors are those that are able to live long enough to reproduce. The majority of trees in a forest setting don't make it. They're either subdominant or in some way defective and unable to compete.

Dead trees are a major source of carbon for soil organisms (fig. 8.1). Modern forestry practices and urban sprawl are taking away substantial portions of this carbon source in a relatively short period of time. A dwindling food supply in the rhizosphere is a form of injury. It adversely affects the natural controls that diverse communities provide to a healthy soil environment. In a healthy forest, successions of living, dying and dead trees and other organisms are the ingredients for its overall well-being. Layers of built-up annual leaves, for example, serve a variety of different populations in each strata. Collectively they benefit from and contribute to the well-being of the rhizosphere (fig. 8.2).

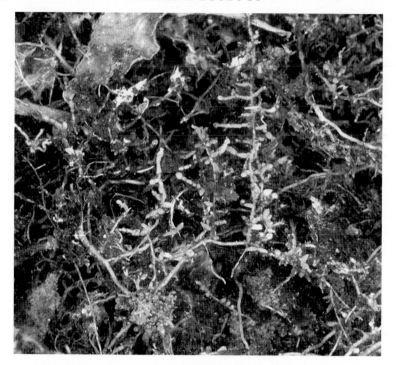

FIG. 8.2 Low-power microscopic view of the rhizosphere showing grada-
tions of living, dying and dead nonwoody roots (including mycorrhizae).
Note white clusters of fungal hyphae and mycelial strands (upper left).
Photo Alex Shigo. Courtesy Shigo & Trees, Associates.

Clearing out too many leaves, too much understory vegetation, or too many
trees depletes the ingredients necessary for a healthy rhizophere.

Nonwoody roots, through secretions and shedding, make a valuable contribution to the soil environment. The hyphae of mycorrhizae contain chitin.
Simular to cellulose, this structural polysaccharide contains a nitrogen group.
Nitrogen is a limiting factor for growth in all organisms. In healthy soil it's
quickly utilized. Soluble nitrogen in groundwater implies there are problems
in the soil environment and with the equilibrium between soil organisms and
plants.

Soil bacteria digest dead mycorrhizae hyphae, leaving minute tunnels that
are about eight to ten microns in diameter. The bacteria colonize these tunnels
and are afforded protection in a life-or-death struggle with hungry protozoa
(usually greater than ten microns in diameter). Unfavorable soil conditions
restrict the development of mycorrhizae. Compacted and saturated soil, for

example, kills mycorrhizae and destroys their microcavity habitat and, in turn, the tunnels for bacteria.

Manual techniques that fracture or punch holes in the ground don't bring back the microcavities or the tunnels. The accumulation or addition of compost, over many years, can help. When soil conditions degrade and beneficial connections between tree and soil organisms break, biological processes in trees decline.

Excessive soil or tree management activities cause tree and soil injuries. Examples include excessive watering, pruning, fertilizing, and compacting soil. Compacted soil changes air and water concentrations in ways unfavorable to trees and soil organisms. Soil microcavities, the spaces where microorganisms live and nonwoody roots grow, are destroyed. Populations of beneficial microorganisms decrease and the development of nonwoody roots is diminished.

Overwatering stalls the processes of absorption and respiration. The formation of carbonic acid is inhibited and ions needed for absorption aren't formed. Overpruning injures the treetop and, in turn, the roots. When the energy (food) source from the top decreases, roots begin to starve. Root disease is a common symptom.

The absorption of fertilizer reduces energy reserves in trees. It initially weakens them and alters soil pH in the rhizosphere. Even if only for a brief period, weaknesses provide an opportunity for pathogens, which also benefit from the introduced nitrogen. Most fertilizers contain nitrogen, which stimulates growth. Should deficiencies for other elements exist, nitrogen fertilizer will make those deficiencies more acute.

FERTILIZER is a salt made up of a lattice of anions and cations that separate and carry electrical charges when in contact with soil water. Mineral elements present in the soil enter and exit nonwoody roots on the molecular level as inorganic IONS (charged particles) in solution. The electrical charge ions carry is either positive in CATIONS or negative in ANIONS. Ions with opposite charges attract; ions with like charges repel. They vary greatly in weight (size), strength of charge and availability.

In general, organic molecules (containing carbon) are too heavy and not in the right form to be absorbed. An exception is manmade urea (a highly polar molecule), but to only a limited extent, because most will be oxidized (broken down) to nitrate. Nitriform fertilizer products bind nitrogen in carbon chains that must be biologically broken apart by soil bacteria. The misuse of fertilizer and pesticide chemicals can cause soil and water pollution and injure or kill plants and soil organisms.

When a cation or anion enters a root, another must exit. Most nitrogen, for trees, is absorbed as a nitrate anion, and as it enters, a BICARBONATE ANION exits. This ion forms from carbonic acid, and is an important compound in nature that helps drive the plant-absorption process. Bicarbonate causes soil pH spikes around the rhizosphere. The increase may only be temporary, but it creates a weak moment for a tree by inhibiting the availability of certain essential elements, offering pathogens an opportunity.

Soils have a natural buffering capacity that minimizes and shortens moderate pH changes (see chap. 15). There are no easy ways to measure pH in the rhizosphere (a 1-mm area). A standard soil pH test may measure 6 when the rhizosphere is at 8. Soil tests showing deficiencies for nitrogen can also be deceptive. Nitrogen is quickly absorbed by soil organisms and plants, or moves through the topsoil by leaching. The presence of nitrogen in a soil test or run-off water can imply a problem of excessive nitrogen, or low levels of soil micro-organisms and absorbing roots.

Fertilizers with urea can increase soil pH in the rhizosphere two or more units and cause the availability of certain elements essential for photosynthesis, especially iron and manganese, to decrease. The elements may be present in soil but not available to the tree as absorbable ions. In a high-pH soil environment, certain elements form molecules that precipitate (separate) rather than ionize.

CHLOROSIS is a generalized term used to describe a condition that blocks or slows photosynthesis. When the energy flow is blocked, trees decline and pathogens enter. The condition occurs because elements and enzymes that form chlorophyll either aren't available or are not in a usable form. Fertilizers with an ammonium-based nitrogen source can reduce rhizosphere pH. The ammonium cation enters a root and a positively charged hydrogen proton (cation) exits, creating a slightly more acidic condition.

Root hairs actively secrete hydrogen protons. These cations are able to bond electrostatically to the negative positions on soil colloids. They replace other cations (cationic exchange), which become available for plant absorption. Colloidal surfaces, common to clay and humus, help to hold cations against the leaching effect of soil water. Anions don't bond and are prone to leaching.

🌳

Several limiting factors are associated with commercial fertilizers. Much of the nitrogen with ammonium- and urea-based fertilizers is converted by NITRI-FICATION (oxidation) to a nitrate. Fertilizers are expensive and often prove wasteful. Quick-release forms leach easily, and slow-release forms are either absorbed by soil organisms or dissipate. Little actually gets to the tree.

In warm temperatures and in low-oxygenated or alkaline soil, nitrogen can convert to ammonia gas. Another loss of nitrogen is through DENITRIFICA-

TION (reduction). Microorganisms in low-oxygenated soil convert nitrate to a nitrogen or nitrous oxide gas. Nitrogen patterns differ between ninety-day agricultural crops and ninety-year-old trees. Trees have a low nitrogen-to-carbon ratio compared to other organisms. This protection feature has contributed to their evolutionary success. Supplemental fertilizer with nitrogen for trees initially depletes energy reserves and stimulates tissue growth. This larger system with a lowered defense capacity benefits the pathogens (see chap. 28).

Specific situations may warrant the conservative application of fertilizers or pesticides for trees. Nursery trees or young trees in low-quality urban soils may need supplementary minerals to better develop. Mature trees with rot or canker infections don't benefit from nitrogen-based fertilizer, although the pathogens may. Pesticides may help to control a periodic insect infestation but won't save a tree if the insects are symptomatic of a greater problem. The excessive use — or any other form of misuse — of chemical products, synthetic or organic, isn't in the best interest of trees or the environment. The residual effects to nontarget organisms and the cumulative effects between different chemical agents aren't well understood.

A holistic approach for tree and soil problems, with minimal dependence on supplemental chemicals, may prove to be more practical. Optimal soil and tree conditions are those that protect trees and afford them ample space. Beneficial soil microorganisms bring about more fertile conditions through the breakdown of organic materials. Healthy soil conditions favor root growth, and root growth helps create healthy soil conditions. Fallen leaf layers or composted mulch protects and benefits soils. Fallen tree trunks and lichen-covered rocks nurse young ferns and saplings (see fig. 31.2).

Natural understory trees and vegetation in wooded areas exist in a mutualistic manner. Planting trees in clusters with groupings of companion species that have similar requirements for soil, light and moisture give each the best advantage (fig. 8.3 & plate 3). Trees and lawns do better when in separated areas. Wooded and garden areas with some weeds and wildness isn't necessarily bad, although aggressive plants can cause problems. Exotic invasive plants, once established, are difficult to control. Native plants are environmentally sensible. They're naturally suited to climate and soil conditions, generally require little supplementary water or chemical products, and benefit native wildlife.

CARBON is a naturally abundant, nonmetallic element and a universal constituent of organic compounds. Trees and all life forms exist because of carbon and its capacity to form long chains of atoms. Organisms manufacture or derive

FIG. 8.3 A cluster planting of Dawn Redwood (*Metasequoia glyptostroboides*) in a low-lying area.

energy through carbon-based molecules within their cells. All living processes are centered around energy management. Energy for trees is acquired from the sun during photosynthesis. It's stored in carbon-based organic molecules for direct use by trees, and indirectly passed to other organisms for their use.

Carbon expenditures are fundamental to life processes. Carbon in the tree is either lost or tied up through actions associated with growth, respiration, absorption or exudation. The energy-releasing process of respiration drives metabolic cellular functions. Carbon dioxide and water are the by-products.

Carbonic acid forms when carbon dioxide dissolves in water. Carbon containing bicarbonate ions form from carbonic acid and are associated with absorption. They exit when nitrate ions enter tree roots. Nitrate ions form compounds, such as amino acids, from reactions with reserve carbon. Carbon compounds released from trees are referred to collectively as exudates. The percentage of exudates released increases when trees are stressed or dying.

Should the rate at which carbon reserves decrease outpace increases, the potential for defense diminishes. Trees manufacture and store carbon-based food in a consolidated period of time, but must budget its use year-round, because metabolic processes are continuous.

The rhizosphere is about little spaces and little living things that are connected and responsible for major life forces. Life exists because of its ability to continually repeat processes and to reproduce. Events that injure the rhizosphere can interrupt life processes and escalate into serious long-term environmental problems. Conditions that respect it allow for healthy diversity and the natural oscillation (rhythm) of nature.

PART II

Parts & Processes

New Light

Rising up and swirling in the breeze,
smoke off the trunk in the morning sun.
Light glimmers from thawing ice,
held by needles and twigs, it drips.
Long shadows of branches lie,
cast into the field, they reach.
Roots pretend to sleep.
A corky coat covers the soul
of the tree by the field,
in this new morning light.

FIG. 9.1 Black Birch (*Betula nigra*), 5 cm diameter, with wound. Open arrow points to reaction zone boundary (wall 2). Discolored area is the reaction zone. Other arrows point to barrier zone boundary (wall 4) and indicate size of sample when wounded.

FIG. 9.2 Red Maple (*Acer rubrum*), 5 cm diameter, with wounds. Open arrows point to reaction zone boundary (wall 3). Other arrows indicate barrier zone boundary (wall 4) of initial wound.

9   Compartmentalization

COMPARTMENTALIZATION is the defense process of trees. It's a method for survival after injuries and infection. Trees form new boundaries and strengthen existing boundaries in order to be resistant to pathogens and to protect their liquid-transport, energy-storage and mechanical-support systems.

Compartmentalization is a two-part process that takes place in wood at the time of and after wounding. When wounded, a tree responds by forming a chemical boundary first, then an anatomical boundary. The first boundary is the REACTION ZONE; wood present at the time of injury is chemically altered to a more protective state. The second boundary is the BARRIER ZONE, which separates wood present at the time of injury from new wood formed after wounding. It provides a protective anatomical layer that pathogens seldom breach (figs. 9.1, 9.2, & 9.3).

Compartmentalization — a dynamic, energy-dependent process — is under moderate to strong genetic control. The process is not completely effective every time, because numerous combinations of factors influence the results. Energy availability leads the list, followed by the severity and the timing of wounds. The tree's age, health condition and species are also factors.

A succession of infecting microorganisms, after injury, challenge the survival of a tree (see chap. 22). The progress of infection and gradual degradation of wood occurs within compartments. Compartmentalization allows trees time to grow new wood and new parts, thus enhancing chances for long-term survival.

Compartmentalization is initiated by a wound or infection. Crushed, severed and broken cells die. Living cells around the margin of a wound begin to chemically convert intracellular materials into protective substances that are resistant to pathogens. Free oxygen combines with cellular enzymes during the process.

The chemical response progresses to adjoining cells within the symplast system. These living cells, growing among dead wood cells, change the region (the reaction zone) to a more protective state. In addition, transport elements (vessels, tracheids, pit openings) are plugged with deposits of materials such as resins, crystals, gums, tyloses or callose.

Boundary patterns vary among trees. Combined factors between the host,

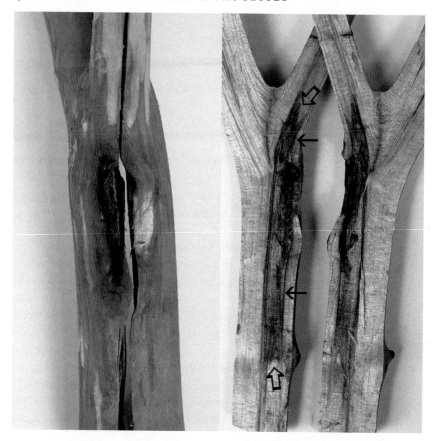

FIG. 9.3 Crapemyrtle (*Lagerstroemia* spp.), 2.5 cm diameter, split lengthwise through wound. Internal column of discolored and decayed wood visible. Open arrows indicate vertical boundaries of the reaction zone (wall 1). Other arrows indicate barrier zone boundary (wall 4).

pathogens and environment affect the outcome. Despite variances, certain patterns are associated with specific species and types of injuries. They can be better understood through profiles and dissections of common local trees.

❦

The barrier zone is characterized as tissue having a great number of axial parenchyma, few conducting elements, low amounts of lignin and, with some tree species, suberin in the tissue. Suberin is highly resistant to breakdown by microorganisms.

Despite strong protective properties, barrier zones have two intrinsic problems. The first concerns energy. The defensive action of building boundaries requires a great deal of energy. Once boundaries are formed, altered wood in the reaction zone no longer stores energy reserves. The depletion of energy reserves and storage space can lead to unhealthy, defenseless trees. A tree can compartmentalize itself to death.

The second problem is structural. Internal separations — CRACKS — may occur along a barrier zone. Circumferential cracks are known as RING SHAKES. Sudden and extreme changes in temperature can trigger separations in the barrier zone. Radial cracks near the margins of a wound may also develop at the barrier zone and spread outward. Regardless of the cause, any internal crack (wound) in sapwood will trigger the formation of a barrier zone and a reaction zone. Cracks are starting points for infections, decay and structural problems. They threaten tree survival and pose public safety issues.

❧

CODIT is an acronym for the Compartmentalization of Decay in Trees. It's not an actual biological process, but a model developed to define the dimensions of a column of infected and altered wood associated with wounding. CODIT has two parts: Part 1 represents the reaction zone containing model walls 1, 2, and 3. Part 2 represents the barrier zone with model wall 4.

Part 1 is a three-dimensional representation of the infected column that forms in wood present at the time of wounding. The wood is altered and resistant to the spread of infection. Wall 1 resists vertical spread above and below the wound. Wall 2 resists the inward spread. Wall 3 resists the lateral (circumferential) spread. In Part 1, wall 1 is often the weakest, wall 3 is usually the strongest, and wall 2 ceases at the pith.

Part 2 represents the anatomical boundary formed by the living cambial zone outside a wound. The physical boundary separates wood present at the time of wounding from wood formed after wounding. Wall 4 is the strongest protective wall of CODIT. The four wall boundaries are visible in figures 9.1 (walls 2 & 4), 9.2 (walls 3 & 4), and 9.3 (walls 1 & 4).

🌳

Trees are a generating system. To survive, they grow new parts in new spatial positions. They regulate their mass by shedding (separating) parts. Outer parts are cast off and inner parts are compartmented (segregated). When wounded, trees can't heal; that is, they can't repair or replace cells in the same spatial position or rid themselves of infection. The injuries that trees receive throughout their lives are permanent.

Animals, by contrast, are a regenerating system. They can heal after an injury or infection. With trees, new growth forms around and over wounds and branch voids. This growth, known as CLOSURE, shouldn't be confused with or referred to as compartmentalization or healing. The closure process isn't an indication of the effectiveness of the compartmentalization (defense) process.

FIG. 9.4 Section (30 × 30 cm) of a 125-year-old Red Oak (*Quercus rubra*) slab. Shows boundary and column patterns of discolored and decayed wood in heartwood. Sapwood wounds are from secondary events.

FIG. 9.5 Fifty-year-old White Oak (*Quercus alba*) limb (12.5 cm diameter) shows vertical column (darker) of discolored heartwood associated with pruning injury.

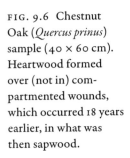

FIG. 9.6 Chestnut Oak (*Quercus prinus*) sample (40 × 60 cm). Heartwood formed over (not in) compartmented wounds, which occurred 18 years earlier, in what was then sapwood.

Compartmentalization occurs in heartwood (genetically altered protection wood). Dissections of trees with heartwood show distinct boundaries and column patterns of discolored and decayed wood associated with wounds, similar to those of sapwood (figs. 9.4 & 9.5). When wounded, a reaction takes place and boundary layers form. The reaction may be associated with oxidation, wood enzymes, or other enzymes introduced by infecting microorganisms. The process isn't fully understood, but dissections show that:

1. Rot confines itself to the wood present at the time of wounding.
2. Decay-causing fungi don't grow at will in heartwood.
3. Heartwood can form over compartmented wounds, but won't form in the reaction zone of wounded wood (fig. 9.6; see chaps. 19 & 20).

Discoloration and decay induced by wounds, infections, or branch death in sapwood and static core wood are sometimes confused with heartwood. The decomposition of dead trees is an essential and normal part of nature, whereas the decay of dead wood in living trees is a serious problem and a destructive disease.

It was once thought that wounds affecting heartwood led to its unrestricted breakdown: the heartrot concept. This idea didn't account for the response of the living tree and confused the results of other processes and conditions. Unlike heartwood (in which color does not derive from wounds, infections or branch death), discolored wood, false heartwood and wetwood are the products of tree processes and, in some cases, the effects of microorganisms. These conditions contain wood that has been altered and can no longer respond or react any further if wounded or infected. They are not heartwood.

FIG. 9.7 Boundaries associated with wound to Red Maple (*Acer rubrum*). Although decay spread inward, the barrier zone boundary effectively separates wood that formed afterwards.

Tree dissections help to clarify the process of compartmentalization. They show basic patterns of internal columns of discolored and decayed wood associated with wounding and the tree's response. The column boundary layers are formed by the barrier zone outside and the reaction zone inside. The greatest diameter of a column is the diameter of the affected tree area at the time of wounding. The barrier zone separates this wood from wood that formed after wounding (fig. 9.7).

Within the reaction zone, the three-dimensional shape of the column is generally conical above and below a wound's point of origin. The length and depth of a column gradually changes over time. The reaction zone, at best, resists the degradation process. Radial (lengthwise) dissections through affected wood show column patterns well. Transverse (cross) cuts alone can cause confusion. Radial cuts must follow the curve of the pith, which is the biological center of a stem.

Trees grow as a somewhat curved cone, wider and older near the base, more narrow and younger near the top (see fig. 18.8). Trunks, branches and roots rarely grow perfectly straight or round, and piths are seldom concentrically centered. Straight cuts through curved cylinders yield artifacts (see chap. 34).

Confusion about compartmentalization can occur from a combination of circumstances: a faintly visible barrier zone, multiple barrier zones, overlapping boundary layers, escalating cracks and cankers, expanding woundwood rolls, and wounds to defenseless wood. Focusing on the basic features of tree anatomy and patterns associated with specific defects helps to clear up confusion.

A barrier zone, prominently visible or not, ultimately results from an injury to wood with living cells (sapwood). Multiple barrier zones and overlapping boundary layers occur from multiple wounds in a localized area. Over time, tree growth can cause cracks to escalate, and the actions of pathogens expand canker lesions. Rapidly growing woundwood often rolls inward, causing pressure cracks or crushing soft tissue. Dead and dying wood is defenseless and can't respond to injuries. Trees are highly ordered living systems and things don't happen randomly. The sequence of biological events are influenced by time, energy reserves, the nature of the wounds, and the virulence of pathogens.

❧

Dating wounds is possible because trees generate new parts in new spatial positions with regularly occurring phenological cycles (see fig. 34.1). Most trees start to grow new wood after the leaves have formed. A wound occurring within the seasonal growth period can be narrowed to an exact date, give or take a week. The date is based on the position of the barrier zone within the growth increment, as the bulk of growth will be completed in about six to eight weeks.

A wound occurring at a time when wood isn't forming can be dated within the year. The barrier zone runs along the annual growth increment (ring). Counting and observing growth rings, in general, provides information about the age of a tree, its condition at the time of death, and also reveals past growth patterns and disturbances. The information can be extrapolated to similar trees living in a comparable setting.

❧

Important points to remember are that trees defend themselves and compensate for adversity to survive. Compartmentalization is an active defense process resulting in compartmented wounds and infections. We can't see it happening, but we can see the results. Trees receive numerous wounds and subsequent infections throughout their lives. Age-related decline, associated with genetics and environmental factors, is a constant force against survival.

Ultimately, all trees die and all wood rots. Compartmentalization doesn't stop biological or structural decline, but it does resist and stall the process. It allows time for a tree to grow new parts in new positions. The concept of compartmentalization is based on the fact that trees are active, responding organisms. Wood in living trees is not dead, because it has living cells among the dead and dying cells; the living parts control the dead parts.

10   Callus and Woundwood

CALLUS is new tissue growth around the margin of a wound. The growth is a response to a traumatic opening (wound) of the vascular cambium. Callus is a mass of living, undifferentiated parenchyma cells and is characterized as soft adventitious tissue. The cells are meristematic and homogeneous with low to no lignin. This means they have the capacity to divide and differentiate, are all the same, and are nonwoody.

Callus grows for only a relatively short period of time. Its rate of development depends on several factors, such as the size, position and time of a wound, as well as a tree's health condition. Wounds occurring during dormancy start callus growth the following spring. Callus forms a thin, protective epidermis with suberin.

A wound releases pressure to the surrounding cambial zone. Crushed and damaged cells die. The uninjured peripheral cells begin to initiate new growth. At first, callus cells are large, round and relatively uniform in size. A probe will penetrate callus with little resistance compared to other kinds of wood tissue because of the low lignin content and the loosely packed cells. It's also the reason why callus will bruise easily if physically disturbed. As accumulating cells continue to divide, building upon themselves, pressure increases and their shape begins to change. Increased pressure and limited space trigger cells to differentiate, marking the changeover from callus to woundwood.

WOUNDWOOD, the growth following callus, is specialized woody tissue growing around and over a wound (figs. 10.1 & 10.2). The cells are lignified, heterogeneous and not meristematic. This means the cells are woody, specialized, and no longer have the capacity to divide and differentiate.

Woundwood protects and strengthens the structural integrity of damaged trees. It differs in a number of ways from normal wood (wood not influenced by wounds). It has a greater mechanical strength, a higher concentration of lignin, fewer vessels, wider growth increments, and a stronger resistance to decay. The bark of woundwood is generally smoother and thinner, and it has an equal to greater amount of chlorophyll than the bark of normal wood.

Annual growth increment bands are discernable on the bark as woundwood grows. When a wound is fully closed by woundwood, then normal wood will

FIG. 10.1 Woundwood growth looking down into sample from fig. 9.5. Sapwood has rotted away, and discolored heartwood is visible. See also figs. 9.1 and 9.2 for interior views of woundwood growth outside of barrier zone.

FIG. 10.2 Nine-year-old Tuliptree (*Liriodendron tulipifera*) sample, 15 cm diameter, with advancing woundwood growth over column of discolored and decaying wood.

form. The outer bark generally remains smoother and characteristically different from normal bark.

In many scenarios, woundwood growth may never fully close over wounds (fig. 10.3). The wound may be too large or the tree too weak to produce enough growth. Woundwood growth patterns can cause defects: internal cracks, barrier zone separations and included bark. In some cases, the lack of pressure over a wound allows woundwood to curl inward. This predisposes the area to cracks and infections. From a transverse (cross cut) orientation, the growth pattern has a rib or ram's horn appearance (fig. 10.4). Wetwood infections are common to wounds caused by internal cracks. Bark stains associated with wetwood are often visible below woundwood.

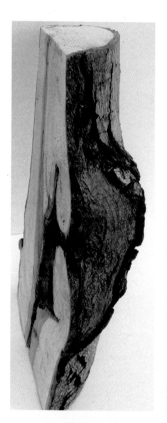

FIG. 10.3 Dissection through woundwood on Red Maple (*Acer rubrum*) reveals wound not fully closed. The inward curl of the growth pattern has initiated small internal cracks. Note that bark characteristics differ between woundwood and normal bark.

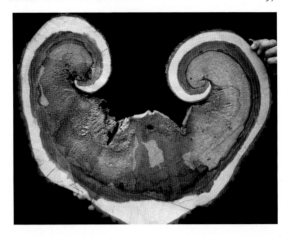

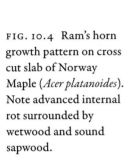

FIG. 10.4 Ram's horn growth pattern on cross cut slab of Norway Maple (*Acer platanoides*). Note advanced internal rot surrounded by wetwood and sound sapwood.

The growth of new wood and bark tissue over a wound is called CLOSURE and shouldn't be confused with compartmentalization. Closure is a generating process, growing new parts in new positions. COMPARTMENTALIZATION — the formation of protective boundaries in response to wounding — is a defense process. Both processes demand energy, but neither are related to the zoological process of healing. Prominent woundwood growth isn't callus and doesn't indicate healing.

Another point needing clarification is the distinction between the terms callus, callose and callous. CALLOSE is an insoluble carbohydrate laid down around perforations in sieve elements, where layers build and thicken, forming blockages that may be seasonal or permanent. Callous is hardening of the skin, or an unfeeling attitude.

11   Branches, Collars and Twigs

BRANCHES are growth extensions—secondary stems—off a central trunk that are made possible by a tree's capacity for multiple meristems. The evolutionary development of multiple growing points gave trees survival benefits enabling them to occupy more space and survive in colder climates. If one point dies, other points can continue. The precursors of trees had only a single growing point, the equivalent of one branch. Branches allowed trees to diversify and migrate to cold temperate regions.

A tree is a collection of branches; each branch is an independent subdivision, much like a tree on a tree. Branches manufacture their own food and export a portion of that food to the trunk and root system below. The roots and trunk provide water, essential elements and support, but only so long as the contribution from the branch to the tree system is greater than its draw.

Photosynthates produced by branches move through phloem tissue in a BASIPETAL direction (towards the base). Water with soil elements move in an ACROPETAL direction (towards the top) from the roots through the most current xylem tissue. Except with first-year primary tissue, no direct conduction occurs to or from trunk tissues above a branch, or from branch to branch.

Branches are held on trees by anatomical collars (fig. 11.1). COLLARS are a series of interlocking structural bands of branch and trunk tissue that support the branches. Branch tissue begins to form and mature before trunk tissue. It doesn't grow out of or into the trunk or parent stem, but turns and grows on the trunk below the branch base. As this growth slows, trunk tissue growth increases and forms a collar over the branch tissue.

The overlapping tissues are collectively part of the trunk system and are technically a trunk collar. The succession of collars, year after year, builds a tightly layered mesh that secures a branch and encases the branch core in compacted xylem (wood) as trees grow (fig. 11.2).

The branch attachment design is strong and resilient while branches are alive, yet weak after they die, which facilitates branch decay and shedding. After branches die, the collar continues to serve as a protective boundary for the trunk. A piece of firewood split around a branch stub (fig. 11.3), or a small limb pulled out of a stem, shows the collar construction. The branch

FIG. II.I Tuliptree at left and Hemlock (*Tsuga canadensis*) at right show the collar design.

FIG. II.2 Twenty-year-old Black Walnut (*Juglans nigra*) shows the succession of annual collars that secured the branch to the trunk.

FIG. 11.3 Split firewood
shows compacted xylem,
branch core and pith.

attachment is a structural phenomenon of nature. This concept was not published until 1985 and is credited to Dr. Alex Shigo.

The BRANCH PROTECTION ZONE is a boundary area within the branch base. It protects the branch core and trunk by resisting the inward spread of pathogens and decay as branches die. Decay outside this zone allows branches to shed. Physiological and anatomical changes occur as branches age and die. Cellular substances are altered to materials with antimicrobial properties that inhibit the advancement of pathogens. Conifers, for example, build terpene-based resins. Angiosperms form phenol-based materials.

Another protection boundary is the PITH PLUG. The branch pith does not connect with the trunk pith. The separating plug is a nonconductive wedge of compacted, thick-walled cells. The BRANCH BARK RIDGE is raised bark at the upper position of a branch/trunk junction (branch crotch). As branch and trunk tissues grow, a raised ridge forms where compacted bark and xylem converge. Staggered branch and trunk growth generally produces a strong fibrous union. The ridge is carried with each year's growth expansion (fig. 11.4).

The branch crotch area can become an Achilles' heel for trees. INCLUDED BARK is an example of a common but serious structural defect, where bark and wood tissues turn inward, trapping branch bark against trunk bark

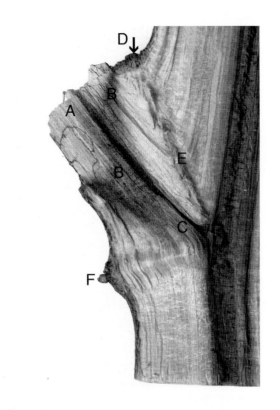

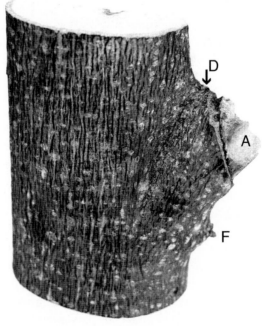

FIG. 11.4 Features of nine-year-old Tuliptree sample: (A) dead branch, (B) branch protection zone, (C; *below*) branch pith, (D) branch bark ridge, (E) compacted xylem, (F) meristematic point.

FIG. 11.5 Dogwood (*Cornus florida*) branch crotch with included bark. Note branch protection zone at base of discolored branch stub (*right*).

(fig. 11.5). The branch attachment will be structurally weak and prone to splitting. Another weakness occurs during the spring growth period when bark expands. Small openings can briefly develop in the crotch and twig/bud areas that allow pathogens access into a tree. This occurs at a time when trees have high energy expenditures and low reserves (low defense). This is the mode of infection for Chestnut Blight (*Cryphonectria parasitica*) and Dutch Elm Disease (*Ophiostoma ulmi*). Canker infections are also common around crotches.

Collars vary in shape and size, but the principle of branch attachment anatomy is still the same for trees worldwide. They generally bulge outward with a shoulder-like shape, although flat or sunken collars aren't unusual, especially on conifers (fig. 11.6). The growth pattern sometimes leaves a V-shaped void below the branch junction when the trunk collar doesn't fully envelop the branch. Collars around dying branches often appear swollen.

When pruning dead limbs, the boundary of live tissue shouldn't be disturbed. Removing or injuring a collar — referred to as a flush cut — wounds the trunk and is the starting point for infections (fig. 11.7). Woundwood growth associated with flush cuts doesn't develop uniformly. It forms from the sides, and a defenseless void is left above and below the cut. This growth pattern is prone to the development of included bark and cracks.

Pruning cuts shouldn't leave protruding branch stubs. Stubs are defenseless and become a food source for pathogens. Perfect pruning cuts aren't always possible, but they should be made as close as possible to the collar without injuring it or leaving stubs (see chap. 33).

🌳

Dying branches live off their own energy reserves until they're nearly exhausted. With depleted nutrients and little moisture, the branch tissue becomes semi-desiccated. False heartwood, a type of protection wood, is associated with the

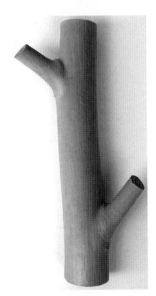

FIG. 11.6 Bark was removed from Tuliptree to show shoulder-shaped collars (*left*). Sunken collar on White Pine (*Pinus strobus*) at right.

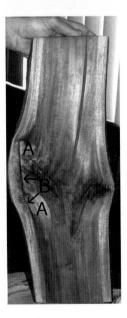

FIG. 11.7 Pruned dead Oak limb. Live tissue not disturbed. Flush cut (*right*, sample prepared by A. Shigo of Shigo & Trees, Associates) injured Mahogany trunk and initiated rot (A) and crack (B).

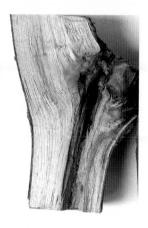

FIG. 11.8 Branch rot patterns (6 cm diameter samples): A type, 22-year-old Pin Oak (*Quercus palustris*) with rotting dead limb; B type, ten-year-old Carolina Silverbell (*Halesia carolina*), note chambered pith; C type, 20-year-old Red Maple (*Acer rubrum*), note spreading rot.

death of branches. Trunk wood in conjunction with the branch ages and discolors, but is not infected. The column of false heartwood will be the diameter of the branch at the time of its death (see chap. 20).

When a branch protection zone associated with a dying branch doesn't form or function effectively or is pruned off, pathogens spread inward. Discolored wood, rot or wetwood will begin to develop in the branch core and trunk wood. There are three types of BRANCH ROT PATTERNS that can occur (fig. 11.8). Type A contains rot at the branch protection zone with no internal spread. Type B contains rot within the branch core. Type C doesn't contain rot, and the rot spreads throughout the branch core into the trunk wood present at the time of branch death. A barrier zone separates new wood that forms after a branch dies.

The branch design allows for pathogens to decay dead limbs at or near the branch protection zone. Branches often break off at the base, and advancing trunk tissue gradually grows over and closes the opening (fig. 11.9). When limbs don't break off evenly, or when a stub remains, the trunk tissue still expands to envelop the remaining stub as it simultaneously rots (fig. 11.10). Many branch openings never obtain full closure.

CODOMINANT STEMS are two stems of equivalent size that initiate from a pair of apical buds off a single parent stem (fig. 11.11). Unlike branches, they have no collar or protection zone at their base. When either stem is wounded or dies, pathogens can spread downward into the main stem with little resis-

FIG. 11.9 Trunk tissue enclosing core of shed Red Maple branch.

FIG. 11.10 Norway Spruce (*Picea abies*) slab is about 60 years old and the branch died about 35 years ago. Trunk growth is gradually enveloping the stub as the exposed portion simultaneously rots.

tance other than the tree's vertical plugging potential associated with compartmentalization (see fig. 9.3). The stem bark ridge of compacted tissue is similar to a branch bark ridge. Its union tends to be stronger when the ridge rises outward, and weaker when it turns inward. A crotch with included bark prevents the formation of a fibrous stem connection (fig. 11.12). As the stems grow they increase in length, weight and diameter, which predisposes the crotch to splitting.

FIG. 11.11 Codominant stems of Elm (*Ulmus americana*) with bark removed to highlight the union. Note epicormic sprout on left.

FIG. 11.12 Dogwood with included bark.

Trees with codominant stems tend to have a spreading growth habit. Young trees in a forest setting that develop codominant growth generally don't compete well against tall, single-trunk trees. They shouldn't be confused with understory trees, which normally form codominant stems, stay short and live in low-light conditions. At the forest canopy level, mature trees tend to develop a codominant growth habit in their crowns (fig. 11.13). This allows them to obtain more light over a greater growing surface and to suppress competition.

Codominant stems are common to urban shade trees. Environmental factors contribute to developmental distinctions between city and forest trees. Contributing influences include wider spaces, more light, and cultural practices (see chap. 3).

TWIGS are small, young stems or branches representing the most recent few years of woody growth. Spring growth of the apical and vascular meristems begins to function in a wave from twig tips towards the woody roots. Prior to the formation of foliage, energy for twig and sprout growth is taken out of stored reserves.

Twig buds are formed during the previous growth season. They don't store starch, but a starch-rich zone exists just behind the bud in the stem (see fig. 14.1). The chemically induced conversion of starch to sugar unlocks bound water and increases osmotic pressure. This provides food and water for buds to initiate growth.

The activation of buds is an important component of the tree's transport system. Water and essential elements are moved from nonwoody roots through the vascular transport elements of the previous year (see chap. 14). At first, new growth is similar to that of an annual plant. With the exception of the cambial zone, there is an abundance of chlorophyll in soft, newly forming tissues. Once formed, new leaves provide trees with food for growth and metabolic functions. Energy reserves are also replenished. Woody features develop in the latter part of the growth period.

The anatomical features of a twig stem (fig. 11.14) include a thin outer boundary layer, the EPIDERMIS. Soft primary tissue behind the epidermis (the CORTEX) contains chlorophyll. The inner bark layer (PHLOEM) is transport tissue with sieve elements (openings) through which materials are moved.

FIG. 11.13 Mature trees with codominant growth habit.

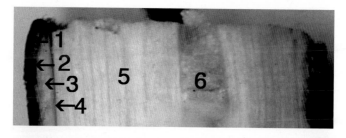

FIG. 11.14 Twig stem internal features: (1) epidermis, (2) cortex, (3) phloem, (4) cambial zone, (5) xylem, (6) pith; Tuliptree (*Liriodendron tulipifera*).

The CAMBIAL ZONE (vascular meristem) produces new phloem cells on the outside and xylem on the inside. Cells of the XYLEM include fibers and vessels (angiosperms) or tracheids (conifers), and parenchyma (axial and radial) in both. Lignin deposits form in cell walls during the latter part of the growth period. Lignified wood is SECONDARY XYLEM. A central cylinder of pulpy primary tissue (PITH) provides support and sustenance for new sprout structures.

Tree species have distinctive twig and bud characteristics. They provide a means to identify trees, especially in the winter when leaves and flowers are not present. External twig features (fig. 11.15), in general, are composed of an apical tip, the TERMINAL BUD. Secondary buds include PSEUDO-TERMINAL, FLOWER and LATERAL BUDS.

Buds are preformed structures containing undeveloped sprouts. Their protective outer coverings are BUD SCALES. After leaves are shed, the marks left on stems in the abscission zone include BUD and LEAF SCARS, as well as BUNDLE SCARS from the xylem/phloem veins. The ring-like nodal position of seasonal growth from one year to the next is a TERMINAL BUD SCALE SCAR.

FIG. 11.15 External features: (1) terminal bud, (2) lateral bud, (3) lenticels, (4) terminal bud scale scars, (5) bud/leaf scar, (6) bundle scars, (7) bud scales; dried Eastern Cottonwood (*Populus deltoides*).

LENTICELS (small, pulpy openings) form along stems and facilitate the exchange of gases (see chap. 13). A leaf-like appendage, the STIPULE, forms in pairs at the base of a petiole (leaf stem) on certain trees. Some trees grow thorns, or STIPULAR SPINES. These woody protrusions provide protection. Seasonal (yearly) growth features along stems mark the age and rate of growth of a twig or branch. They also offer insight into the general vitality of a tree.

NODES are growth positions. On twigs they occur where the terminal and lateral buds form and resulting sprouts grow leaves, flowers and stems. The three basic nodal patterns are ALTERNATE, OPPOSITE and WHORLED (figs. 11.16 & 11.17).

The overall growth pattern and architectural shape of a tree is under strong genetic control. The two general patterns are EXCURRENT or DECURRENT (see figs. 3.1, 3.2 & 34.7). Trees with excurrent growth are under strong apical dominance and have an upright form with straight, central trunks. They include many forest hardwoods and most conifers. Trees with decurrent growth are influenced by apical control and have an open branching form with multiple leaders (trunk stems). They include trees that grow in open areas, such as Elms (*Ulmus*, see fig. 2.3 & plate 14), as well as understory trees.

Available space and light also influence tree growth. Trees clustered together in a dark setting generally are tall with a narrow branch spread. Trees in an open, bright setting tend to be shorter with a wider branch spread. Despite environmental factors, trees with a strong excurrent growth habit, including many conifers, tend to retain the growth pattern even in an open setting.

FIG. 11.16 Opposite and alternate nodal growth positions: at left, opposite, Maple (*Acer* spp.); at right, alternate, Tuliptree.

FIG. 11.17 White Pine (*Pinus strobus*) has a whorled nodal pattern. Note preserved branch cores in hollow (rotted) trunk. Barrier zone boundary indicates tree size when wounded. Subsequent wood growth indicates effectiveness of boundary.

12
Sprouts and Pith

SPROUTS are new growth appendages extending from a given position on a tree. Below ground they are referred to as root sprouts; above ground they are aerial stem sprouts. The latter are the focus of this chapter.

Tree growth originates from the MERISTEM SYSTEM, a continuous layer of living cells with the ability to divide and form new cells. Growth is under strong genetic control and is influenced by the environment. Most above-ground growth occurs during a consolidated phenological period, during which preformed parts function and new parts form. The active growth period is followed by a protracted dormant period. This doesn't mean the entire tree goes dormant. Metabolic processes may slow but they never cease, and the root system experiences continuous stages of activity. Energy production and management is the overriding theme of the tree system. Growing sprouts use energy, whereas developed sprouts provide energy.

BUDS are preformed embryonic structures with a predetermined capacity to form a leaf, flower or stem (fig. 12.1 & plate 4). Buds are the most abundant source of tree sprouts. The majority grow on branch twigs. Roots don't form buds; their growth is from the apical meristem and meristematic points (see fig. 16.10). Buds form during the seasonal growth period. Many, not all, functionally open and grow the following growth season. Bud features are distinctive among tree species and offer a reliable method for tree identification.

A bud at the tip of a stem is the TERMINAL BUD. It expresses APICAL DOMINANCE, a chemical influence suppressing the development of other buds. The terminal bud sprout usually experiences prolific growth, elongating the stem. LATERAL BUDS are the side buds that, in many tree species, are smaller than the terminal bud. Sprout growth of lateral buds is moderate compared to that of the terminal sprout.

Some lateral bud sprouts develop into successful branches. A lateral bud can become apically dominant if the terminal bud is damaged. Lateral buds of certain tree species, such as understory trees, express APICAL CONTROL; that is, the bud sprouts will suppress and outgrow the terminal sprout. Clusters of secondary buds on or behind the terminal bud, and in some cases the lateral

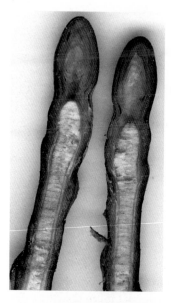
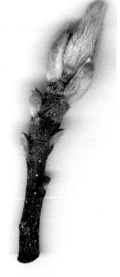

FIG. 12.1 Sliced leaf
bud from Tuliptree.
Note green of chloro-
phyll and pulpy, lighter
colored pith. Flower
and leaf buds on dried
Magnolia stem (*right*).

FIG. 12.2 Epicormic
sprouts on Tuliptree
(*Liriodendron tulipfera*)
associated with wounds
and stress.

FIG. 12.3 Topped
Tuliptree with
adventitious sprouts
growing from the cuts
(wounds).

buds, are referred to as AUXILIARY BUDS. They may open only if the primary
bud or its sprout is injured.

EPICORMIC SPROUTS are sprouts that grow on the trunk but not from a preformed bud (see fig. 11.11). They're often a response to injury or stress (fig. 12.2).
The two kinds are ADVENTITIOUS and MERISTEMATIC, and they are subdivided into two types. Those that grow rapidly and persist are ELITE. Those
which remain small or die young are SUPPRESSED. Adventitious sprouts are
associated with wounds to the vascular meristem (cambium). After wounding,
sprouts form from meristematic tissue of the cambial zone along the margin of
an injury (fig. 12.3). There is no such thing as an adventitious bud.

Meristematic sprouts originate from MERISTEMATIC POINTS: a mass
(bundle) of meristematic cells positioned in the cambial zone. They form the
terminal point of a MERISTEMATIC TRACE: a thick sheet of radial parenchyma, or a macro-ray (fig. 12.4). Meristematic points and traces build with
secondary growth, and in a sense are being carried along in the xylem system
(see fig. 11.4). Their cells in the cambial zone don't store starch, but the connected radial parenchyma cells do.

Meristematic points have the capacity to form stem and root sprouts. Once

FIG. 12.4 Meristematic traces (macro-rays): Crapemyrtle (*top*); Catalpa (*lower right*); Oak (*lower left*).

FIG. 12.5 Bark removed to highlight cluster of meristematic points.

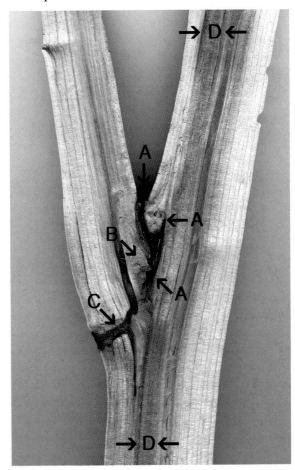

FIG. 12.6 Elm. Growth pattern of four-year-old epicormic sprout branch (*left*) led to structural and health problems: (A) included bark and ensuing cracks, (B) pressure-induced dead pocket, (C) insect gallery. Note that seven-year-old parent stem (*right*) has a wound-induced column of discolored wood (D) that coincides with the initiation of the sprout.

formed, stem sprouts with foliage produce photosynthates (food) for themselves and the tree. The tips of meristematic points often have a protruding nipple shape, but these are not dormant buds (fig. 12.5).

The triggering mechanism for sprouting isn't fully understood, but appears to be associated with stress and induced by growth-regulating substances. Trees with energy deficiencies often produce epicormic sprouts. On older trees, these sprouts are thought of as an allegorical old-age pension plan.

Few epicormic sprouts develop into successful branches or stems. Either they don't succeed biologically, or structural problems associated with their growth habit or stem attachment occur (fig. 12.6). Sprouts growing close together, for example, create pressure against themselves or the trunk. This scenario can cause localized dead spots, infections and fractures.

Horizontal sprout growth that turns vertically increases the chance of failure due to weight and leverage. Sprouts may be squeezed off by trunk growth, or may dislodge because the trunk is rotting. Even when there are no defects, it takes years for epicormic sprouts to become stable branches.

Adventitious sprouts start from injuries, and despite compartmentalization, injuries lead to infections and defects. At best, the tree's defense process resists the spread of decay. In general, elite sprouts growing off rotting stems don't become structurally stable branches.

A sprout will also become unstable if the attachment position develops included bark. The barrier zone at the base of an adventitious sprout separates new growth from defective wood, but the potential for internal cracks and decay increase over time. Diminished space to store energy reserves is also a factor.

Some tree species naturally produce a lot of sprouts while other species don't. The abundance and position of sprout growth from preformed buds on healthy trees is a natural characteristic influenced by genetics and space. Certain individuals within a species are predisposed to produce more sprouts than others.

Conditions and events causing disruptions or stress trigger responses that alter sprouting characteristics. Some burls (an enclosed woody tumor), for example, produce sprout clusters. Epicormic sprouts often form when the survival of the tree or its parts is threatened. Although sprouts, in terms of energy, are expensive to produce, successful ones benefit trees. Foliage increases the absorption surface and manufactures photosynthates for the localized area and the tree system in general.

Recognizing sprout types and understanding their implications provides a means to assess a tree's condition. A structural fracture, bent stem, or dying tree section are examples of events that trigger sprouting (fig. 12.7). The sprouts are symptoms of the event. Sprout clusters develop behind the defects. A few elite sprouts may, over time, succeed as new stems.

Epicormic sprouting is relatively common in city trees. Harsh conditions and management procedures can stimulate sprouting. Curbside trees beneath utility lines offer an example of how trees in challenging locations that have been pruned back on many occasions produce an abundance of stress-associated sprouts.

Injurious pruning practices also tend to stimulate sprout growth (fig. 12.8). Examples include topping trees, internodal cuts, flush cuts, excessive removal of live branches, stripping sprouts off limbs, and cutting into barrier zones. Stress-induced sprouts often grow rapidly, which increases the need for additional pruning.

FIG. 12.7 Serviceberry (*Amelanchier* spp.). Bent and dying trunk stem triggered sprouting.

FIG. 12.8 Internodal pruning cut of Chinese Elm (*Ulmus parvifolia*). Note epicormic sprout cluster.

Practical options for pruning that cause less problems and involve less effort and expense should be encouraged. Start training trees when they are young. Thin sprouts incrementally. The remaining sprouts contain growth regulators that will help to suppress additional sprouting. Summer pruning tends to minimize sprouting, whereas fall or winter pruning tends to stimulates it.

In certain scenarios, pruning an entire limb may be the most practical way to minimize sprouting. Aim to make accurate cuts close to collars without injuring them. Avoid cutting into existing barrier zone boundaries. Tree work can be dangerous and should be performed by qualified professionals. Remember: safety first, never take chances, avoid electric lines, and comply with local laws.

❦

Coniferous trees, with few exceptions, don't form epicormic sprouts. Sprouts develop from preformed buds (see fig. 14.1). Should a terminal sprout be injured or pruned, lateral sprout growth will accelerate. Shearing and tip-pruning techniques, associated with ornamental gardening, exploit this tendency in order to produce bushy trees and shrubs with a desired shape.

Most conifers have scaly buds with evergreen leaves that vary from small scales to elongated needles. Several genera of the cypress family (Cupressaceae) — such as Junipers (*Juniperus*), Arborvitae (*Thuja*), and False-Cypress (*Chamaecyparis*) — produce no conspicuous buds or distinctive nodes. Tips covered with small immature leaves look similar in summer and winter. Immature cones are budlike and preformed on the tips of short branchlets. Distinctive cones (berrylike on Juniper) mature within one to two seasons, depending on the species.

🌳

Epicormic sprouts often grow from the stumps of cut deciduous trees. Stump sprouts can become stable trees (fig. 12.9). Adventitious sprouts grow off the exposed cambial zone. Sprouts from meristematic points develop from the wood of the trunk base or woody roots.

At first, the root system of a cut tree is still alive and able to support sprout growth. New sprouts must develop quickly in order to support the current root system or establish a new one. Starch reserves dwindle within a few years and, without a continued supply of energy, pathogens have easy access to the defenseless (dying) root system.

Other limitations of stump sprouts concern structural issues of weak stem attachments or self-wounding growth patterns. Rot isn't usually a concern, because compartmentalized boundaries resist the spread from the stump into the new sprouts. Sprouts off low-cut stumps, growing most rapidly upright, tend to have the best chance of becoming a successful tree. Twin or multi-trunk trees growing from stump sprouts are common in second-growth forest stands. They have a greater potential for structural failure than single-trunk trees.

Epicormic sprout growth, as mentioned, is a stimulated survival response to stress. The sprouts, once formed, provide food (energy) for the tree. Misleading terminology for this growth creates confusion. The words *sucker, water*

FIG. 12.9 Trees that grew from stump sprouts.

sprout, or *excess growth* are not appropriate terms to describe sprouts or their growth.

✿

PITH is a nonwoody, pulpy, parenchymatous, short-lived tissue in the biological center of aerial stems; roots have no pith. At first, the bulk of new growth from buds is pith tissue. It acts to stabilize newly forming sprout structures that, composed of soft tissues, are simular to annual plants. The large balloon-like pith cells often contain chlorophyll.

As sprouts mature and become woody, pith cells lose their living contents and dry out. The pith is compressed from the surrounding woody growth and shrinks somewhat in diameter (fig. 12.10). The pith of a few tree species disintegrates, leaving a hollow chamber; Princess-tree (*Paulownia tomentosa*), for example. The pith is not continuous through a tree.

A bud sprout has its own pith that doesn't connect with the pith of an associated twig or branch. A protective plug forms at the base of the terminal bud and the lateral buds. The PITH PLUG is a nonconductive wedge of compacted thick-walled cells that contains a high level of phenol or terpene compounds. It's a primary protection boundary in trees, separating the piths of a bud, twig, branch and trunk. A protective sheath (membrane) also surrounds the pith, separating it from the xylem (fig. 12.11).

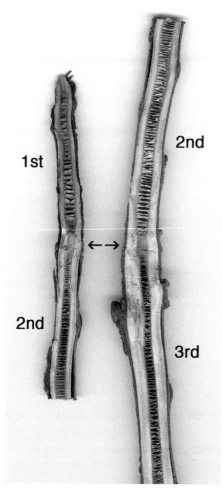

1st

2nd

2nd

3rd

FIG. 12.10 Dried Black Walnut (*Juglans nigra*) sample with three years' growth. Arrows indicate pith plugs (annual partitions). Note pith diameter change during growth period.

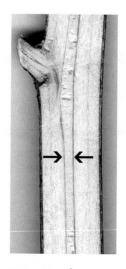

FIG. 12.11 Arrows indicate sheath that separates pith from xylem.

FIG. 12.12 Distinctive red pith, Kentucky Coffeetree (*Gymnocladus dioicus*).

Tree species have distinct and often interesting pith characteristics (fig. 12.12). Oaks (*Quercus*) with a star-shaped pith come to mind, as does Walnut (*Juglans*) with a chambered pith. Dissections through the pith, at a terminal bud or at twig/branch junctions, show the pith plug and contrasting gradations of pith texture, color and size. The pith, or lack of it, indicates where trunk and root tissues meet, because roots have no pith.

13

Bark

BARK is the outer boundary layers of a tree. Made up of living, dying and dead cells, it includes all tissues outside the vascular cambium. Bark is a physical barrier covering and protecting the inner workings of the tree. It keeps moisture in, and is a strong deterrent to insects and other pathogens. Bark is a center for fundamental biological activities, including the movement of food and other organic compounds. It's subdivided into two parts: PHLOEM (inner bark) and PERIDERM (outer bark; fig. 13.1).

Secondary growth in trees refers to expansion in diameter, rather than height or length. The vascular cambium produces a greater volume of secondary xylem than secondary phloem (i.e., trees produce more wood than bark). Wood cells inside the cambial zone are trapped in a permanent position, whereas bark cells on the outside are always on the move. Boundaries formed in wood are more or less stable, while bark boundaries hold for as little as a single growth season.

Stress from seasonal growth causes bark tissues to stretch and tear. New outer bark cells form to compensate for growth expansion. The cells have a physical and chemical composition resistant to moisture, insects, microorganisms, and most natural environmental threats. When bark openings occur, even if small and only for brief periods, they allow pathogens access to the inside of the tree.

The thin, outermost protective bark layer of a young stem or root is the EPIDERMIS. Outer epidermal cells secrete CUTIN, a waxy substance forming the CUTICLE, or the surface layer. The epidermis contains STOMATA (openings for gas exchange), but far fewer than the epidermis of a leaf. The layer of soft spongy tissue beneath the epidermis of a stem is the CORTEX. Defined as primary tissue, it has an outer layer of COLLENCHYMA, which are pliable elongated cells that provide support. The majority of cortex cells are PARENCHYMA, thin-walled cells with living contents. In aerial stems the cortex contains chloroplasts with chlorophyll that are photosynthetic. Parenchyma store, synthesize and transfer intracellular substances. All tree cells start alive and all living cells are connected (see fig. 11.14).

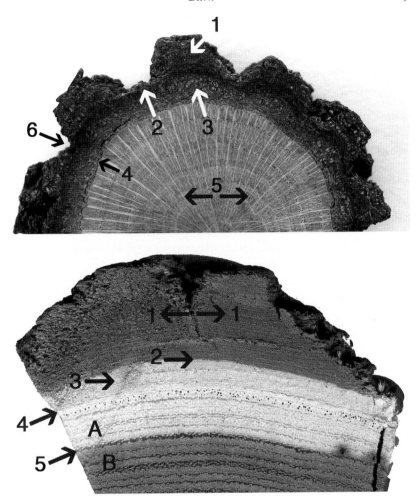

FIG. 13.1 Oak (*Quercus* spp.) at top, and Black Locust (*Robinia pseudoacacia*) below show (1) phellem; (2) phellogen; (3) phloem; (4) cambial zone; (5) xylem, (A) sapwood, (B) heartwood; (6) fissure. Note sclereids visible in bark of Oak.

The vascular cambium is the origin of phloem and its short lived sieve elements. Primary phloem is pushed outward by secondary phloem. Growth pressure causes soft, thin-walled cells — including sieve elements and intercellular spaces — to be crushed and compacted. Supportive thick-walled phloem fibers (SCLERENCHYMA) remain.

Secondary phloem is subdivided into two parts: nonconducting (older) and conducting (younger). Phloem transport moves and unloads photosynthates (energy-containing substances) in a basipetal direction through the current season's sieve elements. This movement demands energy. Materials are pumped and squeezed under pressure into and through connected living cells by their own metabolic actions. Gravity is not a major force in phloem transport.

🌳

The initial epidermis is progressively destroyed and replaced by thicker bark layers, collectively called the PERIDERM (outer bark). This protective group of tissues is composed of three parts: phellem, phellogen and phelloderm. The bark cambium (PHELLOGEN) is the secondary meristem of the periderm. It produces tough, corky bark (PHELLEM) on the outside, and PHELLODERM — a thin, membrane-like boundary layer of parenchyma tissue — on the inside.

RAYS are the thick sheets of radial parenchyma cells (see chaps. 17 & 19). They're produced by the vascular cambium in the cambial zone to form phloem rays on the outside and xylem rays on the inside. Radial parenchyma (rays) form a living connection between wood (secondary xylem) and the inner bark (phloem). Phloem rays thicken and bifurcate (flare) to keep pace with increasing circumferential growth (fig. 13.2). They supply nutrients to the phellogen.

Phellem cells are arranged in compacted rows. They have thick inner walls with alternating layers of fatty acids of suberin and waxes. Phellem is the first line of protection for a tree. It's highly impermeable to water and resistant to decay.

🌳

LENTICELS are a small, pulpy zone of intercellular spaces between the periderm and the phloem (see fig. 11.15). These openings allow for the exchange of gases between internal tissue and the atmosphere. This exchange is required for metabolic processes in living cells containing chlorophyll.

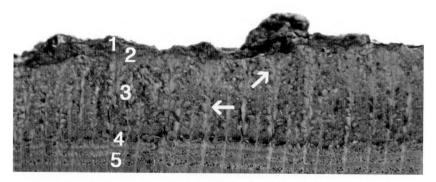

FIG. 13.2 Red Oak (*Quercus rubra*) sample shows phloem rays (*arrows*). Note: cambial zone (4) also produces xylem rays (*below*). Numbers correspond to Fig. 13.1.

FIG. 13.3 Mature White Ash (*Fraxinus americana*) with fissured bark.

Lenticels are common to twigs and trees with thin bark, such as Birch (*Betula*). Lenticels are small, with species-specific characteristics. In general, they're raised, oval-shaped, horizontally oriented areas. Lenticels are produced by the phellogen as secondary growth alters the epidermis of maturing stems. Often they're positioned below the initial site of epidermal stoma openings. Lenticels become less efficient over time. On older stems with thickening bark, they're plugged or shed with layers of exfoliating bark. Lenticels continue in areas of newly forming periderm and along fissures.

FISSURES are narrow, naturally occurring vertical gaps in the phellem, and are associated with growth (fig. 13.3). They're a normal bark feature of mature trunks and branches of numerous tree species, such as Red Oak (*Quercus rubra*) and Tuliptree (*Liriodendron tulipifera*). Regardless of the thickness of outer bark, the maximum depth of a fissure will terminate at the phellogen. Chlorophyll containing tissue is often present in these sites, and contributes photosynthates to the localized region.

Bark cracks are not fissures. They're a generalized condition ranging from superficial exfoliation of outer bark sections to serious structural splits and defects related to health problems or wounds. Dead roots or branches, acute dryness, canker infections and internal trunk defects can cause bark cracks.

Axial cells of both the vascular cambium and phellogen divide in a periclinal and anticlinal direction. Cells building in front of or behind each other (PERICLINAL GROWTH) increases diameter. Cells building side by side (ANTICLINAL GROWTH) expands circumference. Smoother bark patterns occur when periclinal and anticlinal cell division of the phellogen are more or less even and keep pace with the expanding growth of the vascular cambium (fig. 13.4). Fragmented patterns of textured outer bark result where periclinal cell division of the phellogen is more prevalent.

Thousands of tree species exist worldwide, and each has its own bark identity. Characteristics vary during different growth stages and in different environmental settings; however, specific features are consistent enough to offer a method of tree identification. Many trees, as they grow, naturally exfoliate (shed) bark (fig. 13.5). Comparing mature trunk bark to the young bark on branches gives a sense of how aging alters characteristics. Observing color variations and texture helps to distinguish the bark of different trees. Examples of bark patterns range from ridged with furrowed fissures to thick plated slabs, shaggy with fibrous strips to thin curling layers, and coarse with bumps to relatively smooth.

FIG. 13.4 Smooth, lenticellate bark pattern, Birchbark Cherry (*Prunus serrula*).

FIG. 13.5 Exfoliating bark on Paperbark Maple (*Acer griseum*).

Diverse communities of organisms live in association with tree bark. Some of them are pathogenic, but the majority are not. A wide variety of fungi, bacteria and epiphytes grow on bark. Lichens, Mosses and Algae cause no known harm to bark and may offer benefits not yet recognized (fig. 13.6). Crevices and layers of bark offer ideal protection for insects, their eggs or cocoons. Many insects assist with pollination or attract other wildlife that in some way benefit trees. Beetles are provided protection by bark as they help break down weak and defective trees. Tree ecology relies on diversity.

Unanswered questions remain regarding the processes and properties of bark, such as the electrical insulating capacity of bark and how it ties into the overall design of the tree system.

The tissues of secondary phloem are involved in the transport of PHOTOSYN-THATES, organic compounds produced by photosynthesis. Zones of soft, living tissue make up the SIEVE ELEMENTS, or transport cells. The cells often lack a nucleus and are sustained by contact (axial) and radial parenchyma. Sieve elements in conifers are sieve cells with perforated sieve areas. In angiosperms they're referred to as sieve tube elements and have specialized end walls called sieve plates. Both systems have randomly aligned pores. Sieve pores are tiny channel openings linking the transport cells to each other.

FIG. 13.6 Lichens, Mosses and other organisms live on tree bark.

PHLOEM FIBERS (sometimes referred to as hard bast) are composed of an aggregate of thick-walled cells that provide rigidity and strength within the phloem. The two types are fibers and sclereids (see fig. 13.1). Both are from SCLERENCHYMA: support tissue derived from enlarged parenchyma with thick, lignified walls.

Fibers are the primary type. These strong cells are generally long and slender, and occur in strands or bundles. Sclereids (also called stone cells) are generally more stout but less numerous, and they vary in shape (round, box, star, branched). They appear singly or in aggregates and are more prevalent in the outer phloem layers.

Sclereids are also found in nut and seed shells. Depending on species, outer cell walls may contain crystals (calcium oxalate or silicate) or other chemical deposits. Successive phloem layers form patterns characteristic to specific tree species. Increments of annual growth in the phloem can be dated, but unlike wood rings, they're difficult to decipher.

The two major components of bark are the phloem and the periderm (as previously described). They are interconnected and adjust, as a unit, to biological and structural changes caused by growth. The phloem is affected by compression forces, and the periderm is affected by tension forces. Induced by these forces, the maturation of bark involves physiological processes that result in physical change.

Bark cells, under a strong genetic influence, alter their contents to a more protective state. Sieve elements form callose (insoluble carbohydrate) blockages and cease to function. Sieve elements and the spaces between them are squeezed under pressure and collapse. Sclerification of phloem fibers thickens and strengthens cell walls. Tangential stretching associated with growth triggers the dilation of radial phloem rays.

At the time of peak expansion, seasonal growth can cause minute tears in bark tissue. The phellogen produces phellem to compensate for increases. Phellem (cork) cells start alive but are short-lived. They're built of substances with strong structural and protective qualities. Suberin, for example, is a lipid material that resists water and rot. Layers of these cells form tree-specific bark textures and patterns. RHYTIDOME is the technical term for dead layers of outer bark.

Trees are in a state of constant change, and the bark system emphasizes this point. It's on the move, generating new living cells, while at the same time altering aging cells and positioning dead tissue. Contact and radial parenchyma undergo swelling, which aids the collapse of aging sieve elements and the formation of dilated rays. The rays are directly associated with the phellogen and assist in transferring organic compounds.

The concept of waste doesn't apply to the tree system. Trees incorporate by-products to benefit survival. As aging sieve elements cease to function in bark, specialized parenchyma cells sequester and synthesize metabolites into protective compounds. Examples include resins, gums, tannins and crystals, which are resistant or toxic to pathogens. Certain conifers form resin ducts in their bark from enlarged parenchyma, or resins secreted into intercellular spaces.

14   Transport System

TRANSPORT SYSTEM refers to the movement of liquids and materials in solution throughout the tree. It's a complex subject to discuss, because it involves all aspects of the tree's biological system and environmental influences. The system has no beginning or end, and all phases are important for proper function.

The transport system is not a circulatory system, because its contents don't flow. Materials are pumped, pulled or squeezed in a liquid state from compartment to compartment. Transport is an energy-dependent action. The movement of substances in solution towards the base (basipetal) occurs with phloem transport. The movement of elements in solution towards the top (acropetal) occurs with xylem transport. The point of origin for materials is referred to as the SOURCE, and the areas of assimilation are the SINKS.

Tree physiological functions are continuous. The motion (dynamic equilibrium) involves opposing forces and occurs at a steady rate. The tree system adjusts its equilibrium as processes fluctuate. The production and distribution of sugar in leaves, for example, varies between times of daylight and darkness. Energy is required for any movement into, out of, or within the SYMPLAST, the network of connected living cells throughout a tree. The intercellular spaces, static cells and inert areas surrounding the symplast are collectively called the APOPLAST.

ROOT ABSORPTION begins as water with essential (inorganic) elements in solution is absorbed through nonwoody roots and moves by apoplastic loading through the walls of static epidermal cells. The EPIDERMIS of a root is the outer skinlike membrane layer. The cell walls have a waxy cover, but the cover offers little resistance to the passage.

The ENDODERMIS is the inner layer of cells forming a sheath around the vascular tissues. The primary cell walls have a suberin boundary called the CASPARIAN STRIP that makes the cells impermeable to water. These cells are the boundary of the symplastic pathway. Movement into and through living cells uses stored energy. The solution crosses a plasma (cytoplasmic) membrane of endodermal cells attached to the Casparian strips.

Cells have pit openings through which minute cytoplasmic strands of living material (PLASMODESMATA) pass. They connect the protoplasts of adjacent living cells. As the solution moves further into the transport system, it passes through the PERICYCLE (parenchymatous layer within the endodermis) into the STELE (vascular tissue).

PHLOEM TRANSPORT is the movement of photosynthates (organic compounds) in solution from the leaves towards the roots. The source-to-sink pattern transports the sugar-based compounds to sites in tissues for metabolic use or storage. Storage tissues then serve as sources for the export of material to other sites (sinks).

OSMOSIS is an important factor in phloem transport through the movement (diffusion) of water across a semipermeable plasma membrane, from a dilute solution to a more concentrated solution (see chap. 28). Leaves pump material in solution into the interconnected conducting pores of phloem cells called SIEVE ELEMENTS. These living cells are filled with and surrounded by water, resulting in high TURGOR PRESSURE, to the point that the slightly elastic cell walls can no longer expand. Material is moved (squeezed) into the next connecting sieve element. The movements expend energy, as does unloading materials into other areas of the symplast towards and into the roots.

The phloem moves large volumes of water throughout the tree. Concentrations of sugars at the sources cause water to follow. Osmosis can occur into or out of a cell. Higher sugar concentrations in cells are maintained by turgor pressure and OSMOTIC PRESSURE, the pressure necessary to stop osmosis. The removal by use or storage of SUCROSE (the transport sugar) increases water potential at the sink areas. Returned water is reintroduced in the xylem and the transpiration stream.

WATER is essential for all organisms (life) and most biological processes. It provides a fluid environment for cells and transport for molecules in and out of cells. The molecular structure of water is key to its ability to move materials. Water owes its liquid state to the presence of minute hydrogen atoms with lone pairs of electrons on the oxygen atom. The strong power of oxygen to attract electrons causes water molecules to link together by forming HYDROGEN BONDS: intermolecular bonds between polar molecules in which hydrogen is bound to a strongly (stronger) electronegative element.

Water is a POLAR MOLECULE, meaning that the position of shared electrons in a molecule is closer to one atom than to another. This makes it nonsymmetrical, with a partial negative charge and a resulting partial positive charge in its opposite sphere. The molecules cluster together by virtue of a network of hydrogen bonds, and so move as a mobile liquid instead of independently as a gas.

Cellulose is abundant in fiber cells. The FIBER SATURATION POINT is reached when inner walls of the fiber cells become saturated with free water (the liquid state). Apoplastic loading is the force (pressure) moving water into fiber cell walls. BOUND WATER is a chemical state where water vapor molecules bond (hydrogen bonding) to the surfaces of cellulose and hemicellulose microfibrils. Hydrogen on the water molecule bonds to the negative position of the oxygen atom on the hydroxyls ($-OH$) that stick out from cellulose.

FUNCTIONAL GROUPS are chemically active parts of organic molecules (a group of atoms) that impart a certain set of properties to organic compounds. Examples include the hydroxyl group $-OH$ (alcohols) and the carboxyl group COOH (organic acids). In the cell wall, bound water is a storage product with protective and stabilizing properties. Water occupying spaces along and between cellulose makes it difficult for pathogens to become established. The hydrogen bonds of bound water do release but are somewhat tenacious, which helps stabilize shrinking and drying tendencies when conditions become dry from heat or lowered humidity.

Water is a constant component of trees. It's present and continuously processed in the symplast and held and moved in the apoplast. Vessels and tracheids of the xylem facilitate long-distance transport of free water from the soil to the leaf through several forces. COHESION is the connection of water molecules to each other. Water molecules are connected together by hydrogen bonding, and because of the intrinsic characteristics of these polar molecules (nonsymmetrical in shape with partial charges), they tend to clump together, resulting in a strong unit force. The classic teardrop shape or the way water beads up on surfaces after rain are familiar examples of cohesion. ADHESION is the sticking or clinging together of differing substances. Tree vessels and tracheids are small capillaries with textured inner walls in which a column of water, in a cohesive state, adheres.

TRANSPIRATION is the loss of water from the surface of a plant. Most water taken in by tree roots is lost in the air as water vapor through stoma openings of leaves. Stomata open to take in carbon dioxide from the atmosphere and, while open, intercellular water evaporates (transpires). Water molecules adhere to the capillary walls, forming long cohesive columns of water. As water exits the stomata, the columns are pulled (move) intact. These three combined forces, and the small capillaries in trees, are the reasons water stays intact for long distances without (or rarely) developing disabling embolisms, and contribute to the ability of trees to grow tall.

Transpiration creates tension pressure (negative pressure). The transport system is under tension pressure for the majority of the year. This is why

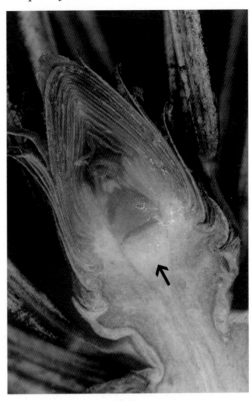

FIG. 14.1 Colorado Spruce
(*Picea pungens*) with dissected
bud. Arrow centered in starch-
rich zone behind bud (not
I_2KI stained). *Photo Alex Shigo.
Courtesy Shigo & Trees, Associates.*

pruned limbs don't usually release water. The water column, under tension,
recedes below the cut surface.

🌳

The startup of buds in the spring is a prime component of the tree's transport
system. Biochemical chain reactions associated with the activation of buds
drives the system, in a sense. The traditional belief assumes roots do. Although
positive root pressure exists in some trees in early spring, it's only an indirect
mechanism of moving water (see below). Conifers don't develop positive root
pressure.

BUDS are preformed structures (fig. 14.1). They don't store starch; however,
there is a starch-rich zone at their base. STARCH is found only in living cells.
It's a polysaccharide, and therefore insoluble in water.

A combination of factors in the spring, including intensified sunlight and
rising temperatures, contribute to the activity of PHYTOCHROME, a protein-
based pigment found in low concentrations in most plant cells. It participates
in the transport of electrons during biochemical reactions. The pigment helps
activate AMYLASE, an enzyme involved with the conversion of starch to sugar.

In this reaction (the hydrolysis of starch), glycosidic bonds holding polysaccharides together are broken (glycolysis), yielding a soluble sugar. The small amount of water present with the sugar makes for a concentrated sugar solution. The more concentrated the solution, the higher the osmotic pressure.

High osmotic pressure pulls bound water off cellulose and free water becomes available. The food (sugar) and water at the base of buds allow them to open and grow. Leaves, in turn, produce photosynthates and facilitate transpiration, which (as previously described) is a primary component of the transport system. Cut stems of *Forsythia*, for example, brought indoors in early spring and placed in water will produce flowers and some foliage without help from the roots.

Few trees move organic molecules (sugars) in the xylem, and those that do, do so only briefly in early spring. (Phloem transport is the primary means by which organic substances are moved.) This interesting phenomenon occurs only in certain deciduous trees, and is restricted to a comparatively short period within the tree's annual cycle. It ceases as phloem transport and tran-

FIG. 14.2 Plastic jugs on Sugar Maples (*Acer saccharum*) collecting sap.

spiration increase later in the spring. The occurrence is more prevalent in diffuse porous trees; for example, Maples (*Acer*) and Birches (*Betula*).

A combination of factors is involved. The relatively closed tree system and saturated ground create a positive pressure gradient. The water continuum in vessel elements is influenced by temperature variances (freezing nights, mild days). Phloem transport is low prior to the formation of leaves, but water pressure is increasing. Buds have not yet opened, but seasonal conversion of stored starch to sugar has begun. The higher concentration of sugar draws water. Contact parenchyma that line vessels secrete sugar during this brief period, primarily in the form of sucrose. Water helps break the glycosidic bond in sucrose to yield glucose (sugary sap). Drilled holes or other stem wounds at this time release apoplastic pressure. Sap flows out of the openings in a manner similar to a pinhole in a water filled ballon.

Tree sap is a generic term referring to fluids inside a tree. Its release from a wound in an outward direction is a protective feature that helps prevent pathogens from entering the tree. Tree sap is primarily water, and its external flow is not injurious to the tree, but the wound itself is an injury. Living cells surrounding a wound respond to defend the tree. Defensive actions include plugging vessels, producing antimicrobial substances, and forming a barrier zone. Contact parenchyma surrounding exposed vessels alter their cellular contents and excrete plugging substances. Chemicals that prolong sap flow, such as paraformaldehyde, do so by killing contact parenchyma. The flow of sap through a wound opening can range from heavy in spring in certain species, such as Sugar Maple (*Acer saccharum*), to nonexistent in others (fig. 14.2).

15   Elements, pH and Soil

ELEMENTS are the basic building blocks of the universe. Composed of one kind of atom, they can't be broken down into simpler substances by ordinary chemical means. There are about 92 naturally occurring elements on earth, each with its own name and properties.

ATOMS are the smallest part of an element that can exist as a stable entity. The science of chemistry examines the arrangements and properties of atoms. MOLECULES are two or more atoms that are chemically bonded together into a definite geometrical arrangement. A molecule of an element is when the combining atoms are the same. COMPOUNDS are chemical combinations of atoms of different elements that form a substance.

Elements are not organic or an energy source, but are fundamental to the composition and function of living organisms. Trees are composed of 16 to 18 elements. Referred to as ESSENTIAL ELEMENTS, they're indispensable for normal growth and maintenance. A macroelement refers to one required in relatively large quantities: carbon (C), hydrogen (H), oxygen (O), nitrogen (N), sulfur (S), phosphorus (P), potassium (K), magnesium (Mg) and calcium (Ca). The others are referred to as microelements. Although small in quantity, they shouldn't be called minor, because the tree's life processes couldn't function without them. These are manganese (Mn), iron (Fe), molybdenum (Mo), chlorine (Cl), zinc (Zn), boron (B) and copper (Cu) plus, in certain trees, sodium (Na) and nickel (Ni).

The first six major elements (C, H, O, N, P, & S) are the basic chemicals of life, making up about 99 percent of a tree's dry weight. Essential elements alone do not provide a source of energy or nutrition. Trees do not derive nutrition from the soil. They acquire nutrients by capturing sunlight and using its energy to combine atmospheric carbon dioxide (CO_2) with essential elements and water from the soil to form carbon-based molecules (see chap. 27). NUTRIENTS are substances that supply energy (nutrition), such as starch and oils.

Elements derived from soil come from organic matter decomposition, weathering of particles, environmental deposits, and nitrogen fixation. All essential elements except carbon and oxygen are absorbed by roots as IONS (charged particles) dissolved in water. CATIONS are ions with a positive charge and ANIONS are ions with a negative charge. Particles with opposite charges attract each other; those with like charges repel each other. Cations and anions, having opposite charges, attract each other and form IONIC BONDS. Ionic bonding is the method by which elements enter the tree.

Ions are absorbed by trees at exchange sites located along the rhizoplane, the root-soil interface. Absorption utilizes stored energy as ions are taken in from the soil; other ions are released from the tree. Soil conditions such as pH extremes (too high, too low) or moisture extremes (too dry, too wet) affect the availability of elements. Ions (elements) don't provide energy.

SOIL is the top layer of the earth's crust that is suitable for the support of biological activity, including plant growth. Soil consists of a vast number of living organisms, dead organic matter, water, air and elements of rocks (sand, silts and clay). The SOIL HORIZON refers to the vertical succession of fairly distinct layers, each with different properties, referred to as the A, B and C horizons.

The A horizon is the uppermost organic layer (forest layer, topsoil) and has the most intense biological activity. HUMUS, part of the A horizon, is decomposing organic matter produced by the action of soil bacteria and fungi on plant and animal substances. Humus enhances the water-holding, air-exchange and cation-exchange capacities of soil.

The B horizon is the subsoil layer containing materials leached down from above or brought up from the level below. There is less biological activity than in the topsoil. The C horizon is the soil base weathered from the underlying rocks.

SOIL TEXTURE refers to the size of particles. SOIL STRUCTURE describes the arrangement and organization of soil particles. CATION-EXCHANGE CAPACITY is a measure of the soil's ability to store positive ions.

SOILS are composed of solid particles and pore space. Up to 50 percent of the ideal total soil volume is pore space, which is occupied by air, water, and a rich diversity of living organisms. Soils are a mixture of particle sizes that are divided into texture classes ranging from coarse sand to fine clay. Plant life is diverse and adaptable enough to grow in soil extremes from dry sand, where water drains out quickly, to wet clays, where water moves slowly. LOAM refers to soils containing sand, silt and clay in proportions ideal for the widest variety of plant growth. The percentage of water that soil can hold against the force of gravity is its FIELD CAPACITY.

Management strategies for agriculture take into account the tolerance of plants for specific soil conditions. Negative environmental effects can result from the misuse or abuse of soil. Erosion, compaction and exposure to toxins are examples of events that alter soil structure and kill beneficial soil organisms.

CLAYS are fine-grained particles composed of alumina, silica and bound water. Kaolite, and most other clays, are a matrix of silica and alumina crystals held closely together with oxygen bonds. Montmorillinite, another type of clay, occurs when alumina lies between two layers of silica. The crystals are small, but the spaces are large with a capacity to readily absorb water and expand. When water is lost, shrinkage occurs rapidly.

❦

Many soil elements in solution form cations. Both clay and humus can have an excess of negative charges on their COLLOIDAL SURFACES (the surface of fine particles in soil solution) where cations can be bound. This helps to hold cations against the leaching action of percolating soil water. The bonds are weak, meaning cations can be replaced by other cations (CATIONIC EXCHANGE) and become available for plant absorption.

Respiring roots release CO_2 along the rhizoplane. Some CO_2 dissolves in soil solution, becoming CARBONIC ACID (H_2CO_3). Carbonic acid ionizes producing BICARBONATE IONS (HCO_3^-) and HYDROGEN IONS (H^+). The hydrated form of carbon dioxide is a bicarbonate ion plus a hydrogen ion $(H_2O + CO_2) = (HCO_3^-)(H^+)$. A hydrogen ion is a hydrogen proton. These protons (H^+) can exchange places with cations on the clay or humus.

Anions, like nitrate (NO_3^-), leach more readily because they don't bond to clay particles. An exception is phosphate, which doesn't leach readily, but forms an INSOLUBLE PRECIPITATE; that is, it chemically separates from a solution. Soil pH has an effect on the availability of elements for plant use. In an alkaline soil, for example, certain cation-forming elements (Fe, Mn, Cu, Zn) precipitate and become unavailable for absorption by plants.

🌳

The symbol pH refers to the concentration of hydrogen cations (H^+) and hydroxide anions (OH^-) in solution: p for power, H for concentration of hydrogen ions. The pH SCALE is the acid (acidity) or basic (alkalinity) strength of a solution expressed in terms of a number. The pH values represent logarithms (log). A log is an exponent; it can't be averaged. The scale is from 0 to 14; a difference of 1 in pH is equivalent to a tenfold difference in acid or base strength. The lower the number, the stronger the acid; the higher the number, the stronger the base.

A pH of 7 indicates an equal amount of H^+ and OH^- ions (neutral). In pure water there are 0.0000007 moles of H^+ (10^{-7} moles). A MOLE is the amount in grams for the molecular weight of a substance. Hydrogen has a molecular weight of one; a mole of hydrogen would be one gram of hydrogen in one liter

of water. A BUFFER is a solution that maintains a constant pH with the addition of either a weak acid or a weak base.

A SOLUTION is a mixture consisting of a solute dissolved in a solvent; for example, salt (solute) dissolved in water (solvent) results in a saltwater solution. It's transparent, homogeneous, and can pass through a membrane. COLLOIDS are mixtures consisting of tiny particles suspended in a liquid (usually water). The particles don't settle, are translucent (milky), and don't pass through membranes; protein is an example. A SUSPENSION is a substance that doesn't dissolve in solution. An example is sand in water; once you stop shaking the sand settles.

16   Roots

ROOTS, the underground portion of a tree, constitute an organ: a specialized system of tissues that provides structural support for the tree, absorbs water and essential elements, transports and synthesizes soluble substances, and stores energy containing substances. Roots are a major part of the entire tree system, in that the top and bottom of a tree are mutually dependent.

Tree root systems affect and are affected by the physical characteristics of the soil and terrain. In a forest setting they share space with a diversity of soil organisms and the roots of other vegetation. They are extensive, difficult to access, and fragile, which makes them technically and physically challenging to study, contributing to confusion and generalizations.

The two basic root types are woody and nonwoody. WOODY ROOTS make up the bulk of the root system. They support the tree and transport and store water with dissolved elements and soluble substances (fig. 16.1). NONWOODY ROOTS are associated with absorption and are located along the peripheral interface with the soil. Two types of specialized structures form on or in them: ROOT HAIRS, which are extensions of single epidermal cells, and MYCORRHIZAE, which are composed of tree and fungal tissue.

Woody roots share basic similarities with above-ground trunk and branch stems: both have an apical and vascular meristem; wood cell walls contain lignin, cellulose and hemicellulose; and bark cells are lined with suberin. There are also distinct anatomical and physiological differences (fig. 16.2): secondary growth starts in roots after it starts in aerial stems; the concentration of cell wall materials varies; and bark thickness below ground is thinner.

The following root characteristics distinguish them from aerial stems.

1. No chlorophyll in the cortex or in any other root tissue, because its production is dependent on light.
2. No buds: roots grow from meristematic tissue, including meristematic points.
3. No heartwood: roots don't form genetically controlled protection wood.

FIG. 16.1 Dried woody root samples (3.5 cm diameter) illustrate how root characteristics vary between species. Oak (*Quercus* spp.) at left, bark layers and rays visible. Tuliptree (*Liriodendron tulipifera*) at right, bark removed, has smaller and more numerous vessels and rays.

FIG. 16.2 Comparison between an Oak aerial stem (*right*) and woody root (*left*). (Not I_2KI stained.)

4. No pith: pith is a specialized primary tissue of emerging aerial stems that assists with support, and is the demarcation indicator between the trunk and roots.

5. Growth increments are not as distinctive in root wood as they are in trunk wood.

6. Lower lignin content: supported by the soil, roots require less rigidity and compression strength.

7. Roots can't make or absorb food: they depend on leaves and translocated photosynthates for nutrition.

8. Root wood has a greater percentage of parenchyma cells and transport elements.

9. Higher concentrations of starch: I_2KI (iodine in potassium iodide) starch test comparisons show darker staining in root wood than in trunk wood, especially around vessels.

10. The root system is active in the fall and winter: even beneath frozen ground, nonwoody roots grow and are functioning.

NONWOODY ROOTS are tree organs that facilitate absorption of water and essential elements in solution. Located in the region of cell elongation and differentiation, they contain little lignin and no corky bark. Nonwoody roots have a two-part boundary layer specially suited for absorption and the selective release of compounds associated with biochemical synthesis and respiration.

The EPIDERMIS is the outermost layer of cells. Water moves through epidermal spaces and cells by apoplastic loading, an abiotic force (pressure). The ENDODERMIS is the inner membrane-like layer that has suberin-lined cells. The protective, waterproof suberin barrier is known as the CASPARIAN STRIP. Absorption at this point moves the solution through the plasma membrane of living cells. Movement of substances in or out of the symplast (living) network is an action requiring the use of stored energy.

The solution next moves through the pericycle into the transport system. The PERICYCLE is a meristematic, parenchymatous layer within the endodermis and forms the outermost layer of the STELE, the vascular tissue of a root (or stem).

🌳

ROOT HAIRS consist of tubular extensions of epidermal cells (fig. 16.3). They greatly increase the absorption surface of nonwoody roots. Root hairs grow when conditions are suitable; they live for only a short time, a few days to a few weeks. They decline, die and shed in place. Sections (sheets) of the epidermis also shed in association with the growth of nonwoody roots (fig. 16.4). Shedding helps to build a healthy soil environment by adding an important source of organic material to the rhizosphere.

FIG. 16.3 Eastern Hemlock (*Tsuga canadensis*) nonwoody root with root hairs and a developing ectomycorrhiza (bulge). *Photo Alex Shigo. Courtesy Shigo & Trees, Associates.*

FIG. 16.4 Epidermal shedding. *Photo Alex Shigo. Courtesy Shigo & Trees, Associates.*

FIG. 16.5 Mycorrhizae
(nonwoody roots) in
winter. *Photo Alex Shigo.*
Courtesy Shigo & Trees,
Associates.

Root hairs are more common in young trees than in mature trees. They're fragile and won't survive or develop in sufficient numbers if their habitat is disturbed. It's inaccurate to refer to small, thread-sized roots as root hairs. Root hairs, which can number in the millions, are cell extensions and not the entire root section. It's also incorrect to refer to nonwoody roots as feeder roots. Roots can't feed as they don't have the capacity to derive nutrition (a food/energy source) from the soil.

Root growth is thought to be a continuous process stalled only by periodic conditions such as drought or the absence of oxygen. Woody root growth occurs in sequence with branch and trunk wood growth. Nonwoody growth is more continuous and becomes particularly active in the fall and winter (fig. 16.5). Trees, in a sense, are on 24/7 with components that undergo dormant cycles.

Root growth is influenced by genetics and environmental conditions. In dry climates with sandy soil, roots are inclined to grow deep. In soils with an organic top layer and a clay or rock-based subsoil, growth tends to be more lateral with relatively shallow absorbing roots. Lateral spread can be several times that of the crown spread.

FIG. 16.6 Surface roots of Red Spruce (*Picea rubens*) in a rocky area.

FIG. 16.7 Girdling root.

Root growth patterns aren't necessarily symmetrically distributed around the trunk. Roots grow where conditions are advantageous, as they compete for space and resources. The presence of woody surface roots can be a result of low-oxygenated soil (fig. 16.6). Compacted and saturated soil conditions foster surface roots.

GIRDLING ROOTS are woody roots that cause constrictions to trunk stems and other roots by growing over or around them. Seasonal woody growth of stems and roots progressively increases pressure at contact positions as they expand in girth (fig. 16.7). Girdling roots occur in any tree setting, including forests. They are particularly common to urban trees, where adverse soil conditions and cultural practices contribute to their development.

The root system of a tree begins with the germination of a seed. This process is associated with water accumulation in the seed, and is influenced by temperature, oxygen availability, and genetic predisposition. The contents of seeds are utilized to fuel growth. The embryonic root, or RADICLE, is also known as the primary root. It provides support and initiates the absorption of water and soil elements. The transition from primary to secondary growth (see next section & chap. 17) increases the diameter of roots as the vascular meristem forms and functions. At this stage, the main root of a tree, or TAPROOT (fig. 16.8), anchors the tree with its downward growth habit and gives rise to lateral roots. The growth and basic role of a taproot is associated with young trees.

PRIMARY GROWTH is associated with the apical meristem. For roots, it initiates from pericycle (meristematic) tissue rather than from buds. All primary growth is nonwoody. New growth comes out of the tip of another root. The parent root is woody and covered by a protective calyx-like structure. The apical sprout is referred to as a PIONEER ROOT (fig. 16.9). It grows and elongates rapidly, and can be a few inches long with a diameter greater than the parent root. The pioneer will eventually become woody and form secondary branching roots. Root hairs seldom grow on pioneer roots.

   The tip of an emerging pioneer root is called the ROOTCAP. It's a mass of living parenchyma cells that helps to penetrate the soil and protect developing root tissue. Growth pushes the rootcap through the soil. It's short-lived peripheral cells are shed as new ones are added. Outer cells produce and secrete pectin or a pectin-like hydrated polysaccharide substance: a moist, gel-like lubricating material covering the rootcap called MUCIGEL. It combines with shed cells and associated soil bacteria attracted to the slimy mix.

SECONDARY GROWTH increases root girth and is associated with the vascular meristem. As apical elongation ceases, a gradual transition from primary to secondary growth occurs. Meristematic procambial cells between primary xylem and phloem initiate the vascular cambium. Suberin layers build behind the endodermis as external tissues begin to shed. Absorption components begin to close as root transport and storage potential increases. Symplastic pathways remain for movement of water and essential substances. Dividing cells in the cambial zone begin to mature and differentiate, forming secondary xylem and phloem. A corky periderm with a phellogen also develops. Lignin forms in the cell walls of xylem cells. Lignification is the quintessential

FIG. 16.8 The taproot is associated
with young trees. It develops from a
primary root (radicle) of a seed.

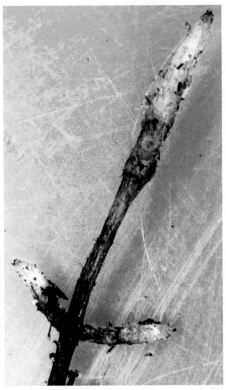

FIG. 16.9 Pioneer root. Note
rootcap at tip. *Photo Alex Shigo. Courtesy
Shigo & Trees, Associates.*

FIG. 16.10 Yellow-wood (*Cladrastis kentukea*) root shows secondary branching from meristematic points on parent stem. (White root unrelated.)

characteristic of secondary growth. Starch deposits build in wood by the end of the first growth cycle and reach full potential the following year.

SECONDARY ROOTS develop from the meristematic tissue of a woody root to form nonwoody roots. New growth that's infected by fungi forms nonwoody roots with mycorrhizae; if it's not infected, it forms nonwoody roots with root hairs. It's possible to have both on or in a different section of the same nonwoody root if the infection occurs after a root hair zone begins.

Nonwoody roots experience active growth in the fall and winter. A natural shedding cycle of mycorrhizae and root hairs occurs in the fall, somewhat in sync with leaf shedding and prior to the onset of new root growth. The process demands energy as it requires building an abscission layer with a protective membrane.

SECONDARY WOODY ROOTS, sometimes referred to as side or branching roots, come from meristematic points within woody roots (fig. 16.10). They begin as a noninfected nonwoody root. The growth process is simular to the previous description of pioneer roots and secondary growth. The rate of growth is slow during the first growth season because these root sprouts are newly developing under apical dominance by the parent root. By the second growth season, roots have formed independent apical tips and can grow a pioneer root and additional secondary roots.

The root growth cycle repeats annually, exponentially increasing the overall mass of the root system. The size of the root system is somewhat contingent on the size of a tree's crown. A dynamic oscillation exists between both areas as each part adjusts to changes in the other.

MYCORRHIZAE are nonwoody structures of nonwoody roots composed of tree and fungal tissues (see fig. 8.2). Mycorrhiza means a fungus root. They develop when fungi of specific mycorrhizal species infect emerging nonwoody roots. The resulting tissues are organized into a structural and functional unit. The structures consist of two basic types: ectomycorrhizae (external infections to the outermost cells) and endomycorrhizae (internal infections of the cells). A third type, ectendomycorrhizae, represents a gradation in characteristics between both.

A mycorrhiza is an organ of the tree that facilitates absorption of water and essential elements. It's also thought to have a protective role against root pathogens. Trees provide the fungi a source of carbohydrates and other organic compounds, such as vitamins and amino acids. The trees receive an enhanced absorption potential for water, and also for elements, especially those that are difficult to access, such as phosphorus, zinc and manganese. The beneficial association between mycorrhizal fungi and trees is an example of SYMBIOSIS: living together in a close mutual relationship. Fossil studies reveal that the mycorrhizal association goes back to the beginning, when plants first colonized land, and is believed to have had an integral role in tree evolution.

The fungal component of mycorrhizae forms HYPHAE (fig. 16.11). The hyphae are fine tubular filaments associated with absorption and bidirectional distribution of essential substances. Most hyphae secrete enzymes to predigest material for absorption. The hyphae of certain species are segmented by SEPTA, or cross-wall membrane partitions. Septa and other morphological characteristics help in identifying fungus species.

The branching hyphae network, called MYCELIUM, forms the vegetative body of a fungus. Mycelial groups of many species form visible, white, mat-like patches. Cell walls of the fungal component of mycorrhizae, and fungi in general, contain CHITIN, which is a tough but lightweight waterproof boundary material resistant to decay. Simular to cellulose, this structural polysaccharide differs in that it contains a nitrogen group. Chitin also makes up the exoskeleton of insects and crustaceans.

ENDOMYCORRHIZAE are the most widespread mycorrhizal type and occur in about 80 percent of all living plants. They consist of three general groups, of which two are small and limited to a few families of Ericales plants and

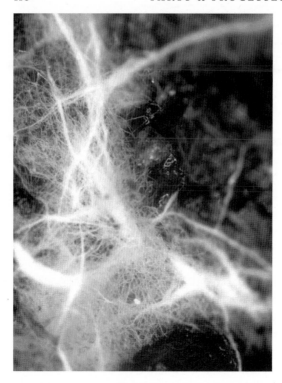

FIG. 16.11 Hyphae in soil.
Photo Alex Shigo. Courtesy Shigo
& Trees, Associates.

Orchids. VESICULAR-ARBUSCULAR MYCORRHIZAE (VAM) are the most prevalent group associated with both trees and the majority of other vascular plants. They develop inside nonwoody root cells and form substructures that support the bidirectional transfer and storage of metabolites and nutrients. Infected nonwoody roots are not changed in external color or shape. Subtle differences may include a smooth surface, from the lack of root hairs, and fine hypha whiskers. Precise identification requires viewing of stained sections with a microscope.

ARBUSCULES are multiple branched, feeding structures of the fungal element of an endomycorrhiza. They form exchange sites within the cell wall and around the peripheral region of the protoplast. They distort but do not breach the plasma membrane enclosing the protoplasm. VESICLES are the associated small vacuoles (spherical, fluid-filled sacks) thought to function as storage compartments.

The fungi associated with endomycorrhizae come from a somewhat limited number of species. Some are host-specific, while many others share multiple hosts. They produce large spores in roots and soil and have no above-ground fruit bodies. Spores are slowly disseminated by insects and other small animals, and to a lesser extent by leaching.

The longevity of mycorrhizae, although uncertain, is thought to be relatively short (a few weeks or months to a year) and tied to the phenological growth cycle of trees. Mycorrhizal fungi are naturally present in healthy soils. The species and population density vary between soil types and plant communities. A poor-quality soil habitat won't adequately support mycorrhizae.

ECTOMYCORRHIZAE are the other major type of mycorrhizae. The fungal element surrounds, rather than penetrates, a nonwoody root cell. Ectomycorrhizae are associated with various tree groups generally found in temperate regions. Member trees seem tolerant of harsh conditions. Tree families include Fagaceae (Beech, Oak), Salicaceae (Willow, Poplar), Juglandaceae (Walnut, Hickory), Betulaceae (Birch, Hornbeam), and Pinaceae (Pine, Spruce, Hemlock). Other tree and shrub groups worldwide have ectomycorrhizae, but the list is short: one of note is *Eucalyptus*. Ectomycorrhizae don't occur on nonwoody plants.

Hyphae of ectomycorrhizae grow between the epidermal cells, forming a fungus–root interface layer called the HARTIG NET. A sheathlike mantle of hyphae also covers the surface. Hypha filaments, extending from the mantle into the soil medium, greatly increase tree absorption potential. Mycelial strands grow between soil duff layers and decomposing leaves (fig. 16.12).

FIG. 16.12 Mycelial strands in decomposing leaves. *Photo Alex Shigo. Courtesy Shigo & Trees, Associates.*

Fungi involved with ectomycorrhizae come from a large number of species, often with a host-specific relationship. Fungal components generate mushrooms and puffball fruit bodies. Billions of spores are produced and disseminated by the wind.

Infected epidermal nonwoody root cells are stimulated to enlarge and thicken. Ectomycorrhizae can be detected with the naked eye, but looking through a low-power microscope enhances the view of their features. They are stout, swollen root structures and generally grow in short, branched clusters. Some resemble miniature elk horns. Most are white to light brown in color, and darken with age-related decline and death. They're relatively short-lived and are tied into annual growth and shedding cycles.

Ectomycorrhizae often form at right angles to a parent root and stand upright in soil microcavities. The base connection holding the structure is cuplike with a central perforation. A protective partition (plug) is formed in association with shedding, which restricts the access of pathogens to the root system.

In addition to mycorrhizal fungi, other microorganisms develop symbiotic associations with trees. ACTINORHIZAE are nonwoody structures composed of root tissue and actinomycetes (fig. 16.13). They're able to fix nitrogen; that is, convert atmospheric nitrogen into a usable form. The ACTINOMYCETES are a group of filamentous bacteria with funguslike characteristics. Along with other types of bacteria, they're the most numerous organisms in soil and are an integral component of soil fertility. The familiar smell of good earth is associated with actinomycetes, as are various antibiotics.

RHIZOBIA, another group of soil bacteria, are also able to live symbiotically in plant roots and fix nitrogen. Bacteria enter through root hairs and, under anaerobic conditions, provide nitrogenous compounds and receive carbohydrates. Infected plants generally produce BACTERIAL NODULES, tumor-like nonwoody structures. They're common to legumes. Symbiotic bacteria are usually host-specific.

OOMYCETES are microscopic organisms of aquatic (water molds) and terrestrial environments. They're nonphotosynthetic protists that range from unicellular to highly branched and filamentous forms; the latter resemble fungal hyphae. Oomycetes are heterotrophs; that is, they can't manufacture organic compounds (food) and instead feed as saprophytes or parasites. Terrestrial species include plant pathogens such as *Plasmopara viticola* (the downy mildew of grapes) and *Phytophthora infestans* (the blight rot of potatoes). Oomycetes have been observed in close association with tree roots in wet, boggy areas, so it's possible that the relationship between oomycetes and trees may be more than just parasitic.

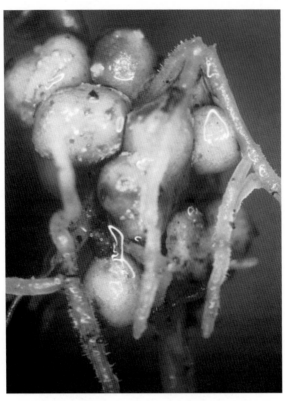

FIG. 16.13 Actino-
rhizae of Alder (*Alnus*
spp.). *Photo Alex Shigo.*
Courtesy Shigo & Trees,
Associates.

Nonwoody roots are shed in place, and are broken down (digested) by soil microorganisms. This contributes an important source of organic material to the soil. It's thought that roots contribute at least as much material as is shed from aerial parts (leaves, flowers, twigs, bark). These materials are fundamental to the health of trees and soil organisms.

Woody roots are spherical or ovoid, and have no pith. The biological center is seldom concentric, but is instead positioned in the lower region of the sphere. Aerial limbs have an opposite arrangement: the biological center (pith) is in the upper region (fig. 16.14). When a branch dies, trunk tissue below it is altered to a more protective state. For dying roots, tissue on the upper side, towards the trunk base, is affected in a similar way. Root decline and death result from injuries, infections or natural aging.

Woody roots receive wounds and infections in numerous ways, including crotch defects, girdling roots, and abrasions against rocks. Healthy trees effectively compartmentalize root wounds by forming and strengthening protective boundaries (fig. 16.15). If boundaries don't form, pathogens can enter roots

FIG. 16.14 Biological center is not usually concentric in roots or aerial branches. Lower region roots (*left*), upper region in branches.

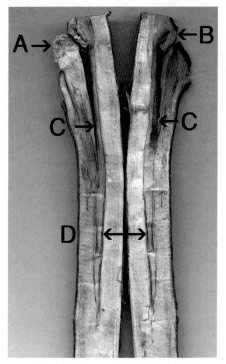

FIG. 16.15 Conifer with (A) dead branching root, (B) woundwood growth, (C) crack, and (D) compartmentalized column boundary.

with little resistance. Infections often spread as root sections die in weak trees. Infection columns may, in larger roots, coalesce together up into the trunk base. Cracks associated with dead and dying roots sometimes develop on the lower trunk. Fungal fruit bodies (mushrooms and conks) are a sign of root infections (fig. 16.16).

Woody roots form three types of protection wood: false heartwood, discolored wood, and wetwood. They don't form heartwood. False heartwood is associated with the death of branching roots. Discolored wood is associated with wounds and infections. Wetwood is associated with bacterial infections and can occur independently or in conjunction with discolored wood or false heartwood.

Protection wood is wood altered to a state resistant to decay. It allows wounded trees time to grow new wood. Canker infections are common to roots and cause biological and structural problems. Trees with root rot, such as *Armillaria* (see fig. 6.1) and *Phytophthora*, often display stress-related symptoms such as wilted foliage, crown die-back, and epicormic trunk sprouts.

🌳

Trees are inadvertently damaged and predisposed to root problems by intensive forestry, construction, and landscaping practices. Enthusiastic lawn-care activities, for example, can injure roots and foster disease through excessive

FIG. 16.16 Fungal fruit bodies are a sign of root infections. *Ganoderma lucidum* conks shown.

irrigation and fertilizing. Mature trees with rotting roots are prone to structural failure. Trees that fail are often exposed or have preexisting defects. City-street trees come to mind as examples. They frequently stand alone, have less than optimal conditions for root development, and receive wounds that induce rot.

The body of exposed roots from a mature uprooted tree may seem modest in size when compared to the trunk and branches. This perception is false, because a large portion of the root network has been severed or previously rotted. Roots form an extensive weblike underground system. The arrangement of multiple branched, interlocking roots with the strong physical properties of the soil provides exceptional structural strength. Roots of surrounding trees also overlap each other. Combined conditions of high wind and saturated soil, especially at times of peak foliage, can exceed mechanical limits and cause trees to uproot.

Root suffocation is a form of injury that diminishes the overall ability of a tree to properly function. Without oxygen, nonwoody roots quickly die and the oxygen-dependent process of respiration stalls. Beneficial aerobic soil organisms are also killed. Examples of events that cause suffocation injuries include flooding, soil compaction, or adding soil over root areas.

Mycorrhizae will naturally be present when a soil habitat is healthy and stable. The soil environment best suited for mycorrhizae consists of organic matter rich with microbes. It's moist but well drained, aerated and weakly acidic (pH 5 to 7). A damaged soil habitat reduces or eliminates beneficial soil organisms and disrupts tree processes. Compacted and flooded soil conditions, for example, inhibit the formation and function of mycorrhizae, as well as the oxygen-dependent processes of absorption and respiration.

Most trees are dependent on mycorrhizae for healthy survival. Referred to as OBLIGATORY species, examples include Beech (*Fagus*) and Hemlock (*Tsuga*). Trees that can live without or with low levels of mycorrhizae for all or part of their lives are referred to as FACULTATIVE species. They often are the first trees to return to cleared land (fig. 16.17 & plate 9). Examples include Ash (*Fraxinus*) and Aspen (*Populus*). Trees chosen for city landscapes are frequently facultative species tolerant of poor soil conditions. Examples include Sycamore (*Platanus*) and Linden (*Tilia*, see fig. 34.7).

Trees that are native to swampy or low-oxygenated soils (see fig. 8.3 & plate 3) are considered to be facultative species, because mycorrhizae are thought to be dependent on oxygen. Observations of nonwoody roots with mycorrhizae-like structures taken from wet areas, however, raise questions as to whether mycorrhizae are more tolerant of low oxygenated conditions than once believed. It's possible that other symbiotic associations are involved with tree

FIG. 16.17 Species facultative for mycorrhizae are often the first to return to cleared land. Birch (*Betula* spp.) and Aspen (*Populus tremuloides*) along field.

roots that are tolerant of anaerobic conditions. The associations and dependent relationships between trees and other organisms can't be over emphasized.

Nonwoody roots grow beneath frozen and snow-covered soil. Frost expands soil layers, creating microcavities for root structures and other soil organisms. How roots and other organisms survive and function in a supercooled environment isn't well understood. Frost resistance for cold-tolerant species involves slowing down physiological and metabolic functions. Factors include changes in osmotic pressure and conduction potential, production of compounds such as abscisic acid, vitrification of the protoplasm through a high concentration of sucrose and other sugars, resistance of symplastic (pure) water and bond water to the formation of ice crystals, and a general capacity to minimize frost plasmolysis (desiccation) from freezing temperatures.

17   Tree Cells and Growth

This chapter is an introductory bio-primer about wood. The next chapter introduces wood structure. These and several other primer chapters throughout the book are designed to give preliminary information necessary to understand trees.

CELLS are the basic unit of structure and function of living organisms, excluding viruses. Cells require energy (sugar), water and essential elements to form compounds (building blocks) that assist with the metabolic processes of life. Cells divide and differentiate (specialize) to facilitate the growth and development of an organism. The cell system has built-in safeguards to ensure survival. Trees are highly compartmented and a cell is the basic compartment. A description of cellular parts and functions follows.

PROTOPLASM: The gel-like living contents of a cell, composed of the cytoplasm and a nucleus.

CYTOPLASM: The living contents of a cell where many metabolic activities take place. It includes organelles but doesn't include the nucleus or large vacuoles. The cytoplasm is about 90 percent water, with ions and molecules in solution.

NUCLEUS: The control center of cell activities, it is a large, spherically shaped organelle with a perforated membrane that has many pores that allow for the exchange of material with the cytoplasm. The nucleus contains thin, threadlike structures of CHROMOSOMES that carry the genes and are made up of DNA molecules. A GENE is a unit of hereditary material located on the chromosome that determines a characteristic in an organism.

DNA (deoxyribonucleic acid): A nucleic acid, mainly found in the chromosomes, that contains the hereditary information of organisms.

ORGANELLE: A subcellular structure with a particular function.

CHLOROPLAST: A photosynthetic plastid (envelope-like enclosed organelle) found in all plants. It contains chlorophyll and other pigments associated with photosynthesis.

MITOCHONDRION: A sausage-shaped organelle having a double membrane, it's associated with aerobic respiration and with the Krebs-cycle.

KREBS-CYCLE: The process by which energy is used in cells. It's a complex cycle of reactions associated with respiration in which ATP (adenosine triphosphate) and electron transport chains are involved.

VACUOLES: Spherical, fluid-filled sacks bound by a single membrane to separate a variety of material from the cytoplasm.

RIBOSOMES: Sites for protein synthesis composed of about equal amounts of protein and RNA.

RNA (ribonucleic acid): A nucleic acid found in the cytoplasm and nucleus that's involved in protein synthesis.

CELL MEMBRANE: A separating structure consisting of lipids and proteins; a selectively permeable barrier controlling the passage of substances. Membranes are also found surrounding cell organelles.

PLASMA MEMBRANE: A membrane surrounding a living cell.

DIFFUSION: To move away from an area of high concentration; the manner by which substances or molecules in solution or gas get into and out of cells.

CELL DIVISION: The process by which cells multiply. Trees grow by cell division and expansion. One parent cell divides and forms two identical daughter cells that, in turn, mature and divide. As cells build up and pressure increases, they begin to differentiate for specialized functions.

PRIMARY GROWTH originates in the APICAL MERISTEM, elongating the outermost tips of aerial stems and roots. It's associated with length, not diameter. Cells form and differentiate but do not have additional cells growing over them. Cells associated with primary growth, like those of herbaceous plants, don't form lignin.

SECONDARY GROWTH occurs in the VASCULAR MERISTEM. Cells are produced on the inside and outside of the cambial zone. The diameter of stems and roots increases as layers of new cells form over old ones. Cells form lignin. Boundaries are set between nonwoody (primary) and woody (secondary) parts.

MERISTEM is the continuous layer of living cells that has the ability to divide to form new cells. The apical and vascular meristems are the origin of all tree parts. MERISTEMATIC is the capacity to divide and differentiate. Once cells (other than parenchyma) differentiate, they are no longer meristematic.

CAMBIAL ZONE is the generating region between wood and bark composed of meristematic cells. It produces phloem cells on the outside and xylem cells on the inside. This zone, the vascular cambium, is seasonally active, has no chlorophyll, and doesn't produce or store energy.

An INITIAL is a meristematic cell of the vascular meristem that can differentiate into a specialized cell. The cambial zone consists of parenchyma cells oriented in an axial or radial direction. As cells divide and mature, the outer and innermost cells differentiate, ending their cell-division process.

FUSIFORM INITIALS are thin, elongated, spindle-shaped axial cells of the cambial zone. They differentiate to form specialized xylem and phloem cells.

RAY INITIALS are radial cells of the cambial zone that differentiate to form radial parenchyma.

PERICLINAL and ANTICLINAL DIVISIONS of fusiform initials influence the formation and multiplication of xylem and phloem cells. In periclinal division, the daughter cells are in front of and behind each other, expanding diameter growth. In anticlinal division, the daughter cells divide side-by-side, expanding the circumference.

All tree cells start alive and are homogeneous. They mature, then differentiate to form specialized cells. Cells common to all wood include PARENCHYMA, which are thin-walled cells with living contents. The two types are axial parenchyma and radial parenchyma (see fig. 18.4). Smaller and far more numerous than fiber or vessel cells, they often live for many years. Parenchyma cells store energy for the tree in the form of starch and oils. They are meristematic and have the capacity to divide and differentiate, but don't because they're locked in place.

CONTACT PARENCHYMA (paratracheal) are axial parenchyma in contact with vessels and radial parenchyma. They have an important role in the symplast network. MARGINAL PARENCHYMA (terminal) are axial cells that form at the end of the growth cycle. They form the familiar growth rings that separate seasonal growth increments.

The following cells are associated with angiosperms. FIBERS are axial cells having thick walls of cellulose and lignin. They live for a relatively short time and provide support for the tree. VESSELS are enlarged axial cells that facilitate liquid transport. Living for a short time, they become functional when they die. The cell contents pull away from the cell wall and the end wall partitions (SEPTA) rupture. Groups of cells are stacked on one another like barrels without tops and bottoms. Tree vessels are tubelike multicellular units with tapered ends. Contiguous vessel units overlap with randomly adjoining pit openings (similar to tracheids) to facilitate liquid movement (see fig. 18.7). Water and elements in solution zig-zag through vessel conduits. The arrangements and

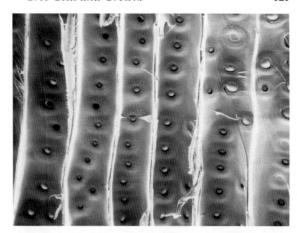

FIG. 17.1 Pit openings
in tracheids of Pine
(*Pinus* spp.). *Photo Alex
Shigo. Courtesy Shigo &
Trees, Associates.*

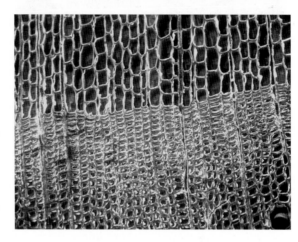

FIG. 17.2 Latewood
fiber tracheids (*bottom*),
earlywood tracheids
(*top*). They're separated
by the seasonal growth
margin (*center*). *Photo
Alex Shigo. Courtesy Shigo &
Trees, Associates.*

functional duration of vessels varies between tree species. Most function for a
full growth season before becoming plugged.

TRACHEIDS are elongated, thick-walled conducting and supporting cells
of the xylem in gymnosperms (conifers). The cells die soon after being formed.
They have tapered ends and pitted walls. Chains of cells are linked to adjacent cells through paired-pit openings with porous membranes (fig. 17.1). Over
time (the amount varies among species) or after traumatic wounding, tracheids
and border pits are clogged with terpene-based substances (resins and gums).
FIBER TRACHEIDS (latewood tracheid) are cells that form late in the growing season and are more compacted, with thicker walls compared to earlywood
tracheids (fig. 17.2). They often have a higher resin content and are darker in
color, which helps to distinguish the annual growth increments (rings).

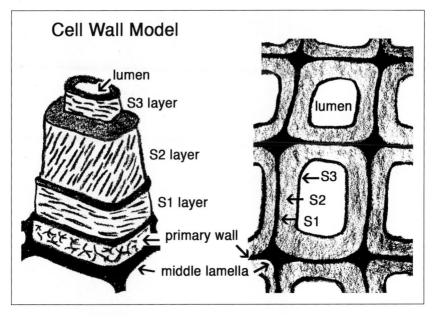

FIG. 17.3 Woody cells have a primary and secondary cell wall. The secondary wall has three layers; S_1, S_2 (thickest with most cellulose), and S_3.

RESIN DUCTS are enlarged parenchyma or large intercellular spaces lined with thin-walled axial parenchyma cells that secrete terpene-based resins (see fig. 18.3). They can occur radially, but are most common in the axial system. Resin ducts are more common in latewood. Certain tree species, such as Fir (*Abies*), have resin ducts in bark but not wood, whereas other species, such as Spruce (*Picea*), have few. After injury, many conifers produce traumatic resin ducts.

🌳

CELL WALLS are the rigid outer layers of plant cells. Rapidly dividing tree cells associated with nonwoody parts or herbaceous plants tend to have only a PRIMARY WALL. Neighboring cells secrete pectin-based material that fuses together their primary walls, creating an intercellular layer, the MIDDLE LAMELLA, which is often difficult to distinguish from the primary wall. A much thicker SECONDARY WALL forms in woody plants after the initial formation of the cell contents and primary wall, and is associated with secondary xylem (lignified wood). The secondary wall usually has three layers: S_1, S_2, and S_3. The layers differ in the orientations of their cellulose microfibrils (strands). This laminated structure increases strength. The middle S_2 LAYER is the thickest and contains most of the cellulose (fig. 17.3).

Cellulose is a key component of both cell walls, but other substances are also present: lignin, hemicellulose, pectin, suberin, enzymes and other proteins. The primary wall contains more pectin compounds and less lignin, making it more hydrated and plastic. The S_2 layer of the secondary wall lacks pectin and contains more hemicellulose and lignin. Lignin adds rigidity and compression strength to the cell wall. The living contents of adjacent cells are connected by strands (PLASMODESMATA or cytoplasmic threads) through pit membrane openings.

WOOD is secondary xylem. It's a highly ordered arrangement of living, dying and dead cells that have walls made up mostly of cellulose, lignin and hemicellulose. Functions include support, liquid transport and protection. It's classified as hardwood in trees with vessels (angiosperms) or softwood in trees with tracheids (gymnosperms). The basic types are sapwood and protection wood (see chap. 18).

SAPWOOD contains living cells and is subdivided into two types, conducting and nonconducting. PROTECTION WOOD is altered to maintain a protective state and doesn't contain living cells. Types include heartwood, false heartwood, discolored wood, wetwood, and noncolored static core wood.

WOOD STRENGTH is indicated by density and specific gravity. DENSITY refers to how closely cells are packed and the thickness of the cell walls. SPECIFIC GRAVITY is the ratio of a cube of oven-dried wood to an equal volume of water. The specific gravity of dry cell-wall cellulose and associated material is about 1.53 in all plants. The thickness of cell walls in relation to the size of cell LUMENS (central spaces) determines differences in specific gravity of wood among tree species. The specific gravity of most wood is less than 1.0. Low specific gravity and the bound air spaces in cell lumens are the reasons why most wood floats.

CELLULOSE is the main component of cell walls in plants and of wood. It's the most abundant organic material in the world. Cellulose is a polysaccharide (an insoluble carbohydrate) composed of long twisting chains of glucose molecules. Glucose molecules are connected by glycosidic bonds to form repeating monomers. Bundles of molecules form microfibrils (strands) that twist together into cellulose fibers, similar to twisting ropes. The chemical arrangement of cellulose imparts strength to wood and makes digestion by pathogens more difficult. Cellulose is an important food source for fungi. Breaking it down requires specific enzymes that animals lack. Cellulose is a source of carbohydrates for herbivores that have microorganisms in their guts that pre-digest the material.

LIGNIN is a unique structural material of woody plants. Its natural cementing ability gives wood its characteristic strength. Second only to cellulose as an abundant organic material, the evolution of lignin allowed trees to increase their stature and develop heavy branches. A complex, three-dimensional, cross-linked polymer, lignin has many variable linkages between the monomers. The chemical makeup and variations serve a protective role, making it difficult for pathogens to penetrate. The bulk of lignin deposits form in secondary cell walls midway into the seasonal growth cycle. The phrase *hardened-off* refers to the lignification of new growth. Lignin fills spaces between cellulose and displaces water in cell walls, adding compression strength and giving a bending rigidity to wood.

HEMICELLULOSE is a group of substances built from more than one type of sugar (heteropolysaccharides). The sugar chains are shorter than those of cellulose. Hemicellulose with pectin forms an interpenetrating matrix in cell walls. Interacting with cellulose and lignin, hemicullulose gives strength while retaining some plasticity. Cellulose microfibrils are cross-linked with hemicellulose molecules. The surfaces are connected by hydrogen bonds that tether adjacent microfibrils, limiting their extension and, in turn, their cell enlargement.

PECTIN is a group of hydrophilic polysaccharide substances having a gel-like characteristic. The water they introduce into cell walls imparts pliable properties necessary for expansion. Pectins are involved in the formation of the primary cell wall and the intercellular cementing of contiguous cell walls.

GLYCOPROTEINS are structural proteins and enzymes contained in cell walls. They are matrix components, particularly in the primary cell wall.

SUBERIN is a natural, waterproofing substance. Suberin, cutin and waxes are unique lipids (fats) of plant cell membranes. Long chain molecules of hydrogen and carbon are connected to glycerol in varied ways that few microorganisms can access as an energy source. Suberin is a structural and protective boundary material. Layers of suberin mix with layers of waxes forming barriers that inhibit the loss or penetration of water and other molecules. Suberized tree parts include corky bark, leaf surfaces, barrier zones, the Casparian strip, and the epidermis of stems, roots and fruits.

GROWTH REGULATORS are a group of essential substances produced in very small quantities that influence growth and development through highly specific chemical signals between cells. (Plant biotechnology and genetic engineering involve growth regulators in the manipulation of plant cells.) Growth regulators are sometimes referred to as plant hormones, although a hormone is a zoological term for a chemical messenger produced by a ductless gland and transported by blood.

AUXINS promote cell elongation in the tips of growing stems and branches. They help the tips to maintain apical dominance and inhibit lateral bud and root development. They're continually produced in the apical meristem. Auxins stimulate the excretion of hydrogen protons. This leads to acid-induced cell wall loosening and, in turn, wall extension. Auxins are transported slowly in the symplast from cell to cell towards the tree's base. They're not transported in sieve elements (phloem) or vessels (xylem). Auxins also affect cell division in the vascular cambium. The principle, naturally occurring auxin is indoleacetic acid (IAA). Synthetic auxins are manufactured for several purposes, including as herbicides.

CYTOKININS are produced in roots; they stimulate cell division throughout the tree. Transported through the xylem from root to shoot, they're essential for the growth of lateral buds and healthy leaves. In leaves they stimulate protein synthesis and slow the senescence process. Cytokinins are abundant in tissue that's actively dividing. In the vascular cambium, they act synergistically with auxins and gibberellins during cell division and differentiation.

GIBBERELLINS are involved in sprout elongation. They stimulate the growth of stems and the germination of seeds. They're present in roots and stem sprouts, but the highest concentrations are found in seeds. It has been shown in grasses that the seed embryo releases gibberellins that help access amylase, an enzyme that breaks down starch to sugars. Low gibberellin levels can result in dwarf plants with low reproductive capacities. This may benefit trees in a competitive or harsh environment, where they can survive longer by remaining small and conserving energy.

ETHYLENE is a gaseous hydrocarbon produced by plants that moves by diffusion and influences many aspects of growth and development. It's involved in fruit ripening, the abscission of leaves and fruit, determining the sex of flowers and has an inhibiting effect on cell expansion.

ABSCISIC ACID is a growth inhibitor that induces dormancy. It's found in dormant buds, fruits and leaves. Except in stress situations, it has no direct role in abscission. Transport is from the leaves through the phloem to developing seeds. It's involved with proteins that prevent premature seed germination. Abscisic acid also induces the closing of stomata, which regulates transpiration (see chap. 25). Its synthesis is stimulated by water deficiencies.

OLIGOSACCHARINS are polysaccharide-based substances in the inner lining of cell walls. Classified as growth regulators, oligosaccharins are though to function as signal molecules in defense reactions.

18

Wood Structure

WOOD STRUCTURE refers to the arrangement of secondary xylem cells. The theme of wood is that cells are produced in an orderly way to best insure biological function, mechanical support and protection (see chap. 17). Although the variations are as numerous as there are tree species, a general theme can be broken into four wood types: diffuse porous and ring porous for angiosperms, and resinous and nonresinous for gymnosperms (conifers). Gradations exist with tendencies that are more or less one way or another.

RING POROUS wood has many large-diameter vessels (pores) that form in the spring, followed by fewer, smaller-diameter vessels later in the growth period (fig. 18.1). The annual growth increments (rings) are well defined. They conduct large volumes of water in the spring and lesser amounts as the season progresses. This growth pattern offers survival benefits to trees in areas with wet spring conditions and drier summers. Examples include Oak (*Quercus*), Locust (*Robinia*), and Elm (*Ulmus*).

DIFFUSE POROUS wood has vessels of approximately equal sizes that are evenly arranged throughout the growth increment (fig. 18.2). It's not always easy to distinguish and count growth increments. This growth pattern offers certain benefits to trees in areas with relatively consistent seasonal moisture conditions. Examples include Maple (*Acer*), Sycamore (*Platanus*), and Cherry (*Prunus*).

RESINOUS AND NONRESINOUS woods have a different cellular arrangement. They form tracheids, which are involved with both transport and support (fig. 18.3). Thin layers of parenchyma cells contact and line the sidewalls of tracheid cells. Latewood cells, called fiber tracheids, differ from earlywood tracheids. They're tightly packed, have thicker walls and, in certain trees, have a higher resin content. The size and color contrast between early- and latewood tracheids makes the growth increments easy to see. Pine (*Pinus*) is an example of a resinous conifer; Hemlock (*Tsuga*) is an example of a nonresinous conifer. RESIN DUCTS are an arrangement of cells or intercellular spaces that contain terpenoid compounds.

CONIFERS are cone-bearing trees and shrubs, usually evergreen, with leaves that are either needles or scales. The male and female reproductive structures are contained in cones (see fig. 26.1). Conifers are the most numerous, wide-

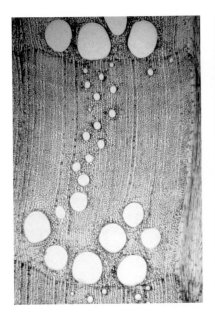

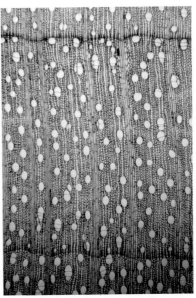

FIG. 18.1 Ring porous, Oak (*Quercus* spp.). *Photo Alex Shigo. Courtesy Shigo & Trees, Associates.*

FIG. 18.2 Diffuse porous, Maple (*Acer* spp.). *Photo Alex Shigo. Courtesy Shigo & Trees, Associates.*

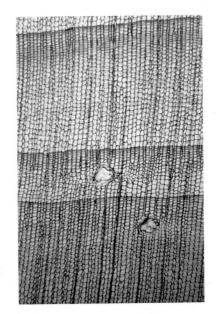

FIG. 18.3 Tracheids, Pine (*Pinus* spp.). Note two sets of resin ducts and contrast between early and latewood cells. *Photo Alex Shigo. Courtesy Shigo & Trees, Associates.*

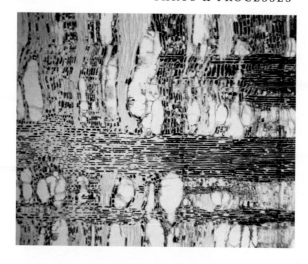

FIG. 18.4 Elm (*Ulmus spp.*), axial (vertical) and radial (lateral) parenchyma cells. Note basketweave pattern.
Photo Alex Shigo. Courtesy Shigo & Trees, Associates.

spread, and ecologically important members of the gymnosperm phyla. They include individuals of the world's most massive, tallest and oldest organisms, such as Redwood (*Sequoia sempervirens*).

Trees are highly compartmented. Wood is produced in an orderly way during every growth period. A single cell is the most basic compartment in wood. Cells within the boundaries of marginal and radial parenchyma form another compartment. All the cells within an annual growth increment also form a compartment. These basic compartments are natural boundaries and form the structural pattern of wood.

The bulk of wood (on a volume basis) consists of axially aligned fiber and vessel cells in hardwoods, and tracheid cells in conifers. Axial and radial parenchyma weave in between (fig. 18.4). Wood cells gradually change throughout the growth period. Earlywood and latewood cells, for example, differ in size, cell wall thickness, and chemical contents. Although the visible change is subtle, the contrast becomes obvious when comparing the abutting sides of an annual growth margin (ring).

Growth rate is not a measure of health. During drought years, or in times of stress, tree growth may slow and only earlywood will form. White Oak (*Quercus alba*), for example, grows more sapwood and delays heartwood when wounded. The specific arrangement of cells give tree species their individualized wood characteristics. The effects of aging, infections and environmental stress alter the amount of growth, but these effects won't change basic wood characteristics.

WOOD DENSITY refers to the size, content and concentration of cells in relationship to the spaces in and between wood cells. Density is the weight of a substance per unit volume. The specific gravity (see chap. 17) and weight of wood varies with different concentrations of cell wall substances compared to the size of the cell lumen. Wood with thick-walled fiber cells and narrow lumens will have a higher specific gravity and be heavier than wood with thin-walled fibers and wide lumens.

From a wood product perspective, wood density is an important indicator of strength. The term *hardwood* refers to an angiosperm with vessels, and the term *softwood* refers to a gymnosperm with tracheids. They have little to do with wood density.

WOOD GRAIN refers to the alignment of axial components in wood: fibers, vessels, tracheids and axial parenchyma. The alignment reflects the orientation of the original fusiform initials and the influence of environmental factors. When parallel to the longitudinal axis, a piece of wood is said to be straight grained. When not parallel, it's described as cross grained. A twisted pattern has a spiral grain.

WOOD TEXTURE refers to the relative size and variation of the elements in a growth increment of wood. Coarse or fine describes wide bands of vessels and broad rays compared to small vessels and narrow rays. Texture (even versus uneven) is the degree of uniformity in the arrangement of cells between early-wood and latewood.

FIGURED WOOD refers to the grain and texture patterns found on the surface of the wood. Woodworkers use figure to describe valued decorative features of wood such as bird's eye or curly (fig. 18.5).

JUVENILE WOOD refers to wood that forms early in the life of a tree. It's characterized by wider growth increments and lower-density wood. Early formed wood usually doesn't have the strength properties of wood that forms later. Juvenile wood is prevalent in trees with rapid early growth, such as trees grown in plantations, nurseries, or cities. It's not as common in forest-grown trees because many don't start with rapid growth, except in exposed areas after a blow-down, fire or clear-cut.

The three dimensional orientations of wood surfaces are transverse, radial and tangential (fig. 18.6). Sample sections of wood from these three perspectives allow for a comprehensive study of wood anatomy (see fig. 34.5).

TRANSVERSE is a cross section at a right angle to the long axis of a stem or root.

FIG. 18.5 Violin with straight grain Spruce top and curly Maple back.

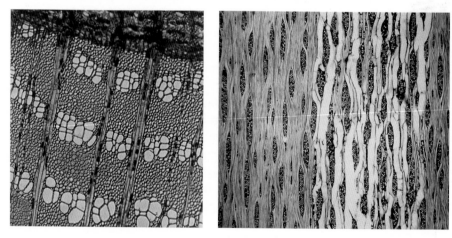

FIG. 18.6 Elm (*Ulmus americana*), orientation of wood surfaces. Transverse (*left*), Tangential (*right*), Radial (see fig. 18.4). *Photo Alex Shigo. Courtesy Shigo & Trees, Associates.*

RADIAL is an axial section along a radius of a stem or a root, parallel to
   the ray.
TANGENTIAL is an axial section perpendicular to the radius.

Anatomical features of wood tend to not be geometrically regular, neither
circular, square, nor straight. The biological center of a trunk, branch or root
is seldom its concentric center (see fig. 16.14). Growth increments (rings) are
rarely perfectly round, but tend to undulate (see fig. 16.2). Vessel and ray units
aren't straight, but generally curve slightly and have tapered ends. Vessel units
overlap and ray units don't (fig. 18.7).

   The structure of a tree is a three-dimensional curved cylinder, wider and
older at the base and tapered and younger towards the top. Like a cone over a
cone, a new tree grows over itself every growth season (fig. 18.8). Trees form a
layer of dynamic mass over an ever-expanding core of static mass. The CORE/
SKIN HYPOTHESIS addresses this change. Equivalent to a multiple plant, the
young living tree becomes a skin over the aging core.

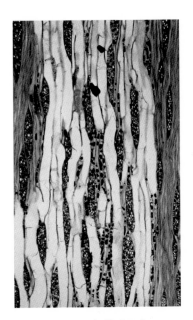

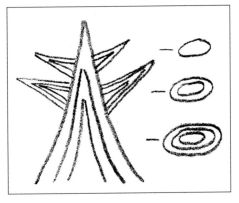

FIG. 18.8 Like a cone over a cone, a new tree
forms over itself every growth season.

FIG. 18.7 Vessels (lighter)
overlap, ray units don't overlap.
Fiber strands outside right and
left. Elm. *Photo Alex Shigo. Courtesy
Shigo & Trees, Associates.*

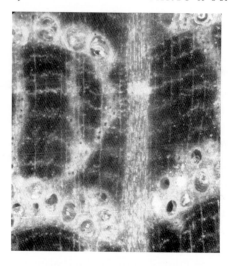

FIG. 18.9 Tyloses plugged vessels,
White Oak (*Quercus alba*). *Photo Alex
Shigo. Courtesy Shigo & Trees, Associates.*

The following are a few additional points on topics related to wood structure.

Transverse dissections (cross cuts) of tree trunks show the growth increments (rings) of wood. Counting them is a method to determine the age of a tree. The width of a single increment is formed during the yearly growth period. Groups of growth increments often form patterns associated with the growth stages of a tree (see fig. 4.4). Early juvenile wood forms a group. Another group is related to the declining years of a tree's life. The width of growth increments decrease when a tree is stressed, and aging is a form of stress. Genetics, competition and environmental factors control most aspects of growth. Tree dissections and associated observations help to illustrate aspects of wood characteristics and growth patterns.

VESSEL CLOSURE is a defensive action protecting wood and the tree in general against the vertical spread of pathogens. Vessels are plugged in several ways: by gums, granular materials, pit closure or embolisms. TYLOSES is a form of vessel closure of certain ring-porous trees. Axial parenchyma cells (contact parenchyma) surround vessels. Cells displace their contents, through pit pores, into vessels. Triggered either by normal genetic aging or by injury and infection, tyloses form thin but permanent balloon-like boundary layers. When viewed through a microscope, they resemble cellophane. Tyloses-forming trees often conduct only in their most current growth increment. Whiskey barrels and wooden ships have been built from White Oak (*Quercus alba*) because its wood forms tyloses (fig. 18.9). The blocked vessels are resistant to leaks and rot. Vessel closure traps air, which is one reason why wood doesn't sink.

PETRIFIED WOOD is a mineralized artifact of wood that no longer contains organic matter. While the wood lay undisturbed in anaerobic conditions over thousands of years, the original wood molecules were replaced, one by one, by minerals. As the bark and the hard and soft parts of the wood attracted different concentrations of minerals, the original arrangement and structures were preserved. The different colors visible are a result of the mineralization process.

Petrified wood allows comparisons between ancient and modern tree species. As many present-day genera have existed for millions of years (see fig. 32.4), this illustrates how genetic traits were established long ago for tree characteristics. The distribution of petrified wood can indicate past geologic and climatic conditions. Evaluation of their growth increments enables us to observe ancient seasonal and weather patterns, as well as insect and animal activities. In order to make observations, petrified wood samples must first be prepared by cutting and polishing.

19

Sapwood, Heartwood, and Reaction Wood

SAPWOOD is wood with living cells (fig. 19.1). WOOD is lignified xylem with a highly ordered arrangement of living, dying and dead cells having walls made up of cellulose, hemicellulose and lignin. Sapwood is divided into two types: conducting and nonconducting. Its major functions include transport, storage, support and defense.

Sapwood has more living cells than dead cells. The living cells are small, thin-walled parenchyma. The dead cells (fibers, vessels, tracheids) are large, and on a volume basis make up the bulk of sapwood. The living parts control the dead parts. Sapwood has a connected network of living axial and radial parenchyma cells. Strands and sheets of parenchyma weave among the other wood cells. They contact transport elements and the vascular cambium (fig. 19.2).

This system of connected living cells throughout the tree, the SYMPLAST, stores energy reserves in the form of starch and oils. The storage, conversion and transfer of energy-containing substances occurs within and between the cytoplasm of living cells. Cytoplasmic threads, PLASMODESMATA, extend through cell openings (pits) to connect adjacent cells. Tree defense is an active response to injuries or infections initiated by the living cells of sapwood (see chap. 9).

Sapwood transport is the movement of water and elements in solution from the roots to the trunk and branch stems (see chap. 14). Transport at the beginning of the growth cycle is through the transport elements of the previous year. During the growth cycle, new transport cells (vessels, tracheids) form, live for a short time, and then become functional. Axial groupings of vessels and tracheids overlap with a random alignment of pit openings. Transport cells are closed off after the functional period, which for some tree species is only a single growing season. The pit openings, and in some species the cell conduits, are plugged. This reduces the loss of moisture and protects against infectious agents.

Support is a result of the structure and arrangement of wood cells. Cells have tough walls with integrated layers of cellulose, hemicellulose and lignin (see chap. 17). Twisted strands of cellulose and hemicellulose are, in a sense,

FIG. 19.1 Red Oak (*Quercus rubra*) block, 49 years old, dipped in diluted bleach to highlight sapwood (darker). Note: growth rate declined during last five years.

FIG. 19.2 Radial dissection through a ray (*bottom*) of same sample as in fig. 19.1. Note impression of vessels where ray overlaps.

like ropes within a cement chimney of lignin. Each individual wood cell is capable of self-support. In angiosperms, short-lived, vertically aligned fiber cells provide mechanical support. In gymnosperms, short-lived tracheid cells serve a dual role of mechanical support and transport.

The VASCULAR CAMBIUM (cambial zone) is the meristematic layer from which cells are produced. Xylem cells are produced on the inside and phloem cells on the outside of this zone. New layers build over older ones, increasing the diameter of aerial stems and roots. Wood cells are trapped in place, whereas the cambial zone and the bark are on the move. The cambial zone produces a succession of identical daughter cells that divide and differentiate into cells with specialized functions. Xylem is the principle water-conducting tissue in plants. It also functions for protection, support and storage.

In temperate regions, the cambium is active only seasonally. In spring, after leaves form, the production of new xylem and phloem tissue begins. The cambial zone in spring is a moist, gel-like layer. Lignification of xylem cells starts midway through the growth cycle. Wood is lignified (secondary) xylem. The bulk of annual wood growth occurs in about six to eight weeks. The bulk of starch deposits (storage) in living cells of new wood takes place during the latter part of the seasonal growth period.

🌳

HEARTWOOD is an age-altered protection wood (see chap. 20). It contains no living cells and is nonconductive (fig. 19.3). Heartwood helps the tree maintain strong mechanical support. The result of genetically controlled aging, heartwood is not caused by wounds or infections, nor is it a wood in gradations. It does not change over time. Specific species of heartwood-forming trees will undergo a relatively uniform transition from sapwood to heartwood. Wound-

FIG. 19.3 Heartwood of Red Cedar (*Juniperus virginiana*). Sample is 10 cm diameter, 43 years old with 30 years heartwood.

ing of the sapwood may cause a delay in the formation of heartwood in certain tree species, such as Oaks (*Quercus* spp.).

All heartwood starts as sapwood and goes through transitional changes. Nitrogen-based chemicals are altered or cycled out of dying cells. The cell moisture content is low, yielding a higher electrical resistance than in normal sapwood. Protective substances, collectively called EXTRACTIVES, form as cells die. They often impart a darker color to the wood. Altered chemical substances in cell walls, and in some cases the cell lumen, help make heartwood highly resistant to infections and decay. Heartwood refers to trees that form extractives.

Decay-forming fungi do not grow at will in heartwood. A boundary-forming reaction takes place in heartwood when it is wounded. Injury-altered heartwood (DISCOLORED HEARTWOOD) forms within the boundaries. The column of discolored heartwood is the diameter of the exposed wood at the time of wounding. The mechanism by which this happens isn't well understood, but is thought to involve several factors: genetic predisposition, chemicals in heartwood reacting as oxygen becomes available, and reactions triggered by the enzymes of microorganisms.

Dissections of trees with wounded heartwood show distinct boundaries and column patterns of discoloration and decay similar to sapwood (see figs. 9.4 & 9.5). Heartwood is the only type of protection wood in which a reaction to injuries occurs. The others have been altered and can't be altered any further if wounded. Heartwood does form around compartmented wounds that occur in sapwood (see fig. 9.6), but won't form in the reaction zone or in other forms of protection wood (see chaps. 9, 20 & 22).

REACTION WOOD is wood altered as a response to the lean of a tree trunk, stem or branch. It compensates for the forces of an inclined position by strengthening wood and, in doing so, protects the mechanical integrity of the tree. COMPRESSION WOOD is reaction wood of conifers produced by increased activity of the vascular cambium on the lower (down) side of a lean (fig. 19.4). TENSION WOOD is reaction wood of angiosperms associated with increased activity on the upper side of a lean. Compression wood is characterized by visibly wider and darker-colored growth increments. The pith is not located in the concentric center of the stem. As with tension wood, the pith is located on the upper side of the lean.

On a microscopic level, compression wood cells are thicker and have more resinous substances in comparison to normal wood. The secondary cell wall layer contains an excess amount of lignin and a lower amount of cellulose, which increases the resistance of the wood to downward pressure. Unlike compression wood, tension wood has more cellulose and less lignin than normal

FIG. 19.4 Compression wood in Norway Spruce (*Picea abies*). Note wider, darker growth increments (*bottom*) that formed on the leaning side.

wood and is more resistant to tension forces. Tension wood contains gelatinous fibers, called the G layer, which is nonlignified cellulose. It develops between and on the inside of the cell's secondary wall.

Tension wood is only visible on a microscopic level. It's more susceptible to decay than normal wood, whereas compression wood, because of its high lignin content, is more resistant to decay. Wood products (lumber) from tension wood can have a sheen and fuzzy finish from pulled fibers. Although it doesn't shrink much, twisting is a problem. Lumber from compression wood shrinks a great deal and is prone to twisting and cupping.

PLATE 1 Trees capturing sunlight.

PLATE 2 Juniper (*Juniperus virginiana*) saplings resulting from birds roosting in Oak stand.

PLATE 3 Top: conifers nurtured by rotting log.
Bottom: Dawn Redwoods (*Metasequoia glyptostroboides*).

PLATE 4 Left: Preformed buds open in spring (*Fagus sylvatica*).
Above right: Tuliptree (*Liriodendron tulipifera*) bud.
Note green of chlorophyll and lighter pith.
Below right: Magnolia flower and leaf buds.

PLATE 5   Top: Rhododendron (*R. maximum*) in flower.
Bottom: Flower with pollinator and fruit
(*Rosa rugosa*).

PLATE 6 Fall color in forest stand.

PLATE 7 Fall leaf color. Top: cultivar of *Acer palmatum*.
Bottom: *Ginkgo biloba*.

PLATE 8 Pitch Pine (*Pinus rigida*).

PLATE 9 Birch (*Betula* spp.) and Aspen (*Populus tremuliodes*) along field.

PLATE 10 A variety of niches result from the breakdown of decaying wood.

PLATE 11 Indian-pipe (*Monotropha uniflora*).

PLATE 12 Epiphytic ferns and mosses on conifer trees.

PLATE 13 Conifer stand, Portland, Oregon.

PLATE 14 American Elm (*Ulmus americana*).

PLATE 15 Venerable Oak (*Quercus alba*).

PLATE 16 Tree evolution has shaped the diversity of life.

20   Protection Wood

The two types of wood in trees are sapwood and protection wood. Sapwood contains living, dying and dead cells. The network of living cells (symplast) stores energy reserves. Sapwood, because of the living cells, has the capacity for dynamic defense; it responds when wounded.

PROTECTION WOOD is wood altered to maintain a protective state. It no longer has living cells and is nonconductive. The altered wood is in a state more protective than sapwood. When wounded, it's resistant to infections because of the strong cell wall boundaries and chemically altered substances produced within cells prior to their death. There are distinct types of protection wood.

HEARTWOOD is genetically altered protection wood. It's a result of the normal aging process in many (not all) tree species (fig. 20.1). Heartwood is not a wood in gradation; it doesn't change over time. Substances with protective qualities, collectively called extractives, accumulate in aging cells and usually impart a color. The altered wood has low amounts of moisture and nitrogen containing compounds. When heartwood is wounded, a boundary-setting reaction occurs that follows the CODIT (Compartmentalization of Decay in Trees) model. Discolored heartwood, and infections associated with wetwood and rot, are confined to the wood exposed to wounding within the set boundaries (see chap. 19).

FALSE HEARTWOOD is associated with the death of branches, where trunk tissues connected to a branch age and discolor but are not infected. It occurs in many tree species. Wood is altered to a more protective state characterized by exhausted nutrients and a lower moisture content. The pattern of false heartwood is set by wood anatomy, not by wounding. Branches generally decline (die) from the tips towards the trunk. When branches die, a central column of false heartwood forms down the branch core into the trunk. It will often coalesce with other false heartwood columns. The column of false heartwood will be the diameter of the branch at the time of its death. Unlike heartwood, a boundary-setting reaction does not take place when false heartwood is wounded. Wetwood bacteria often infect the base area of dead or dying branches, and the infection follows the pattern set by false heartwood (fig. 20.2).

FIG. 20.1 Black Walnut (*Juglans nigra*), a classic example of a heartwood-forming species.

FIG. 20.2 Colored wood in Elm (*Ulmus americana*) core is associated with false heartwood and wetwood.

FIG. 20.3 Red Maple (*Acer rubrum*) with a
column of discolored wood below rotted limb.

DISCOLORED WOOD is injured altered wood associated with wounds and
the tree's response. It forms in the reaction zone (see chap. 9). After wounding, the tree responds by chemically changing the wood to a higher state of
protection. Colors vary from lighter to darker than sapwood, and result from
an alteration of cell content, with slight to no loss of strength. Color change is
triggered by the response of the tree to injury, effects of microorganism infection, or the combination of both. Discolored wood is wood in gradations; it
gradually changes over time and within its space (fig. 20.3). Central columns
of discolored wood developing in heartwood forming trees will not be altered
to heartwood, and usually decay before heartwood.

WETWOOD is a disease of wood and a form of biological protection wood
(see chap. 21 for a description and discussion).

NONCOLORED STATIC CORE WOOD is the nonliving, uninfected, central wood of certain tree species (fig. 20.4). The wood is in a protective state
characterized by exhausted nutrients and a lower moisture content. It doesn't

FIG. 20.4 Spruce species don't form heartwood. The static core wood is not colored.

form heartwood (extractives), nor does it have the capacity for either a dynamic response or a static reaction when wounded. False heartwood, which is associated with dying branches, can develop. When a tree is wounded, infecting agents can cause the development of discolored wood or wetwood.

21

Wetwood

WETWOOD is a disease of wood. Bacteria are the primary agents, but yeast and other fungi may also be involved. The source of sustenance for wetwood pathogens comes from the contents of wood cells. Bacteria digest cell pits (the opening between wood cells), causing cell membranes to become leaky. The affected wood is altered, and some general features that may be present include high moisture content, low oxygen levels, high pH, and low electrical resistance.

These pathogens thrive in a wet, anaerobic environment. They alter conditions in the wood so as to secure a habitat and food source, and to deter other organisms that might threaten or compete with them. Bacteria recycle minerals from infected wood. The elements build up and contribute to the rise in pH. The altered wood condition improves their survival chances and doesn't support aerobic pathogens, including decay-causing fungi.

Stalling decay pathogens protects a tree's structural stability. Wet conditions also allow wood to be more flexible and less prone to mechanical failure. Wetwood often develops along internal cracks (fig. 21.1). Cracks create a scenario of two beams (wood sections) side by side. The moist state allows both to slide and bend under load forces (weight and motion). Dry wood is brittle, whereas in the wet state it's flexible. When conditions in wood that support wetwood change, wood dries and the probability of fractures and decay increase (fig. 21.2).

The term *wetwood* refers to both the disease and the wood condition. Wetwood is bad, in the sense that a tree has a defect, but it's also good in that wetwood delays worse problems. The association of wetwood organisms with trees is thought to have existed throughout the course of tree evolution. It's so common that the condition is considered a normal trait of certain trees (fig. 21.3). Reactions between bacteria and wood chemicals cause specific odors and wood colors characteristic of specific tree species, such as American Elm (*Ulmus americana*), Boxelder (*Acer negundo*), and Pin Oak (*Quercus palustris*). These close relationships benefit the trees and wetwood organisms mutually.

Wetwood can occupy wood altered by aging or from an injury. Wetwood infections often follow anatomical patterns formed by tree branches, roots,

FIG. 21.1 Pin Oak (*Quercus palustris*) with escalating cracks and successions of wetwood infections.

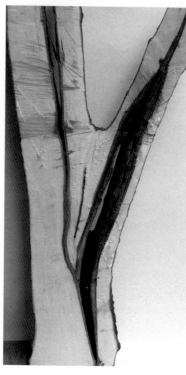

FIG. 21.2 Sugar Maple (*Acer saccharum*) limb with cracks that opened. Wetwood is drying as aerobic fungi cause decay.

FIG. 21.3 Wetwood is a common condition for Tuliptrees (*Liriodendron tulipifera*).

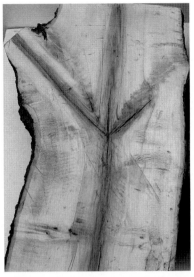

FIG. 21.4 False heartwood and wetwood occur in Boxelder (*Acer negundo*). Rose color thought to result from chemistry between tree and bacteria.

and patterns set by false heartwood (fig. 21.4). Branch anatomy, with its associated series of annual collars, lends itself to wetwood infections. The extent of an infection is generally limited within the core wood present at the time a branch dies. The color gradations of infected wood modify with age. Wood may initially be bleached and darken latter.

Misconceptions persist concerning wetwood and the means by which bacteria enter a tree. The chances of a tree without wounds is impossible, as they receive many throughout a lifetime. The chances of the wounds not becoming infected is equally impossible. Microorganisms are throughout the air and soil environment. They enter trees through wounds and natural openings, no matter how temporary, and tend to infect in successions. Many of the pioneers, which include bacteria, do not cause decay.

Isolating and identifying specific wetwood-causing bacteria is difficult. Several or more species inhabit a single tree, and they interact with each other, other microorganisms, as well as with the tree. For the most part, wetwood bacteria remain unidentified and the ecological relationships between associated organisms remain unrecognized. Trees will always be hard to study.

Pockets of water inside a trunk or standing in a hollow are not causes for

FIG. 21.5 Wetwood
fluids build pressure and
escape through openings
of trunk wound on White
Oak (*Quercus alba*).
Note dark stain from
sooty-mold growing on
wet bark.

wetwood infections or rot. Standing water generally retards the growth of decay-causing organisms. Water pockets exist because of boundaries. Drilling holes or inserting tubes to drain water allows pathogens and infections to spread into otherwise protected areas. It ignores the compartmented design of trees by breaching boundary walls.

Water is not taken into stem wood from rain or by standing in hollows. It doesn't freely move into fiber cells of healthy sapwood or heartwood. Forcing water into stable fiber cells isn't easy, even in a lab setting, because it disperses into vessel and tracheid openings first. Water can move into fiber cells of defective wood. For example, wood products from trees that had areas of rot or wetwood, even when kiln dried, allow for continued wetting and drying. Dry rot and insects (ants or termites) in lumber follow defect patterns formed in wood when trees were alive.

🌳

Wetwood bacteria or other infectious pathogens can access dead or defenseless tissue. Pathogens, for example, can enter dying sections of nonwoody roots. They seldom enter through functioning absorbing roots, and are not spread through transport elements of healthy trees. Infections trigger an immediate response and are compartmentalized. Transport cells are plugged and infections are contained in this protective state.

The wounds on woody roots, as with branches, are infected by wetwood bacteria and other pathogens. Infections can spread inward. Columns of discolored wood sometimes converge (coalesce) into larger roots and spread vertically into the lower trunk (see fig. 16.16). Infections are compartmented within reaction zone boundary layers of the wood present at the time of the infection. Healthy trees continue to grow new wood over compartmented wounds.

🌳

Yeast are involved in some wetwood infections. Anaerobic conditions lead to fermentation, especially in warm weather. The process can produce methane, a colorless, odorless gas. Rancid odors associated with wetwood are from the breakdown of fatty acids in organic compounds. Wetwood gases and fluids may build up pressure and escape through preexisting openings such as branch crotches, cracks, and wounds, but they don't cause cracks, kill the cambial zone, or enlarge wounds (fig. 21.5).

The fluids on bark surfaces associated with yeast and bacterial infections won't kill bark, but they may kill bark-inhabiting organisms, such as epiphytes, and leave bleached patches. Fluids range from clear to brown, and they darken (oxidize) when exposed to air. Fermentation causes a brown, bubbly, alcoholic froth known as *slime-flux*. Sugary moisture on bark surfaces attracts other organisms, such as sooty-mold. Certain fungi associated with canker infections also cause malodorous oozing.

22 Decay and Microbial Succession

DECAY in trees refers to the breakdown of wood cells. It results in a loss of mechanical strength and biological function in localized areas. Decay is a major disease of trees that causes injuries and threatens survival. Wounds and natural openings allow decay-causing microorganisms access. The rate at which decay develops depends on a combination of factors involving the tree, microorganisms, and the environment. The relationships between organisms are usually contentious and competitive, although some involve mutualism (living together cooperatively).

The progression of decay in trees is relatively orderly and results in patterns associated with the succession of microorganisms and compartmentalization. The succession of infectious agents over time alters wood conditions in ways that allow succeeding microorganisms to survive against the protective forces of a tree. Trees resist decay by strengthening existing boundaries and building new ones. The effect of compartmentalization helps contain decay-causing organisms and allows time for trees to grow new wood in new positions. Tree responses are under strong genetic control. Certain tree species and individual trees respond to and resist decay more effectively than others (fig. 22.1).

Cells at the surface of a wound are severely injured or killed. Crushed and broken, they exert little to no protective force. Intact living cells below the surface and surrounding the wound margin respond by initiating a chemical chain reaction. Their contents are altered, making wood more difficult to invade. Antimicrobial compounds form that are phenolic-based in angiosperms and terpene-based in gymnosperms. Cells also produce plugging materials such as, gums, resins and crystals.

Tree decay starts at the microscopic level. Minute wood splinters and droplets of moisture support many colonies of microorganisms. Cracks, no matter how small, offer a way inside trees. The organisms most associated with tree decay are fungi. Bacteria also interact to advance, stall or live off the process.

After wounding of the tree, microorganisms colonize rapidly. A progression of species infect the tree as conditions change and become favorable for them. Although each competes with others to maintain a niche for as long as

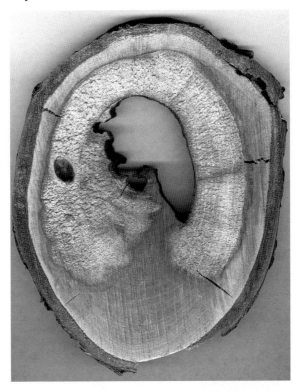

FIG. 22.1 Cherry (*Prunus* spp.) limb (15 cm diameter) sustained two wounding events. Decay organisms survived in boundary layers as tree grew new wood. Note remnants of ant tunnels in center decayed area.

possible, they seldom spread freely. Pioneer pathogens deal with both the tree's defense system on the inside and other competing pathogens on the outside. They alter tree substances in order to provide habitat and food, but generally cause little decay.

🌳

The conditions associated with a wound continually change. The pioneer pathogens, along with the altered wood, become food for succeeding microorganisms. Boundaries called ZONE LINES form where pathogens meet, or they can indicate the cyclic progression of a single pathogen (fig. 22.2). Hard and black in color, zone lines are not tree-induced boundaries.

Dissections through infected tree areas provide a perspective of decay patterns, tree boundary layers and zone lines. The effects of decay and compartmentalization are multidimensional, and the patterns form over time (fig. 22.3). Because trees, microorganisms and the environment are constantly changing, there are no absolutes. When changes occur faster than adaptation, trees and their associates are in trouble. The grand paradox is that wood-inhabiting organisms survive as long as they digest trees, and trees survive as long as they aren't digested (fig. 22.4).

FIG. 22.2 Pathogen-induced zone lines (black boundaries) in reaction zone of dying Beech (*Fagus* spp.) limb.

The general ways microorganisms alter and decay wood are classified as white rot, brown rot, soft rot, pit digestion and discolored wood. The early stages of wood decay are difficult to detect because wood still appears sound. One preliminary indicator is that wood goes into a high state of ionization before it decays. Decay-causing pathogens usually infect altered wood first and follow patterns of wood anatomy. These patterns, set in trees prior to death, influence the susceptibility and advancement of decay in dead trees and wood products.

FUNGI are most associated with the decay of wood (fig. 22.5). A diverse group of heterotrophic organisms, they don't make their own food and they lack chlorophyll. They may feed directly on living organisms, or — in the case of SAPROPHYTES — get energy from dead organisms or other decaying organic matter. Tubelike fungal filaments called HYPHAE grow loosely or join together to form the vegetative body of a fungus, called MYCELIUM (see figs. 16.11 & 16.12). Enzymes facilitate the breakdown and absorption of food materials by hyphae.

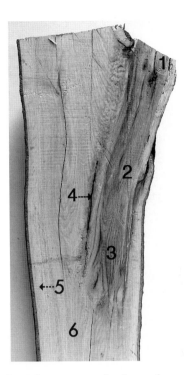

FIG. 22.3 Tree and pathogen boundary patterns develop and change over time. Core of dead stem enclosed in Red Oak (*Quercus rubra*): (1) decaying stub, (2) discolored wood, (3) wetwood, (4) included bark, (5) sapwood, (6) heartwood.

FIG. 22.4 Cherry (*Prunus* spp.) tree continues to survive as do the microorganisms causing rot. Note sprouts.

FIG. 22.5 Decay in trees is
primarily associated with
fungi.

Fungi can reproduce asexually or by means of sexual spores. Fruit structures
called SPOROPHORES, including conks and mushrooms, hold and distribute
spores (fig. 22.6). Mycelia mats and fungal wedges of hardened tissue grow
in trees between bark layers, along the cambial zone, in branch cores, and in
altered wood.

> WHITE ROT: Cellulose and lignin in wood are digested at about equal
> rates (fig. 22.7). It's mostly associated with broadleaf trees (angiosperms).
> Hyphae filaments penetrate and grow in LUMENS, the central spaces of
> cells that have lost their living contents. The internal degradation of cell
> walls progresses outward to the MIDDLE LAMELLA, a layer rich in pec-
> tic compounds cementing the primary walls of neighboring cells. Wood
> affected by white rot generally has a bleached appearance. Many vari-
> ations on the theme occur, some with self-descriptive names such as
> pocket rot and string rot. Hollows in trees are a result of white rot.
> BROWN ROT: Cellulose is digested and lignin is altered only slightly.
> It is mostly associated with conifers (gymnosperms). Infected wood
> has a dry, burnt, cubical appearance and is often referred to as dry rot

FIG. 22.6 Sporophore of *Phellinus robiniae* on Black Locust (*Robinia pseudoacacia*). Young conk left, mature right.

FIG. 22.7 White rot spread throughout trunk core of Black Locust.

FIG. 22.8 Brown rot (dry rot) in conifer.
Photo Alex Shigo. Courtesy Shigo & Trees, Associates.

(fig. 22.8). The wood becomes brittle with a characteristic brown color caused by the altered lignin. The rot-causing fungi follow CODIT patterns that represent column boundary layers associated with compartmentalization. Their enzymes cleave cellulose chain molecules. Fungi can survive a long time in a dormant state and grow rapidly when conditions are suitable. Infected wood is altered in ways that maintain moisture, although moisture in the air is enough to keep the fungi alive.

SOFT ROT: The S_2 layer of a cell wall, which contains most of the cellulose, is digested (see fig. 17.3). Hyphae grow primarily in cellulose microfibrils. Bacteria and nondecay fungi also grow in this layer and are thought to be associated with the soft-rot fungi in living trees. Infected wood can have a water-soaked or burnt look similar to brown rot. The electrical resistance in rotting wood is low. Soft rot is associated with moisture-saturated wood products (usually hardwood) and softwood utility poles. Little is known about it in living trees. It may have a role in accelerating branch shedding.

🌳

PIT DIGESTION is associated with bacteria (see chap. 21). Pits are the openings between wood cells (see fig. 17.1). The valve action regulating their opening and closing is destroyed when pit areas in living cells are digested. In dead wood, bacteria digest pit plugs that were formed as living cells aged or were injured. Wood is left with many openings.

DISCOLORED WOOD is the result of a tree's response to wounds and the effects of microorganisms (see chap. 20). Organisms associated with discolored wood follow the boundary patterns associated with compartmentalization (see chap. 9).

23   Cankers and Canker Rot

CANKERS are necrotic lesions (localized dead spots) with defined borders. They're a disease of trees that causes injury and threatens survival. Cankers are infections usually associated with fungal pathogens. Canker-causing pathogens primarily inhabit bark, although many can live in wood. They form mats and wedges of fungal tissue that kill localized bark and cambial zone areas (fig. 23.1). These areas serve as sites of entry into sapwood.

The pathogens often infect and become established along the marginal perimeter of wounds and branch junctions (crotches, collars, and dead stubs). Dying wood, especially in trees with a diminished defense capacity, is most vulnerable. Many other microorganisms, insects and larger animals live in or around cankers. The three general categories of cankers are annual, perennial and canker rot.

ANNUAL CANKERS are small, short-term cankers that are either contained or shed. They occur on small twigs, roots, and annual parts such as leaves, flowers, and fruit. Pathogens generally infect natural openings, shallow wounds and soft tissue, but their spread is limited by the tree's defensive actions. Small wounds from bird and insect activities are a common site for infections. Fungal spores on leaves or fruit also spawn canker growth, causing circular necrotic lesions. These appear as leaf spots (fig. 23.2) or blemishes on fruit.

PERENNIAL CANKERS are long-term cankers. They grow first and primarily in the bark, and secondarily in the wood. They have seasonally active and dormant periods. Infections are usually in stem wounds, branch stub areas, and in wounded or dying root areas. Perennial cankers can have rot but are more frequently associated with discolored wood. In high density, discolored wood resists rot.

Pathogens start by spreading in the bark, which causes trees to form bark boundaries, then wood boundaries. This stalls the pathogen, but the cambial zone beneath the infected bark is killed. A reaction zone begins to form in the wood behind the dead cambium. The following season, often before annual leaf and wood growth starts, the cycle repeats and infections spread. Wedges of hardened fungal material expand deeper into corky bark, break protective tree boundaries, and expose more tree tissue to infection.

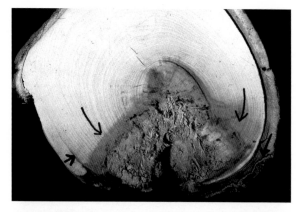

FIG. 23.1 *Populus* spp. with canker infection. Fungus wedge in bark, lower right arrows. Reaction zone, curved arrows center. Barrier zone, lower left arrow. *Photo Alex Shigo. Courtesy Shigo & Trees, Associates.*

FIG. 23.2 Necrotic lesions (annual canker) caused by *Rhytisma acerinum* on Maple leaf.

Natural breaks in the phellogen (bark cambium) occur in the spring when trees grow. Tree energy reserves (defenses) are low during this growth stage, and pathogens can spread rapidly. As trees respond by forming protective boundaries, and as energy reserves increase, pathogens lie dormant in the tissues of dead bark, cambium or surface wood. Trees continue to compartmentalize pathogens in the wood. Fungus and the tree's responses often form target-shaped concentric bands of woundwood (fig. 23.3) or swollen areas in wood that are dense and burl-like in appearance (fig. 23.4). These areas eventually become structurally weak.

CANKER ROTS are perennial cankers able to rot wood. They become established, first in wood and later in bark. Pathogens enter trees through wounds

FIG. 23.3 Pattern of woundwood dieback and growth associated with progression of canker.

FIG. 23.4 Perennial canker (*Nectria galligena*) caused burl-like growth on *Prunus* spp. Inside, infection compartmented with little rot. Outside, necrotic area surrounded by woundwood bands. Epicormic sprouts below infected area.

FIG. 23.5 Canker rot
(*Inonotus obliquus*) in
Yellow Birch (*Betula
alleghaniensis*) forms
black fungal mass.

or natural openings. Dead or dying branch and root stubs are common access
sites. Canker rot pathogens live in compartmented areas and form hard tissue
masses that keep wounds open, cut into bark, and kill the localized vascular
cambium (fig. 23.5).

Some wood beneath the cambial zone is killed beyond compartmented
boundaries, which allows pathogens to spread. They kill by pressure and isolation and expand by repetition. Basically, canker rot pathogens grow around
old boundaries and enlarge wounds from the wood to the bark and back into
new wood. Trees can die from girdling or breaking at the rotting infection
sites. Certain trees, even within the same species, respond to and resist canker
rot infections better than others through compartmentalizing and by the production of wood around bark wedges.

Understanding the effects of canker infections in trees can be confusing. Vari-
ables between trees, pathogens and the environment influence the process.
The point of this discussion is that trees actively resist infections for as long
as possible to survive, using compartmentalization and by growing new wood.

As pathogens advance, trees respond by forming a reaction zone to help contain the infection and a barrier zone to separate the infection from woundwood outside and around the canker lesion. Multiple barrier zones or dead woundwood layers often result from long-term canker infections. The accumulated layers form alternating patterns of dieback and growth that expand from the canker core.

The growth patterns that develop as a result of tree and pathogen interactions over time can be investigated through dissections. Both radial (lengthwise) and transverse (crosscut) views help to minimize confusion. A crosscut view of a sample with center rot, for example, may appear to have no outside connection. A radial cut, bisecting a wound or infected branch stub, helps to clarify the source of rot and progression of infection.

🌳

Once an infection is established, the wood defect associated with canker rot generally becomes worse. As a pathogen gains space, woundwood structurally strengthens areas around infections. It's tough and resistant to decay, but expensive for the tree to produce and maintain. Unhealthy and energy-stressed trees have a diminished ability to produce woundwood or form effective barrier zones, thus they are more susceptible to infection. Many young trees die from girdling canker lesions. Large trees with canker rot infections often become structurally unstable. Safety is a concern when they're situated in high use public areas.

Canker rot pathogens often specialize. They reduce competition by surviving in places or ways others can't. An example is *Phellinus pini*, which is able to grow in resin-soaked wood. Resin is a protective material associated primarily with conifers that is virtually uninhabitable for most other organisms.

Perennial cankers often produce sporophores on bark around canker lesions. Strategies and seasons for the production and distribution of spores vary. Spore distribution can involve wind, rain, insects, birds and other animals. Some canker rot organisms don't produce sporophores until a tree is down and in contact with the ground.

24

Burls, Galls, and Witches-broom

BURLS are enclosed woody tumors (growths) on tree trunks and branches (figs. 24.1 & 24.2). They generally have swollen, hemispheric shapes and are associated with excessive stimulation of the vascular meristem. Burls are usually benign and consist of wood tissue with a swirly, dense grain pattern. The causes of burls aren't well understood. They start from a disruption or cell mutation in the cambial zone that triggers an abnormal production of cells. The condition then continues for the life of a tree.

The wood surface of burls under the bark often have clusters of meristematic points (see fig. 12.5) that may or may not sprout. Those that do almost always persist and grow back if injured or pruned. The epicormic sprouts that develop from these points form buds at their tips with the ability to grow the following season (see chap. 12). Burls with sprouts are informally referred to as bud burls or bud fasciations. Certain tree species, such as Linden (*Tilia*) and Birch (*Betula*), are more inclined to grow burls and burl sprouts.

GALLS are another type of swollen tree growth, and are sometimes confused with burls and cankers. Cankers are localized necrotic lesions (dead areas) with defined borders that are usually associated with an infection from a fungal pathogen. Galls are pathogen-induced, tumor-like swellings on stems, roots and leaves. The pathogens are, in some cases, parasitic. They stimulate abnormal tissue growth through the secretion of chemical irritants.

Gall growths vary in size and shape. Their structure can be enclosed or open, woody or nonwoody. Many galls are associated with mites, wasps or other insects (fig. 24.3) as the gall provides a protective environment for their developmental stages. Most gall growths are thought to cause their host minimal damage or few problems with normal functions.

The galls that cause tree diseases are associated with specific microorganisms (bacteria, viruses, fungi). CROWN GALL, for example, is a tumor-like swelling triggered by a bacterial agent. Infections by the soil-borne pathogen usually start on the lower stem or roots but can progress throughout aerial stems. The gall growths inhibit the flow of water and minerals, which results in stunted and generally unhealthy trees.

FIG. 24.1 Burl growth (tumor) on Spruce (*Picea* spp.).

FIG. 24.2 Multiple burls on mature Tuliptree.

FIG. 24.3 Mite-
induced galls on leaf.
*Photo Alex Shigo. Courtesy
Shigo & Trees, Associates.*

WITCHES-BROOM is a condition with multiple causes (pathogens, parasites, cell mutations, environmental wounding) that leads to an abnormal, dense cluster of twigs growing from a common location.

MISTLETOE and dwarf mistletoe are shrubby, photosynthetic, parasitic, aerial eudicots from different genera. They obtain water, essential elements and organic compounds from their hosts. Mistletoe species are primarily associated with broadleaf trees (fig. 24.4). They produce fruit with sticky seeds that are often dispersed by birds.

An embryonic root, called a RADICLE, pushes into the tree. Secretions from the branching radicle harden to attach itself and push small infecting string cells through lenticels and bark fissures into the phloem and cambial zone. Mistletoe establishes itself by mimicking tree growth-regulating signals to avoid triggering a defense reaction. The sinker organs, called HAUSTORIA (not roots), interface with the tree to draw resources from it.

FIG. 24.4 American Mistletoe (*Phoraden-dron serotinum*) on Red Maple (*Acer rubrum*).

Once vascular connections are functioning, mistletoe leaves develop rapidly and generate much of their own food. Infected trees, or their parts, are stressed and generally decline biologically and structurally, and are also exposed to secondary infections from other pathogens.

DWARF MISTLETOE is a small, leafless seed plant that parasitizes stems of gymnosperms. Their nonwoody sprouts and stems contain chlorophyll but lack central vascular tubes. Seeds, when ripe, explode and are discharged to neighboring trees. They adhere because of a sticky coating. The symptoms of dwarf mistletoe are witches-broom, loss of vigor, and a general decline of the host.

25   Leaves and Fall Color

Leaves (including needles) are the major energy-trapping organs of trees. Flowers are modified leaves. A leaf is a lateral appendage of the stem produced by the apical meristem and composed of an orderly arrangement of primary tissue. The following is an introductory overview of the leaf system. Tree identification books offer species specific information about leaf characteristics.

LEAF BUDS are preformed, embryonic leaves. Their waxy, scale-like outer layers enclose and protect soft tissue over the winter dormancy period (see fig 1.2 & plate 4). The stalk holding the leaf is a PETIOLE. Certain tree species with compound leaves have a side extension, a RACHIS, off the petiole (fig. 25.1). A stalkless leaf (i.e., without a petiole) is said to be SESSILE.

The UPPER EPIDERMIS of a leaf is the outer protective (membrane) layer. The epidermal cells secrete a waxy coating, the CUTICLE, that protects leaves from losing water. The inner PALISADE LAYER and SPONGY MESOPHYLL both are parenchymatous tissue containing chlorophyll, where most of the photosynthetic activity takes place (fig. 25.2).

Vascular veins are the support and transport network throughout the leaf. They include a large MIDRIB that branches out into smaller veins. XYLEM and PHLOEM BUNDLES, transport structures surrounded by a membrane-like BUNDLE SHEATH, distribute water and substances to adjacent tissues. The underlayer of a leaf, the LOWER EPIDERMIS, contains STOMATA, openings that facilitate the exchange of gases. A pair of cells called GUARD CELLS regulates the stoma opening to take in CO_2 and transpire (release) water vapor when open, and to retain moisture when closed. A leaf has thousands of these tiny openings, which are generally closed during daytime and open at night.

Most leaf shedding occurs during regular cycles. For deciduous trees, this occurs mostly in the fall, although many tree species shed primary leaves in midsummer, when temperatures are high and most of the woody growth has been completed. Broadleaf evergreens tend to shed older, inner leaves as new foliage forms in the spring. Most conifers have needles or scales that function for more than one growing season before shedding (fig. 25.3).

Phenological (seasonal) changes, including chemical processes, induce

FIG. 25.1 Compound leaf of
Yellowwood (*Cladrastis kentukea*).

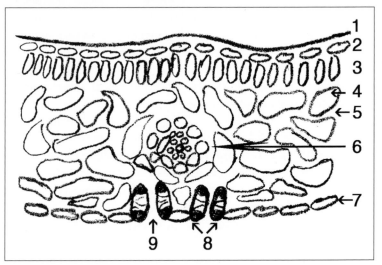

FIG. 25.2 Leaf Model: (1) cuticle, (2) upper epidermis, (3) palisade layer,
(4) spongy mesophyll, (5) cellular spaces, (6) phloem/xylem bundles and
vein, (7) lower epidermis, (8) guard cells, (9) stoma opening.

FIG. 25.3 White Pine (*Pinus strobus*) is a needle-bearing conifer.

shedding. A two-layer ABSCISSION ZONE, composed of a separation layer and a protective membrane layer, forms at the base of a leaf and closes it off from the stem. Certain compounds, such as amino acids and sugars, are translocated prior to abscission. Enzymes aid in the breakdown of the cell walls at the separation layer. The protective membrane layer, called a LEAF SCAR, remains visible on the stem surface (see fig. 11.15). Shedding is also influenced by environmental factors (wind, rain).

Leaves capture energy from the sun in chlorophyll molecules; however, the molecules are also broken down by the sun and must be continually generated. It's an energy-demanding process. Leaves are said to be loaded as they form sugar, and unloaded as they move sugar out. The sugar molecules, soluble in water, are pumped into the phloem transport system. Cytokinins help reverse the movement. Some sugar is reloaded into leaves, which extends their production time and prolongs leaf senescence. Organic compounds produced in leaves are used to run tree processes and build structural parts. They also form protective and toxic chemicals that are difficult for pathogens to digest.

After leaves are fully formed in the spring, new buds for following year begin to form in the leaf axils (fig. 25.4). If young leaves are damaged by frost or insects, a second flush of leaves can usually grow during the late spring, but not in summer. They grow from either preformed auxiliary buds or newly forming buds. Defoliation restricts energy trapping, and new growth depletes energy reserves. Periods of leaf formation and senescence demand energy. When energy reserves are low, defense is low, and insect and fungal pathogens often act at these times. Fully formed and functional leaves replenish energy reserves (fig. 25.5). The sugars are converted to starch and oils and stored in

FIG. 25.4 *(Left and above)* Protective tannins of Oak produce brown color. Note preformed buds in leaf axils. Southern Red Oak (*Quercus falcata*).

FIG. 25.5 Functioning leaves replenish energy reserves. When energy is low, defense is low. Northern Red Oak (*Quercus rubra*).

living cells throughout the tree to power the yearly requirements for metabolic functions and growth.

🌳

The seasonal color change of tree foliage in the fall occurs primarily with broadleaf deciduous trees in temperate regions (see plate 6). It's associated with leaf senescence and shedding as the warm summer growing season ends and the cold winter approaches. Several factors are involved: the physics of visible and reflective light, the concentration of the plant pigments, seasonal changes in leaf physiology, geographic location and weather conditions.

The autumn colors are caused by sunlight striking leaf pigments. The optical wavelength is the portion of the electromagnetic spectrum we see as visible light. Leaves, like anything else, selectively absorb or reflect certain wavelengths of light, which determine the visible colors.

Environmental factors influencing shedding and color include water supply, cooler temperatures and decreasing daylight. Biological factors include the formation of an abscission zone, enzyme actions, and a drop in the production of protein-based compounds, including the growth regulators auxin and gibberellin. As an abscission zone develops, trees recycle a percentage of organic compounds containing essential elements such as nitrogen and phosphorus from leaves. Leaves are segregated from the tree and gradually dry out. They snap off from their own weight and the forces of wind and rain.

CHLOROPHYLL and CAROTENOIDS are photosynthetic pigments (see chap. 27). The synthesis and breakdown of chlorophyll is an ongoing process that occurs in the chloroplast organelles of leaf cells. Chlorophyll produces dominant greens during the growth period. The underlying oranges and yellows of carotenoids become visible in the fall when chlorophyll production declines.

ANTHOCYANINS are leaf pigments synthesized in the fall. Carbohydrates trapped in leaves are necessary for forming the pigments. Anthocyanins are water soluble and react with various sugars in cell vacuoles. They give a red to purple range of color, and mix with remaining carotenoids to produce oranges and yellows. Influenced by pH, they give more red in an acid solution, and purple to blue in a basic solution.

TANNINS are a phenolic-based compound in the cell vacuoles of most plant parts. They cause brown color in leaves and become visible after the production of chlorophyll ceases (fig. 25.4). They form yellow colors when mixed with carotenoids. Tannins are a static form of chemical protection. They tend to make leaves tougher and less hydrated. Plants tan leaves by adding tannin compounds to proteins and chemically removing (oxidizing) hydrogen bonds, causing the protein molecules to collapse. Enzymes of pathogens can't easily fit into these altered molecules to digest the leaves.

The intensity of fall leaf color is influenced by a combination of several factors, such as available soluble carbohydrates, good soil fertility, and bright light (see plate 7). Trees in sun often produce more reds, and trees in shade conditions yield more yellows. Weather conditions with temperatures below 45° F but above freezing help reds and purples. Yellows and browns will always appear.

Rainy or cloudy days can decrease color by limiting the amount of light that strikes pigments. Rain doesn't wash out color, but heavy rains and wind may sweep leaves off trees early. Freezing temperatures and heavy frost can injure or kill leaves before color fully develops. In general, warm sunny days with cool nights are the best conditions for bright fall foliage color.

26   Flowers and Reproduction

The success of trees and all other living systems lies in their ability to reproduce. ASEXUAL (without sex) reproduction in organisms produces offspring that are genetically identical. Cellular division involves MITOSIS, a process in which a cell nucleus and cytoplasm divides in two with the full genetic makeup of the parental cell. It occurs with trees through grafts or cloned sprouts.

SEXUAL reproduction is the dominant method for trees and involves meiosis and fertilization. MEIOSIS is a form of cell division in which half the genetic complement (chromosomes) is provided by each parental cell. FERTILIZATION is the fusion of two gamete nuclei to form a ZYGOTE (embryonic cell), and is the means by which the different genetic combinations of two parents are brought together. The reproductive sex cells, the GAMETES, may be either male or female. They're produced in specialized reproductive organs: a CARPEL in females, a STAMEN in males.

The union of gametes, the sperm and the egg, doubles the number of chromosomes (hereditary information) in the resulting zygote cell. The HAPLOID number is the single set of chromosomes of each gamete. The DIPLOID number is the double set of chromosomes of the zygote and of the resulting SOMATIC (body) cells as the embryo develops into a plant. Sexual reproduction produces offspring that differ slightly from their parents. Genetic diversity in natural populations allows for adaptation to environmental change.

Prior to DNA testing, the classification system of organisms was largely based on reproductive characteristics. Trees have many variations of reproductive structures and strategies. The two basic groups of trees are gymnosperms and angiosperms. GYMNOSPERM means naked seed; they lack an ovary (a protective case) around their seeds. Instead of flowers, they have CONES; that is, reproductive structures with seed-bearing woody fruit (fig. 26.1) that are either STAMINATE (male) or OVULATE (female).

ANGIOSPERM means covered seed. The seeds are borne within a matured ovary. The OVARY is a structure within the flower containing the OVULE: the egg-containing unit that, after fertilization, becomes the seed. A FLOWER is a nonwoody reproductive structure of angiosperm plants (fig. 26.2 & plate 5).

FIG. 26.1 Conifer cones. Clockwise from top: Austrian (*Pinus nigra*) and an unopened Loblolly Pine (*P. taeda*), Tamarack (*Larix laricina*), Red (*Picea rubens*) and Sitka (*P. sitchensis*) Spruce, Red Pine (*Pinus resinosa*).

FIG. 26.2 Rhododendron (*R. maximum*) flowers are monoclinous with stamens and carpels.

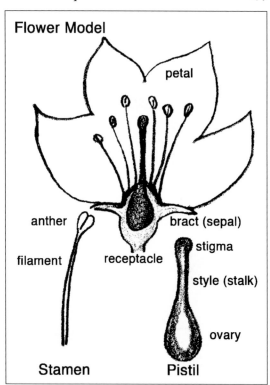

FIG. 26.3 Parts of a
perfect flower.

Angiosperms are subdivided into two groups. MONOCOTS (monocotyle-
dons) initially produce a single leaf from the seed, and they do not produce
secondary growth; examples are palms and herbaceous grasses. EUDICOTS
(eudicotyledons) initially produce two leaves from the seed, and they do have
secondary growth. They include trees and other woody perennials. The seed
is a protective structure for the EMBRYO, the earliest stage of a new organism
resulting from a sexual union. Trees disperse their seeds through shedding,
wind and animal vectors. Survival factors influence the success of germination,
but in general over 99% of seeds don't develop into successful trees.

Flowers can either be MONOCLINOUS — perfect flowers with functioning stamens and carpels (ovaries) — or DIOCLINOUS — imperfect flowers with stamens only or carpels only (fig. 26.3). Trees with imperfect flowers are either
MONOECIOUS — with male and female flowers on the same tree — or DIOE-
CIOUS — with male and female flowers on separate trees. Polygamous species
have some combination of male, female, or perfect flowers on the same tree.

The female reproductive organ of a flowering plant is the CARPEL. The
female seed-containing structure located on the carpel is a PISTIL, which

FIG. 26.4 Developing nut of
Black Walnut (*Juglans nigra*),
2.5 cm × 2 cm. Leaves removed
to highlight preformed buds.

usually consists of an OVARY containing one or more OVULES, a STYLE
(stalk), and a STIGMA (receptive surface). A SEED is a ripened ovule and a
FRUIT is a ripened ovary and its parts (fig. 26.4).

The STAMEN, consisting of a FILAMENT (fine stalk) bearing the pollen
producing-ANTHER (pollen sack), is the male reproductive organ of a flower.
Pollination is the transfer of pollen from an anther to a stigma. Pollen grows
down the pistil, meeting and fertilizing the eggs (ovules). Most tree flowers
have a RECEPTACLE, the structure supporting the ovary. They also tend to
have PETALS that are often within BRACTS (or sepals). These outer layers
help contain and support the internal flower parts, and help to receive pollen
or attract pollen-carrying insects. The CALYX is the outermost protective covering of a flower bud during the developmental and dormant stages.

27 Photosynthesis and Respiration

PHOTOSYNTHESIS is a highly ordered energy-trapping process in plants. Energy from the sun, in the presence of plant pigments, is used to convert carbon dioxide and water molecules into complex organic molecules. An elaborate series of reactions splits the water molecule, a part of which then bonds with carbon dioxide to form sugar compounds. During the process of FUSION under high pressure and temperatures on the sun, mass is converted to extremely high amounts of energy. Four hydrogen atoms with a relative atomic weight of 1.008 are fused to form one helium atom weighing 4.026. The difference is converted to light energy and emitted from the sun in waves/photon particles. Only a small amount (about 1%) of the solar energy that reaches the earth is captured; of that, about 50 percent is trapped by trees (fig. 27.1 & plate 8).

PIGMENTS are substances that selectively absorb visible light. Colors appear because of the physics of sunlight striking pigments. Objects absorb or reflect certain wavelengths of the visible light spectrum, and the reflected light determines what we see. Visible light is only a small portion of the vast ELECTROMAGNETIC SPECTRUM (gamma, x-rays, ultraviolet, optical, infrared, microwave, radio).

Light energy must first be absorbed to be used in living systems. Chlorophylls and carotenoids are the principle photosynthetic pigment molecules. They're found and function in CHLOROPLASTS, which are specialized cell organelles. When sun light waves/photons are absorbed by pigment molecules, electrons are temporarily moved to a higher energy level (an excited state). As they return, energy is either released and transferred to neighboring molecules, or the electron itself is transferred. The molecular structure and absorption properties vary between the CHLOROPHYLL *A* and *B* types. The *a* type is for the oxygen-generating aspect of photosynthesis. The *b* type is an accessory pigment not involved in energy transfer, but which broadens the range of usable light.

The CAROTENOIDS are accessory pigments that capture light at different wavelengths, after which the energy is transferred to the chlorophyll-*a* molecule. An anti-oxidant, its principle function is preventing photooxidative

FIG. 27.1 Trees trap solar energy through photosynthesis. Pitch Pine (*Pinus rigida*).

damage to the chlorophyll. The two groups of carotenoids are carotenes (orange to reddish) and xanthophylls (yellows). The colors are disguised by the ongoing synthesis of chlorophyll (green) and appear when leaf senescence occurs. Leaves are the most active, but not the only, site of photosynthetic activities in trees. In the bark, chlorophyll occurs in epidermal cortex tissue and in the phellogen along fissures.

Chlorophyll molecules contain one essential magnesium atom held by four nitrogen atoms in a PORPHYRIN RING (cyclic structure) making up the molecule's hydrophilic head. A long chain arrangement of carbon and hydrogen atoms make up the hydrophobic hydrocarbon tail, which is anchored to the THYLAKOID (lipid) MEMBRANE in the chloroplast. The chloroplast organelle is a principal type of PLASTID, a component of plant cells bound by an envelope of two membranes. It's the site of food manufacturing and storage. Inside the plastid, a subsystem of thylakoid membranes transverse the STROMA, a homogeneous, gel-like matrix substance.

Pigment molecules of the chloroplast are imbedded in the thylakoids in organizational units called PHOTOSYSTEMS. The two components consist of an ANTENNA COMPLEX, which gathers light energy and funnels it into the second component, a REACTION CENTER that converts it to chemical energy used by a centrally located special pair of chlorophyll-*a* molecules. These two photosystems, 1 and 2, work together simultaneously and continuously. The optimal absorption peaks are designated as P_{700} in 1 and P_{680} in 2. The P stands for pigment, and the subscript is the wavelength measured in nanometers (one-billionth of a meter). The process of photosynthesis is also affected by temperature. It's most efficient in temperate zone trees from 20 to 30 degrees Celsius (68° to 86° F). Regardless of the light intensity, the process drops off with higher temperatures.

Light drives photosynthesis. Carbon fixation depends on the chemical energy harvested. The complexities of photosynthesis are divided into two major processes: the light and dark reactions. In the LIGHT REACTION, energy trapping is initiated as light waves/photons strike electrons and force them into a higher orbit. Light energy is used indirectly to power the synthesis of the oxygen-dependent adenosine triphosphate (ATP) from adenosine diphosphate (ADP). ATP is the major source of usable chemical energy in biological systems. Energy is held in its two high energy phosphate bonds.

PHOSPHORUS is an element essential to ATP and the light reaction of photosynthesis, as well as to other protein-based and hydrocarbon molecules. Mycorrhizae are important in phosphorus absorption (see chap. 16). The energy held by ATP is used in the dark reaction process of photosynthesis to link carbon dioxide covalently (carbon fixation) into organic compounds. In concurrence with ATP, an associated reduction coenzyme synthesizes molecules to a sugar suitable for transport or for storage as a starch.

When either of the chlorophyll-*a* special pair molecules in the reaction center absorb energy, one of its electrons is transferred to an acceptor molecule, initiating an electron flow. The chlorophyll is now oxidized and positively charged. By a reaction not well understood, chlorophyll is able to replace its electrons one at a time from water molecules. As four electrons are removed from two water molecules, the water molecules are split, yielding four electrons, four protons, and oxygen gas (O_2). This water-splitting process — called PHOTOLYSIS, which requires oxygen with the essential cofactor manganese — generates ATP during photosynthesis.

In the DARK REACTION during carbon fixation, atmospheric carbon dioxide is synthesized into carbohydrates. Carbon dioxide reaches the chloroplast of photosynthetic cells through stomata (openings in the leaves) or lenticels (openings in the epidermal cortex). The reduction of carbon occurs in solution through a series of enzyme-dependent reactions called the CALVIN CYCLE.

The metabolic actions of the Calvin cycle, also known as the C_3 pathway, are powered by energy from ATP. The Calvin cycle's fixation of carbon dioxide for subsequent reduction of fixed carbon ultimately yields sugar and starch. Most of the fixed carbon is SUCROSE, the transport sugar, or STARCH, the storage carbohydrate. While glucose is generated in the cells, little remains free. Starch grains are temporarily stored in chloroplast during daylight periods, and converted at night to sucrose for export, via vascular bundles, to other sites.

Biological oxidation and reduction occur simultaneously during photosynthesis and respiration. These processes transfer electrons (electron transport chain). OXIDATION refers to a loss of electrons by atoms or molecules. REDUCTION refers to the gain of electrons. During oxidation, oxygen is gained and hydrogen is lost; in reduction, oxygen is lost and hydrogen is gained.

During photosynthesis through the presence of plant pigments, plant systems incorporate energy from the sun with carbon dioxide from the atmosphere and water from the soil to form organic compounds. During respiration, these compounds are broken down into carbon dioxide and water. On a worldwide scale, these processes produce the CARBON CYCLE.

RESPIRATION is the oxidation (breakdown) of sugar molecules (carbohydrates), and is an energy-releasing process. The energy is utilized to run biological processes such as metabolic functions and growth. Photosynthesis builds up carbohydrate molecules; respiration takes them apart. Both processes begin and end with carbon dioxide and water.

An overview of respiration starts with glucose. Glucose is split (oxidized) and hydrogen atoms (electrons, protons) are removed from the carbon atoms and combined with oxygen (reduced). Energy is released as electrons move. Cells capture a portion of the released energy in phosphate bonds of ATP (adenosine diphosphate), the energy carrier.

Plants are AUTOTROPHS (self-feeders); they make their own food. Sucrose (a disaccharide) and starch (a polysaccharide) are energy-yielding carbohydrate molecules stored in plants. The hydrolysis of these storage molecules yields GLUCOSE (a monosaccharide). Glucose contains energy in chemical bonds that are like links holding it together. These links are released through a series of steps involving ATP and enzymes. The oxidation of glucose is the primary source of energy in most cells. The energy is systematically released to power processes within cells. Some of the energy released is captured in high-energy phosphate bonds attached to ADP to form ATP.

The first of four primary stages in respiration is GLYCOLYSIS. The 6-carbon glucose molecule is split to form two 3-carbon pyruvate molecules. This process, in association with specific enzyme catalysts, occurs in cytosol (cytoplasm solution).

The KREBS CYCLE is the next stage, and takes place in the mitochondrion (a cell organelle with a double selectively permeable membrane). A cyclic series of reactions completes the metabolic breakdown of glucose into carbon dioxide and water. In the course of the cycle, some energy released by the oxidation of carbon atoms and the reduction of coenzymes (electron carriers) yields molecules of CO_2, ATP, and reduced electron carriers.

The next stage is the ELECTRON TRANSPORT CHAIN. A series of electron carriers (containing iron) and enzymes in the inner membrane of the mitochondrion help pass along high-energy electrons to combine with oxygen. Free energy released during the passage down the chain powers hydrogen protons (H+ ions) out of the mitochondrion matrix, creating a potential energy gradient across the inner membrane. As the protons pass through the ATP synthase (enzyme) complex, they go down the gradient and back into the matrix.

The energy released is used to form ATP from ADP and phosphate. This process (chemiosmotic coupling) is the mechanism by which OXIDATIVE PHOSPHORYLATION, the final stage of respiration, is accomplished. At the end of the electron transport chain, electrons accepted by oxygen combine with hydrogen protons to produce water. In the course of aerobic breakdown of glucose to carbon dioxide and water, thirty-six molecules of ATP are generated (most in the mitochondrion). ATP is not transported, but is made within the cell where it is required.

The Krebs cycle is the metabolic hub, and glucose is the primary substrate for respiration, but fats and oils can also be broken down to yield energy. Plant respiration is aerobic, requiring oxygen from the environment. In anaerobic conditions, lacking oxygen, certain bacteria, fungi and yeast organisms extract energy from organic compounds by the process of FERMENTATION. Two forms of fermentation are lactate (with bacteria and fungi) and alcohol (with yeast). Although the energy yield is not as high as with aerobic respiration, it's adequate for these organisms, which suggests that anaerobic respiration was involved in primitive organisms before free oxygen was present in the atmosphere.

28 Enzymes, Nitrogen and Osmosis

Trees trap energy through photosynthesis and release it through respiration. Cells perform the various work tasks of moving, storing, altering and utilizing life-affiliated substances. The processes must be carried out by the most efficient methods in order to survive.

ENZYMES are proteins that act as specific biological catalysts. They increase the rate of chemical reactions in living systems without being consumed by the reaction. Enzymes facilitate reactions efficiently at low temperatures, using as little energy as possible. They can be thought of as chemical keys that unlock doors along chemical pathways, or as chemical knives that cleave molecules (or chains of molecules) into smaller ones.

Enzymes are usually selective to the molecules (called the SUBSTRATE), in which they react to form a given product or result. That is, their particular structures and chemical properties are receptive only to certain specific molecules. In a hypothetical reaction of compounds A + B with an enzyme, the product compound AB is formed and the enzyme is available to react again. In the opposite reaction, the compound AB with an enzyme is cleaved, resulting in compounds A + B, and the enzyme is able to react again.

Most enzymes have names that end with *ase*. Some are named for the type of reaction they catalyze; for instance, carbohydrase or lipase. Others are named for the substrate they act on; for instance, sucrase or lactase. Some enzymes are proteins only. Others have a protein part, the APOENZYME, and a nonprotein part, the COENZYME. Both must be present before the enzyme can function.

Certain vitamins act as coenzymes. VITAMINS are organic compounds essential in small quantities for metabolic functions. Each one influences a number of vital processes, but vitamins are not an energy source.

Enzymes contains an ACTIVE SITE, the part of the enzyme that combines with the substrate. An earlier concept assumed that the active site was rigid and that substrate molecules fit into the site like a lock and key in order to react. In the newer induced-fit model, the active site varies and changes its shape when binding to the substrate.

Enzymes can be destroyed by extremes in temperature and pH. Their reactions can be blocked if nonfunctioning substances build up in or around the active sites. In these situations, enzymes can no longer function normally. Disrupting natural chemical pathways can lead to biological failure. When reactions are blocked or altered, a ripple effect blocks other vital biological processes. This is the method by which some herbicide and pesticide chemicals work. They're designed to kill by inhibiting enzyme-induced reactions.

An INHIBITOR is a substance that fits into an active site, preventing the substrate from reacting with the enzyme. A COMPETITIVE INHIBITOR competes for a place on the active site of an enzyme. A NONCOMPETITIVE INHIBITOR alters the active site by reacting with the enzyme at some point other than the active site.

NITROGEN is an essential element and a limiting factor for growth in living organisms. It is absorbed by trees in three forms: NITRATE ANION (NO_3^-), AMMONIUM CATION (NH_4^+) and UREA. Ammonium and urea will usually oxidize to nitrate. Urea is a manmade, organic, highly polar molecule often used in commercial fertilizer products. Nitrogen stimulates growth in plants.

Trees absorb nitrogen in solution through nonwoody roots (see chaps. 8 & 16). The absorption and processing of nitrogen-containing ions into the symplast system requires the use of stored energy. Once in, a chain of chemical reactions take place forming nitrogen-containing compounds such as amino acids, peptides, enzymes and other proteins. The reactions take place in living cells and stimulate growth, resulting in more protoplasm, DNA/RNA, chlorophyll, larger leaves, and more tissue.

At first, growth processes take energy out of the system. If all goes well, this energy debt will be repaid; however, the system will then be larger and energy reserves must be greater than the amount present when stimulation of growth started.

Orderly growth requires a surplus of potential energy. Should the energy required for growth begin to exceed the available supply, the overall energy reserve of a tree is less than what is needed to maintain other functions. A larger tree system with a low energy reserve has a diminished ability for defense.

Trees have a low nitrogen-to-carbon ratio compared to other living organisms. They've evolved for millions of years with low levels of available nitrogen. Should deficiencies of other essential elements occur in a tree, supplementing nitrogen (stimulating growth) can make those deficiencies worse. When a tree becomes less healthy, pathogens gain an advantage as well as a source of nitrogen. Young trees respond to nitrogen like annual plants, but little is known about nitrogen requirements for healthy growth in mature trees. As trees age, the ratio of dynamic mass to static mass changes, and they're unlikely to need supplementary nitrogen. A low nitrogen level is a protection feature for trees, because they have less nitrogen to offer pathogens.

SALT INDEX is the rate at which materials will ionize (dissociate) in water. Sodium nitrate ($NaNO_3$) is the accepted baseline and is assigned the number 100. For those materials that ionize more rapidly, the number goes up; more slowly, the number goes down.

HIGH SALT INDEX refers to a high amount of materials in fertilizer that will form ions rapidly when in contact with groundwater. An excess of salts in the soil will injure root cells and restrict water uptake. A high salt index increases the probability of PLASMOLYSIS of cells at the rhizoplane, the tree's absorbing interface. During plasmolysis, water moves out of a living cell and its protoplasm shrinks, breaking away from the cell wall and causing the cell to die.

On herbaceous plants this is easily seen as a browning or burnt look, but on mature trees it is not so easily recognized. A familiar example of plasmolysis is the way in which bacteria are killed when they land on a salted ham. Water moves out of the bacteria to the salted surface and the bacteria die.

OSMOSIS is the movement of a solvent from a dilute solution to a more concentrated one through a membrane. Osmosis is associated with the movement of water across a plasma membrane. Water molecules can pass through a selectively permeable membrane from a dilute solution to a more concentrated one. Osmosis will continue between two solutions until they have the same concentration.

Osmosis can occur into or out of cells. Water moves out of cells by increasing OSMOTIC PRESSURE, the pressure necessary to stop osmosis. The more concentrated a solution, the higher its osmotic pressure. Water moves into a cell by decreased osmotic pressure, called the DIFFUSION PRESSURE DEFICIT. To move away from an area of high concentration is DIFFUSION. Osmosis is a special case of diffusion, a natural phenomenon, where water moves across a selectively permeable membrane that permits the movement of water but inhibits the passage of solutes.

Osmosis is a fundamental process of plant and animal biology. It's a driving force in the phloem and other liquid-transport systems of plants. Osmotic pressure makes cells TURGID (rigid), a state in which the protoplasm is exerting pressure on the slightly elastic cell wall to the point that the bulging cell can no longer expand. Turgor pressure (water content) is the main means of support of herbaceous plants and is an essential force in woody perennials (see chap. 14).

Water is the principle solvent in plant cells. The movement (diffusion) of water across cell membranes occurs from an area of higher water potential to one of higher solute concentration. The effect of solutes (particles ranging

from larger sugar molecules to small ions) on water potential is referred to as
OSMOTIC POTENTIAL. The concentration (not size) of solute particles in
water is what affects osmosis.

A high solute concentration, for example, increases turgor pressure in the
stomatic guard cells of leaves, causing them to open for transpiration (see chap.
14) and the exchange of gasses (see chap. 27). A decrease in solutes reduces turgor pressure and guard cells become flaccid and close. A sequence of ongoing
processes regulates the varying concentrations of solutes. Potassium ions (K^+)
are one of the solutes that influence the osmotic processes in guard cells. For
example, the conversion of starch to sugar increases osmotic pressure and the
availability of potassium ions, causing guard cells to be turgid and expand
(opening stomata). Conversion of sugar to starch decreases osmotic potential
(pressure) and closes stomata.

29   Tree Chemistry Introduction

Trees are a chemical system, and chemical processes underlie all biological functions. CHEMISTRY is the science of the arrangements of atoms and their properties. It's the fabric connecting all parts and processes of living systems. Atoms combine through chemical bonds in definite geometric arrangements to form molecules. In a molecule of an element, the combining atoms are the same; in a compound, the combining atoms are different.

Living systems are centered around carbon and its capacity to form long chains of atoms. It's the basis of all living material and the backbone of organic molecules. Organic chemistry is the chemistry of carbon. Carbon connects with hydrogen and oxygen to form thousands of chemicals. These elements — combined with nitrogen, phosphorus and sulfur — make up about 99 percent (by dry weight) of most living things.

The following section on tree chemistry is meant to be a general introduction to the topic. The more advanced aspects of chemistry probe more deeply into the molecular arrangements and three-dimensional structures of compounds, as well as the specifics of reactions, their properties and products. Introducing chemistry allows for a broader perspective on the inherent qualities and functions of the tree system (see chaps. 8, 14, 15, 17, 27 & 28, and Appendix B). Additional references are given in the bibliography.

Carbon occurs as the basic chemical skeleton for the four principle types of organic molecular compounds: CARBOHYDRATES (CHO), PROTEINS (CHONS), NUCLEIC ACIDS (CHONSP) and LIPIDS (CH). These are the building units associated with growth, reproduction and maintenance processes. Although carbon is by far the most common and abundant organic chemical, its primary source for the tree is through photosynthesis. During this process, light energy is captured from the sun and used to chemically combine inorganic atmospheric carbon dioxide (CO_2), soil water, and other essential elements to produce glucose (biological fuel). Oxygen is a by-product of the process.

Water, the most abundant molecule in living systems, is the medium by which chemical synthesis and its resulting substances occur and move. All life is dependent on the fixed carbon and stored energy from photosynthesis.

Much of the excess energy from photosynthesis is stored in the phosphorus-containing compound ATP (adenosine triphosphate), the energy carrier of cells. Oxidation (breakdown) of organic compounds releases stored chemical energy through the process of respiration. Carbon dioxide and water are also released. When trees die, the remainder of its chemical elements are released through decomposition and become available again for new life (fig. 29.1 & plate 10).

A cell is the basic compartment (unit of structure) of a tree. Biochemical processes are continuous in living cells. Energy powers the processes, and if it's lacking, the cell system crashes. Growth occurs by cell division. After the development stage, most new cells differentiate to become specialized cell types.

Metabolic respiration utilizes a large portion of the stored energy from photosynthesis. Most growth occurs at times when the rate of photosynthesis exceeds respiration. Metabolic activities also include the chemical synthesis of compounds (secondary metabolites) into numerous substances for storage and defense.

Wounds, stress, or dying parts trigger cells in localized regions to chemically alter their contents to substances that are biologically and structurally protective. Compounds are phenol-based for an angiosperm, and terpene-based for a gymnosperm. The carbon framework, with attached molecules, in these compounds are altered in ways that are difficult or toxic for pathogens to penetrate.

ELEMENTARY PARTICLES are the components of an atom; that is, protons, neutrons and electrons. They're held together by their inherent electromagnetic charges. The nucleus consists of protons with a positive charge and neutrons that are neutral. Electrons have a negative charge and orbit in an electron cloud outside the nucleus of an atom. The electron cloud is subdivided into different energy levels that hold a given number of electrons.

When the outer energy level (valence shell) is full, the atom has reached its most stable state and is inert (nonreactive). Atoms combine to form molecules and, in doing so, share electrons. The union is referred to as a chemical bond. A common example is water (H_2O). Bonds occur because of an ELECTROSTATIC ATTRACTION, the uniting force between the atoms of a molecule.

ELECTROMAGNETIC refers to the transmission of energy in waves but without the exchange of particles. ELECTROSTATIC refers to the exchange of electrons from one thing to another as electrons and protons are separated. This is the case with chemical bonds in biological processes. The rule associated with electromagnetic force and electrostatic attraction is that opposites attract and likes repel.

FIG. 29.1 *All these molecules were somewhere else before . . . From stars to trilobites to trees the energy makes its rounds.* — S. Murray.

Three major types of chemical bonds are associated with molecules in living organisms. These bonds are essential for life because their properties allow substances to form and break apart. The bonds, based on shared electrons, determine the physical strength and electrical charge of a molecule.

COVALENT BONDS are the strongest because molecules share electrons more or less evenly. When shared electrons are no closer to one atom than the other, molecules are NONPOLAR; they're nonreactive and can't conduct electricity. When shared electrons are closer to one atom than the other, molecules are POLAR and will have a small partial charge because there is a difference in

ELECTRONEGATIVITY, the attraction of an atom for an electron. Water is a polar molecule, meaning that the position of shared electrons in a molecule is closer to one atom than to another, making it nonsymmetrical, with a partial negative charge and a resulting partial positive charge in its opposite sphere. The general rule of solubility is likes dissolve likes; that is, polar liquids dissolve polar compounds, nonpolar liquids dissolve nonpolar compounds.

IONIC BONDS are bonds formed between IONS, which are charged particles that have acquired an electrical charge by gaining or losing electrons. Atoms of certain elements and compounds don't have a full outer energy level (complete shell). They have a strong tendency to lose or gain electrons to form a complete shell. By gaining, the overall charge becomes negative, and by losing it becomes positive.

A negative ion is an ANION and a positive ion is a CATION. Because of their charges, the ions in a substance such as table salt or a fertilizer granule arrange themselves in a pattern called a LATTICE. When put in a liquid environment, electrons and protons are separated and the ions become reactive (conduct electricity) by the flow of their charges. Tree absorption relies on ions to move elements in and out of roots.

HYDROGEN BONDS are intermolecular bonds between polar molecules. They're the weakest of the three bonds, but their weakness is what makes them so important to biologic processes. They hold things together, but come apart easily when pressures are applied. Hydrogen bonds, for example, are responsible for water being a liquid, as well as giving DNA and proteins their functional structure.

Hydrogen is the smallest atom, containing only one proton and one electron. It needs two electrons to reach its most stable state, and in theory forms only a single bond. Hydrogen seems to break that general rule by forming a bond within one polar molecule and a second intermolecular bond (the part referred to as the hydrogen bond) between another polar molecule with a stronger electronegative element. Although small, hydrogen does big things in living systems, making life possible.

Living systems are never in a stationary state. Biochemical processes (actions) of living cells are in a state of constant motion. The constant back-and-forth operational rate (motion) of opposing forces, known as DYNAMIC EQUILIBRIUM (including chemical equilibrium), is a major principle of biology and chemistry. Living systems are constantly changing in association with growth, seasonal activities, aging and stress. As conditions change, the position of equilibrium shifts to minimize the change. Conditions include the concentration of reactants and their products, as well as the effects of temperature and pressure that influence chemical reactions and their resulting compounds. The equilibrium shifts compensate for fluctuations in the concentration of substances (products) in ways that either increase or decrease reactants, so as to minimize change and maintain or reestablish equilibrium. An analogy to this is the addition or subtraction (adjustment) of weight to the opposing ends of a see-saw to allow for the oscillation (uninterrupted rhythm) required for its operation.

LE CHATELIER'S PRINCIPLE addresses change in the equilibrium of a living system. It implies that when a change is made in conditions, the system adjusts so as to maintain equilibrium. Natural systems, including trees, are in a constant state of dynamic equilibrium. With trees, the top supplies photosynthates to the bottom, and the bottom provides the top with water and essential elements. Overpruning the crown or removing portions of the root system can offset this natural motion. Dynamic equilibrium shouldn't be confused with balance, which is the equalization of opposing forces. In a natural system, balance means to stop motion. It's a state of stasis associated with death.

ENERGY is the force that moves matter, and for trees it comes from the sun. Enormous amounts of heat and pressure on the sun convert matter (through fusion) to energy that radiates as light. Organisms containing chlorophyll trap light energy and use it with $CO_2 + H_2O$ through photosynthesis to form sugar compounds. The protons and electrons of water molecules are separated (split), with oxygen as a by-product.

The energy stored in sugar compounds is released during respiration. Oxygen is required for the breakdown (oxidation) of glucose, and $CO_2 + H_2O$ are by-products. Energy is the power for life, and carbon dioxide, water and oxygen are the major components. They start, run and finish the process, coming out unchanged and ready to participate in new life again and again. Life is about energy and orderly processes. It exists because of its ability to continually repeat processes.

A fundamental feature of tree biology is BOUND WATER. It occurs by a chemical process in which free water is altered, through hydrogen bonding, to a different chemical state. Bound water occurs when hydrogen on water molecules attaches (bonds) to the negative position of oxygen atoms on the hydroxyls (−OH units) that protrude from cellulose. Cellulose is abundant in the thick S_2 layer of the secondary wall of fiber cells. When the inner wall layers of a fiber cell become saturated with free water, the condition is referred to as the FIBER SATURATION POINT.

Molecules of free water squeeze into and saturate every available space. Some of this water is then converted to bound water. This condition has a protective role, because pathogens can't easily enter fiber cells. Bound water also serves as a storage product for trees. Hydrogen bonds are weak and, when released from cellulose, free water becomes available. Released bound water is involved during the onset of spring growth activities, when stored starch is being converted to simpler sugars (see chap. 14). Another feature of bound water is that it doesn't freeze as liquid water does, a factor for survival when temperatures are below freezing.

Most water in wood is liquid. It also occurs as a vapor (gas) and as bound water. Water occupies open spaces between and along the surfaces of cellulose fibers. The bipolar property of the water molecule and the nature of hydrogen bonding allow water molecules to bond to exposed hydroxyls on cellulose.

CELLULOSE is a long linear polymer (repeating monomers, molecular units) consisting of glucose units with glycosidic linkages that form bundles of parallel aligned molecules. The wood cell framework consists of a macropolymer of cellulose, hemicellulose and lignin. HEMICELLULOSE is a variable branching polysaccharide (sugar chain) providing a binding matrix component in and around cellulose microfibrils. LIGNIN is a large amorphous polymer interpenetrating between hemicellulose and cellulose. It provides stiffness, strength and a protective barrier for cell wall carbohydrates. Lignin waterproofs cell walls by limiting the outward movement of cellular water. Conifers generally have more lignin and less hemicellulose than hardwoods.

🌲

The molecules necessary for life found in all living cells are PRIMARY METABOLITES. They include simple sugars, amino acids, proteins and nucleic acids. SECONDARY METABOLITES also form important compounds, but are less evenly produced and distributed. They may be produced at one site in a cell and transported to another for storage or use. Concentrations of these compounds may vary on a 24-hour basis. They may only occur in certain tissues or at certain periods of development. Growth regulators (see chap. 17) are an example. They influence growth through specific chemical signals. Secondary metabolites include compounds that deter predators, attract pollinators and suppress competitors.

ALLELOPATHY is the production of toxic chemicals to inhibit other plants. Black Walnut (*Juglans nigra*), for example, produces juglone. Allelopathic ability is also used to suppress competition between individuals of the same species. The evolution of toxic chemicals has played a significant role in tree success. Poison substances in thorn tips or leaves form natural chemical deterrents. PHYTOALEXINS are antimicrobial compounds produced in tree cells after wounding that are used against infecting bacteria and fungi.

Secondary metabolites are divided into three major classes; alkaloids, terpenoids and phenolics. ALKALOIDS are bitter-tasting, nitrogenous plant compounds familiar to humans, including caffeine, nicotine and morphine. TERPENOIDS (terpenes) are the largest and most complex group. All terpenoids are composed of ISOPRENE (hydrocarbon) units. Isoprene is made in chloroplasts and emitted from leaves during daylight. It's thought to help plants cope with heat. Terpenoid examples include carotenoids, gibberellins, taxol, rubber and essential oils. PHENOLICS, present in all plants, are another large group of compounds. They include anthocyanins, flavonoids, tannins and flower pigments. Most phenols are stored in cell vacuoles, but some, such as lignin, are found in cell walls.

Indigenous peoples have long used plant compounds in their pharmacopoeia. Many have found pain relief in salicyclic acid, a phenolic acid compound found in Willows (*Salix*).

TANNING is a metabolic process altering the mature leaves of many broadleaf evergreen trees and shrubs. Protein molecules bond with phenol-based compounds within a leaf, and the intermolecular hydrogen bonds holding the protein spirals in place, are oxidized (pulled apart). The spiral structure of the protein molecules collapses like a slinky toy. The enzymes of insects and microorganisms are virtually unable to digest the altered (tanned) leaves as a food source.

Chemical pathways leading to the synthesis and breakdown of molecular compounds are made possible by the obligatory assistance of ENZYMES, a group of specific proteins. They are biological catalysts that bring about chemical reactions in an efficient way, without being consumed or changed by the reactions (see chap. 28).

CARBOHYDRATES are substances made of varying amounts of carbon, hydrogen and oxygen (CHO). The ratio is usually two hydrogens to one oxygen. They form a wide array of organic compounds ranging from active cellular fuel to tough structural material.

GLUCOSE is the major fuel for living processes. Its molecules also form structural cellulose. Glucose ($C_6H_{12}O_6$), a monosaccharide, is a simple sugar that is soluble in water, making it mobile. In living cells it's oxidized (broken down) to provide energy for living processes. SUCROSE, a disaccharide, combines two monosaccharides. It's the transport sugar.

STARCH, an insoluble polysaccharide, is the combination of more than two monosaccharides: $(C_6H_{10}O_5)n$ (where *n* is some larger number). An enzyme facilitates the reaction and water is released. In the reverse reaction, starch is broken down to many glucose molecules: $(C_6H_{10}O_5)n + (H_2O)n$ (plus an enzyme) $= (C_6H_{12}O_6)n$. Starch is the storage carbohydrate and a major source of potential energy for trees.

PROTEINS are a large group of substances important in the structure and function of all living organisms. They're compounds of amino acids that contain carbon, hydrogen, oxygen, nitrogen, and sometimes sulfur and phosphorus. Twenty basic amino acids, arranged in many ways, serve as the building blocks for proteins. Amino acid molecules are linked by PEPTIDE (protein) bonds. Proteins are also the central molecules of enzymes.

Nitrogen is a key element for the formation of proteins. Nitrogen, as an ion, is brought into the tree from the soil in an inorganic state to form amino acids from reactions with reserve carbon. With nitrogen comes the potential for increased growth. Proteins form regular recurring arrangements of amino acid chains and have specific molecular structures that allow for their biological activity. Hydrogen bonds between amino acids are involved in holding three-dimensional structural units together.

FUNCTIONAL GROUPS (atom groups) define structures and are the chemically active parts of organic molecules. They impart a certain set of properties to compounds. If the hydrogen bonds in a protein are broken, the protein is said to be DENATURED and therefore can't react. The activity of many proteins, including enzymes, depends on the presence of an active site fitting into a specific substrate. If denatured, the active site is no longer in proximity to react. Strong acids, heat, alcohol, and certain salts can cause the denaturation of proteins. Reversible denaturation is possible if the hydrogen bonds can reform.

NUCLEIC ACIDS (CHONPS) are polynucleotides consisting of chains of many linked nucleotides (polymers). NUCLEOTIDES are compounds formed by the reaction of a nitrogen-containing base with a sugar (pentose) and a phosphoric acid. Two linked nucleotides are called a dinucleotide. These compounds are involved in fundamental biological processes such as cellular oxidation and reduction reactions.

ATP and ADP are nucleotides associated with high-energy phosphate bonds, a form of chemical energy used within cells. DNA and RNA are well-known nucleic acids. DNA is a double helix (two parallel coils) of regular recurring polynucleotide chains (the backbones) of alternating sugar and phosphoric acid groups, with nitrogen-based sides (rungs) held together by hydrogen bonds. DNA and RNA are found on CHROMOSOMES, threadlike protein structures that contain hereditary information. The sequence of the bases makes up the GENETIC CODE. The codes within a species are similar in theme, but have countless variations that produce differences between individuals. RNA is involved with the transfer of information in protein synthesis.

LIPIDS are fats, oils and waxes. They consist of long chains of carbon and hydrogen connected to a glycerol molecule that has three oxygen atoms. Because of branching, the chains take on many forms that are difficult for pathogens to break down and use as a energy source. Lipids are not water soluble, and they serve as a primary boundary material; for example, suberin in bark, barrier zones, and the Casparian strip and waxes on the epidermis of bark, leaves and fruit. They help waterproof the outside and retain moisture on the inside. Lipids in the form of oils and fats are stored in tree cells and used as a reserve energy source.

PART III

Associations & Evolution

Unaware

Unaware of someone gone,
reminded of another as I read,
called by science, poetry, and birds.
Thoughts wander,
What life makes for success?
To be large and bold,
or steady and small?
Millions of species, trillions of cells,
cooperation and clashes.
"Essentially it's a microbial world,"
he said, and the other knew.

30

Pathogens

PATHOGENS are organisms capable of causing disease and a toxic response in another organism. Biotic factors affect tree life. Well-established, long-term relationships exist between trees and many other organisms. Most of these associations are beneficial, although some bacteria, fungi, viruses and insects are pathogenic. Pathogens are always present, but in most cases they're opportunistic and cause few problems for healthy trees. When a prospective host is in a weakened condition, pathogens are attracted and often able to infect. The loss or suppression of certain trees within a group, through biotic agents, is a normal part of nature. Survival, for tree species, favors the group and not the individual.

DISEASES are abnormal physiological or anatomical processes that cause injury or death to an organism. VIRULENCE is a measure of the capacity of a agent to cause disease. TOLERANCE is the capacity of an organism to withstand the adverse effects of an infectious disease or of environmental conditions. VECTORS are the carriers of a disease-causing organism. PARASITES are organisms that live on or in organisms of other species, from which they derive their nutrition. The relationship benefits the parasite and is harmful to the host. Obligatory parasites are those that can live only in association with a specific host. Facultative parasites can exist in other ways; for example, as a saprophyte. SAPROPHYTES are microorganisms that live on and degrade organic matter (fig. 30.1 & plate 11). EPIPHYTES are organisms growing upon another organism, primarily for support, without harming its host (see fig. 13.6).

❦

VIRUSES are extremely small (submicroscopic) infectious agents that can live and reproduce only in the living tissue of a host organism. They are systemic pathogens that are often parasitic. Viruses occur in various shapes, which range from rodlike to polyhedral (i.e., with multiple geometric sides). They're composed of a protein cover surrounding a hollow nucleic acid core, and they have no membranes, cytoplasm or nucleus.

The inert extracellular viral form is a VIRION, consisting of a core of DNA or RNA surrounded by a protein coat called a CAPSID. Virions penetrate host cell membranes and liberate the viral nucleic acid into the cell. The nucleic acid is usually translated in the host cell by ribosomes in order to produce enzymes

FIG. 30.1 Indian-pipe (*monotropha uniflora*), a saprophytic angiosperm, lacks chlorophyll. It grows in the shade of conifers and is associated with their mycorrhizae through fungal hyphae connections.

necessary for the reproduction of the virus and the formation of daughter virions. Virions become active with the lysis (i.e., the death and subsequent breakdown) of the host cell.

Viruses may lie dormant in host cells before cells reproduce and die, allowing the viral nucleic acid to become integrated with that of the host. Viruses are adaptable, and under favorable conditions are able to reproduce rapidly and mutate in ways that increase their survival potential over that of a host.

Little is known about viral relationships with trees, especially forest trees.

Viral diseases with fruit and nursery trees have been researched more. Viruses can occur in any living tree tissue. They spread from infected trees through wounding and transmission by insect vectors. Infected trees often have an unhealthy look. Leaves may be chlorotic and have necrotic spots or mosaic patterns.

Trees respond to viral infections, as they do to any infection or wound, by forming and strengthening boundaries. The coupled effect between trees and viral agents may result in abnormalities ranging from stunted, slow growth to swollen, tumor-like growths. Certain gall, witches-broom, and burl-like growths are believed to be caused by viruses. Little can be done to cure infections. Sanitation measures through pruning or culling make sense, particularly with cultivars.

BACTERIA are a large, diverse group of microscopic organisms. Based on sheer numbers and variety of habitats, they may well be the most successful form of life. Most bacteria, even as pathogens, are beneficial and essential in nature. Important in the carbon and nitrogen cycles, they decompose organic matter and some are able to fix nitrogen.

Compared to plants and animals, bacteria have a simple cell structure. They have an outer cell wall, but they don't contain complex organelles such as chloroplasts and mitochondria. The cell wall is generally composed of a polymer of glucose derivatives attached to amino acids. Some bacteria have an additional outer layer consisting of a lipopolysaccharide, a polymer of lipid and sugar monomers.

Many bacteria secrete polysaccharides that form a gelatinous material that allows them to adhere to things. The inside cell wall of certain bacterial species has a MESOSOME, a plasma membrane of coils and loops associated with respiration and cell division. Protein synthesis occurs on RIBOSOMES, which are cellular structures composed of RNA and protein. Many bacteria are motile by means of FLAGELLA, long slender whiplike appendages. These extend singly or in tufts, which propel cells through a medium.

Bacteria are usually unicellular and reproduce by simple cell division, or BINARY FISSION. The shapes of different species vary between rodlike (bacilli), spherical (cocci), or spiral (spirilla). What they lack in size is made up for by an amazing reproductive capacity: under optimal conditions a population can double in 20 minutes. Bacteria demonstrate remarkable versatility with an ability to live practically anywhere, under extreme conditions, extending from icebergs to hot springs.

Most bacteria are dependent on oxygen, although many species are anaerobes and live in low-oxygenated conditions, such as in saltwater or fresh water. Certain bacterial species form ENDOSPORES, or dormant resting cells, that allow them to survive unfavorable conditions for long time periods. Their adaptability extends to reproduction. Most cell division produces clones, but when survival conditions change, bacteria have the ability to adjust by cellular mutation and change inheritable genetic material.

In many bacteria, the cells remain together in chains, clusters or colonies. They hunt prey in groups and secrete chemical trails to direct movement. The more complex colonies consist of thousands of members.

All bacteria are PROKARYOTES: organisms with genetic material (DNA) that is free in the cytoplasm and not enclosed by a membrane. They're from a very ancient lineage. Plants and animals are EUKARYOTES: genetic material is enclosed by a membrane in a nucleus (a nuclear envelope). Most prokaryotes are HETEROTROPHS: they don't manufacture their own food, but consume organic compounds as saprophytes from external sources. Others are AUTO-TROPHS, synthesizing food out of simple inorganic compounds in a way similar to plants. The high degree of genetic variability in prokaryotes, combined with a rapid reproduction cycle and ability to mutate, allow for evolutionary changes that outpace all other organisms.

CYANOBACTERIA (formerly named Blue-green Algae) and PURPLE-GREEN BACTERIA (formerly Sulfur Bacteria) are examples of the remarkable diversity of the metabolic pathways of bacteria. They have internal membranes containing photosynthetic pigments that synthesize organic compounds from inorganic material. The origins of chloroplasts in early eukaryotes are thought to have been symbiotically associated with Purple-nonsulfur Bacteria. Mitochondria came about in a similar way. Bacteria, which are anaerobic and don't require light, trap released energy from the breakdown of materials that include various carbon, nitrogen and sulfur compounds. Indirect evidence based on isotope ratios indicates they have possibly existed for 3.8 billion years.

❈

MYCOPLASMAS are a distinctive group of small bacteria. They're the smallest free-living cells that grow and reproduce without needing a living host. Little is known about these microscopic organisms; it has been only a few decades since they were first discovered. At that time they were thought to be a viral agent. Mycoplasmas are motile pathogens that include a number of disease-causing parasites. They can also exist as a saprophyte. Mycoplasmas vary in appearance, which, combined with their small size, makes them difficult to identify. They lack a cell wall and can assume various forms, ranging from rod-like to branched-spiral filaments. They have a plasma membrane with cytoplasm and strands of DNA. Cell division is through binary fission, and they're capable of forming colonies. Even though they lack flagella, movement is accomplished by undulation and slow rotation.

In trees and other plants, mycoplasmas can affect photosynthetic processes. Leaf chlorosis is a characteristic symptom caused by their activities. In this condition, foliage tends to have a generally unhealthy yellow appearance, and the related diseases are sometimes called *yellows*. Mycoplasmas are also believed to interfere with the movement of sugars through the phloem transport system, resulting in a general starvation syndrome. Phloem blockages are likely tied to a coupled effect between the infecting mycoplasma and a tree's defense response.

Mycoplasmas are thought to be transported within the phloem system of individual trees and are intoduced (spread) to other trees primarily by insect vectors and, to a lesser extent, by root grafts. Disease problems associated with mycoplasmas seem to be more prevalent with cultivated trees and trees predisposed to environmental and biological stress.

Bacteria have no piercing or puncturing apparatus to penetrate tree tissues, but enter through wounds and natural openings. Insects are known to spread bacterial pathogens. Bacteria are present in the soil and carried on airborne particles. They cluster on plant surfaces below and above ground. Conditions causing weaknesses in trees — whether genetic, cultural or environmental — allow bacterial pathogens easier access. Once disease symptoms are visible in trees, the pathogens are usually well established and little can be done. The emphasis for controlling bacterial diseases should focus on prevention through conscientious cultural practices and general sanitation measures, such as culling infected trees.

BLIGHT is a general term for a condition characterized by rapidly developing necrotic areas on stems, leaves, flowers and roots (fig. 30.2). WILT is a blight that interferes with the vascular movement of water and essential substances. Drooping foliage is a common symptom of wilt diseases. Wilts and blights can be caused by either biotic or abiotic factors, and ultimately can cause plants to die.

Microorganisms associated with trees, for good or ill, seldom occur or act independently. Beneficial, predatory and parasitic relationships have evolved in ways that provide natural controls. Some bacteria infect and live off other bacteria. Viruses that infect and live off bacteria are known as bacteriophages. Survival requires an organism to establish and defend a food supply and a space.

Microbial succession in trees — associated with decay, disease and aging — is an orderly process influenced by tree responses, environmental factors, and microbial interactions. Microorganisms must protect their position against other organisms and the forces of the tree. Certain tree-inhabiting bacteria do this well by altering conditions in ways that protect wood and suppress

FIG. 30.2 American
Chestnut (*Castanea
dentata*). Chestnut
blight (*Cryphonectria
parasitica*) girdled stem
without killing roots.
Note base sprouts.

other microbes from advancing. The bacteria that cause wetwood in trees are
an example of beneficial pathogens.

FUNGI are a large, diverse group of mainly terrestrial organisms distinct from
plants and animals. The lack of chlorophyll or any other pigments is a primary
factor distinguishing them from plants. Fungi are nonmotile filamentous
eukaryotes. The cells have a membrane-bound nucleus containing DNA and
membrane-bound organelles. As heterotrophic organisms, fungi are generally
saprophytic, parasitic or symbiotic. Nonphotosynthetic, they obtain nutrition
by absorption through the secretion of digestive enzymes to break down large
molecules into smaller ones.

Fungi such as yeast can be unicellular, although most are multicellular and
composed of filamentous structures called HYPHAE. These small, tubular
organs are associated with absorption and transport. They may be branched
and may have cross-wall SEPTA (partitions) between cells.

Hyphae grow loosely or form a compact mass called MYCELIUM, the vegetative body of a fungus (see figs. 16.11 & 16.12). Mycelium produces the SPO-

ROPHORES, the reproductive organs of a fungus that give way to defined structures such as mushroom and conk fruit bodies. The rigid cell walls of fungi include a matrix of CHITIN, a structural polysaccharide similar in composition to cellulose, except that the monomer contains a nitrogen component. The preferred living environment for fungi is dark and moist. They're somewhat delicate and can dry out in sun and heat.

Abundant almost everywhere on earth, most fungi are a beneficial part of nature. Great recyclers, they decompose and break down dead and living organic matter. Fungal species can cause tree disease and are the most common tree pathogens.

The majority of pathogenic species live in or on dead organic material first, and are attracted to a living host only when conditions are favorable. Opportunistic and patient, they're capable of lying in a dormant state for long periods of time, and spreading when conditions are favorable. They enter trees through wounds and natural openings by both physical and chemical means.

Trees resist pathogens by forming strong physical and chemical boundaries. Fungal pathogens must negotiate protective tree barriers in order to obtain food and defend themselves from becoming food for other microorganisms. The relationships between organisms are complex and competitive. Fungi are susceptible to many microparasites and pathogens.

Fungi reproduce through the formation of spores. SPORES are minute, nonembryonic propagule units associated with reproduction. Fungal reproductive cycles can involve both sexual and nonsexual processes. Produced by the millions, spores literally float on air. They're dispersed from fruit structures that often extend above their food source. Wind, rain and animal vectors also aid distribution.

Spores are durable in that they survive temperature extremes and desiccation. The fruit structures are complex, as are fungal reproductive cycles. Characteristics of reproductive methods help to determine the identity and classification of different species, but specific identification of a fungus is often difficult and requires microscopic examination by mycologists. Sometimes a fungus can be recognized by its fruit structure (fig. 30.3), vegetative material, or by a symptomatic condition of its host. Most fungi are referred to only by scientific names rather than common names. The nomenclature is being adjusted based on new findings. Equivalent synonyms are often connected to names to help with clarification.

INSECTS are the most abundant group in the animal kingdom and in the phylum Arthropoda. A half-million described species are thought to represent only a fraction of their total numbers. Arthropods are subdivided into a

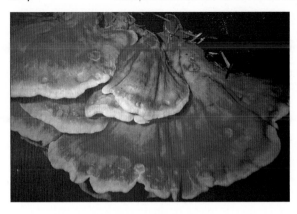

FIG. 30.3 *Ganoderma* spp. (possible *tsugae*) found on conifers. Hoh rainforest, Washington.

half dozen classes, including hexapods and arachnids. The latter includes spiders, mites and ticks.

General insect characteristics include segmented bodies, jointed appendages, and a strong but flexible external skeleton containing chitin. Most insects are terrestrial and can fly. The body is divided into a head, thorax and abdomen. The head has a pair of antennae and eyes, with mouth parts modified according to diet. The thorax has three sets of five jointed legs and, usually, two sets of wings.

Arachnids have a body divided into two parts, with four pair of legs and no antennae or wings. Spiders most often are carnivorous and have spinnerets on their abdomen for web spinning (see fig. 4.3). Arthropods breathe through segmented spiracles (openings) that lead to a smaller series of branching trachea tubes. A specialized system of malpighian tubules and secretory glands function for waste and to regulate water and salt balance.

Arthropods develop from eggs in distinct stages (instars). Between stages, exoskeleton molting (shedding) allows for changes in form and size. META-MORPHOSIS is the process of transformation from larval to adult form. Morphological change is generalized as either simple or complete. The simple pattern starts with an egg, proceeds to nymph instars, and then to adult. Adults are sexually mature.

The majority of insect species experience the complete pattern, in which more specialized functions occur between the stages. The immature stage is a larva (or grub, caterpillar, maggot). Several larval instars follow and culminate in a unique pupa stage. Maturing larvae generally seek out a protected site to form an inconspicuous cocoon for pupation. The adult emerges with a distinctive appearance and habit that differs from other stages. Adults seek out mates and a site for the female to lay eggs (fig. 30.4).

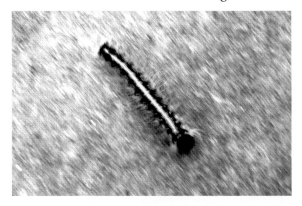

FIG. 30.4 Mature Eastern-tent caterpillar (*Malacosoma americanum*) at top, and empty egg case below.

Nowhere is the versatility of nature more apparent than with insects. The main method of reproduction is sexual, but a few species don't need separate sexes. They reproduce asexually, without fertilization. Some insect species live for only a matter of hours. Most, on average, live three to eight weeks. In temperate regions, life cycles can take a year and experience a long hibernation period. The longevity record may belong to the Seventeen-year Cicada (*Magicicada septendecim*, fig. 30.5).

The overwhelming majority of insects are beneficial and essential. Insect life is closely associated with trees, and trees depend on the activities of diverse

FIG. 30.5 Egg deposit sites from Seventeen-year Cicada. Note discolored pith and wood. A barrier zone separates the wood formed after wounding.

FIG. 30.6 *Rosa rugosa*
flower with pollinator
and a mature fruit.

insects; an example is pollination (fig. 30.6 & plate 5). A minority of insects
are tree pathogens. Opportunistic insects are attracted to trees with low vigor,
and their presence is often a sign of a greater problem (see fig. 12.6). Trees have
strong protective features and aren't an easy target. Insect activities often are
based around tree phenological periods. They sense weaknesses in trees. How
they know is not clear. Insects frequently follow boundaries predisposed by
pioneer pathogens and have close associations with specific fungi and bacteria.
Insect populations rise and fall, although the reasons aren't well understood.
They have survival challenges from predators and nature.

TERMITES and ANTS, although quite different from each other, are closely
associated with trees and for the most part aren't pathogens. In trees they share
a common characteristic of following CODIT patterns and the fungi associated with decay (see fig. 22.1). Microorganisms help access and predigest wood
cells.

   Termites and ants are social insects within family units, but are generally
territorial and don't tolerate other insects. They live in colonies with a caste
system of specialized workers. A difference between them is that ants live in
trees and eat out. Termites feed in trees and usually live out. Careful miners,
termites and ants leave pillars and boundary supports in wood. They don't
mine into the sound wood formed after wounding.

   Termites are blind and white in color. They have a flat, soft body with a
fused head and thorax. In the adult stage, they have beaded antennae and
opaque, equal-sized wings. Adults mate in flight and then drop the wings. Ter-

mites generally build galleries from the nest to the food source. They're quite sensitive and need to maintain conducive oxygen, moisture and temperature levels. Termites ingest cellulose, but can't process it without the assistance of digestive microorganisms.

Ants have strong, segmented bodies and elbowed antennae. The wings on adults are unequal and transparent. They mate in flight. Ant nests are kept clean and dry. Wood frass particles are discarded outside the tree. The activity benefits trees by controlling the spread of microorganisms. Ant diets vary. They feed on other insects (live and dead) and farm insects for honeydew.

Ants are food prey for other insects and animals. Woodpeckers will peck through live or dead wood to get at ants. Carpenter ants are common in trees with decay pockets, but they don't damage or eat sound wood. Termites and ants are an important part of nature, but they can pose a threat to wooden houses. They will follow the pattern of defects in lumber that originated in wood while trees were alive.

NEMATODES are small animal invertebrates (lacking an internal skeleton) that inhabit terrestrial and water environments in large numbers. These slender, transparent, soft-bodied organisms are sometimes referred to as roundworms. They inhabit many ecological niches. Most are free-living saprophytes, but many are parasites and some vector serious diseases. Those inhabiting the soil are short and feed on microscopic organisms. Mouth parts may be tubelike to suck, or spearlike to puncture. They can inhabit columns of decayed wood in trees.

Nematodes have been reported to infest mycorrhizae and to vector tree viruses. Low vitality and a general decline are symptoms of infected trees. Specific diagnosis of many nematode species and infections requires microscopic examination. Nematodes aren't a substantial threat to healthy trees.

SLUGS are mollusks, terrestrial relatives to clams and mussels. Their bodies are soft, nonsegmented, and have no skeleton. Movement is by muscular actions. They have two pair of front tentacles: shorter ones for sensing odors and longer ones for eyes. Many slugs are hermaphrodites with male and female stages. They generally reproduce a single generation per year. Slugs chew plant foliage by a rasping motion with fine teeth, and they usually feed at night to avoid detection and drying out. They leave a trail of mucus that can have an afterglow. Slugs that eat Algae growing on trees cause irregular, bleached patches on trunks. Symbiotic, internal microbes make it possible to digest Algae. Slugs cause little serious damage to trees.

31

Epiphytes

EPIPHYTES are organisms, usually plants, that grow on other plants or objects, primarily for support. In contrast to organisms that grow in a host for sustenance, such as saprophytic fungi or parasitic mistletoes, they're not parasitic and cause no known harm to their host. Epiphytes are sometimes referred to as air plants since they're not in contact with the ground (fig. 31.1 & plate 12). They obtain water and minerals from rain and materials that collect around them. Orchids and ferns are common tree epiphytes of tropical regions. Epiphytes in temperate regions include lichens, mosses, liverworts and algae.

LICHENS are a composite organism. They're a symbiotic combination of a fungal element enclosing cells of either a Green Algae or a Cyanobacteria. The photosynthetic element of lichens, PHOTOBIONT, sometimes lives independently, whereas the fungi component MYCOBIONT usually doesn't. Algae and Cyanobacteria contain chlorophyll and trap energy through photosynthesis. The fungi absorb water and essential elements, and provide support and a suitable physical environment to grow.

The body of a lichen is a THALLUS: an undifferentiated body type lacking stems, roots, and leaves. Lichens have rootlike organs, called RHIZINES, which help penetrate rocks. The fungal hyphae, HAUSTORIA, are projections that penetrate host cell tissue in order to access organic compounds and distribute water and essential elements. Lichens secrete chemicals (acid-based metabolites) that slowly erode and decompose rocks. Soil accumulates and enables plants to root in crevices (fig. 31.2).

Lichens are from ancient lineages and believed to be some of the first organisms to colonize land surfaces. Thousands of species have been identified. Lichens are important autotrophs (self-feeders). They grow slowly and come in many varieties of shape, size and color. The scientific names given to lichens are based on fungi. They colonize inhospitable sites and surfaces (stones, exposed soil, logs) and tolerate extreme conditions (heat, cold, dry). The ability to survive desiccation and remain dormant has allowed lichens to occupy practically every land area in the world.

FIG. 31.1 Epiphytic ferns and mosses on conifer trees. Ecola State Park, Oregon.

Cyanobacteria convert atmospheric nitrogen to a usable form. The production of fixed nitrogen is an important contribution for local ecosystems. Lichens are a food source to many animals, from caribou to minute mites. Squirrels and birds use lichens to build nests and, inadvertently, help to disperse them. Lichens reproduce by fragmentation and by fungal spores contacting appropriate Algae.

FIG. 31.2 Lichens slowly decompose rocks, enabling ferns, mosses and other plants to become established.

Highly sensitive to air pollution, lichens are thought of as the canary in the cage for monitoring atmospheric pollutants. Unclean air minimizes their ability to survive. No evidence indicates that lichens harm trees. Trees support many species of lichens and vast communities of other organisms (see fig. 13.6).

ALGAE are eukaryotic organisms from various unrelated protist phyla. The photosynthetic protists (Algae) are autotrophic and were once classified as plants. They need an aquatic or moist environment to live. Globally, Algae trap large quantities of solar energy. Like plants, they release oxygen and fix carbon that would otherwise exist as carbon dioxide, a greenhouse gas.

The thallus body form of Algae has no true roots, stems or leaves. Green Algae (phylum Chlorophyta) are a large, diverse group. Most of the thousands of species are aquatic and found in fresh water. They're thought to be the ancestors of modern plants, and they contain photosynthetic pigments, store starch as food, and contain cellulose. Modern genera have cell division, along with reproductive and other features that link them to bryophytes (mosses and liverworts) and to vascular plants.

Certain land species of Algae are associated with tree communities as epiphytes. Some that grow on trees are filamentous and, along with chlorophyll,

FIG. 31.3 Algae and
Mosses tend to grow on
the north side of trees.

produce carotenoids (accessory pigments) to aid in screening strong light. Thin
layers of Algae can often be found covering the trunks of trees in moist locations,
and tend to be most prominent on the lower, north side of a trunk (fig. 31.3).

Mosses are seedless (nonflowering) terrestrial plants that grow in carpetlike
colonies and require a moist habitat. Mosses and liverworts are BRYOPHYTES,
which includes thousands of known species. The ancient lineage goes back
four hundred million years. They represent a step in the evolutionary transition of plants from water to land by their aquatic algal ancestors.

Mosses have remarkable dispersal capabilities and the ability to survive in
harsh environments. Together with lichens, they're important colonizers of
open rocks and soil surfaces. Mosses contribute to biodiversity and collect
large amounts of global carbon. The mosses (phylum Bryophyta) are far more
widely distributed than leafy liverworts (phylum Hepatophyta). Mosses are
abundant on and around trees in moist forest settings (fig. 31.4). Their presence implies healthy conditions, because they don't thrive in polluted air or
soil environments.

FIG. 31.4 Stump
colonized by Mosses and
decomposed by fungi.

Structurally simple, mosses have pseudostems and leaves, but no vascular system to transport food and water. Without a xylem or phloem, transport conduction is accomplished osmotically from cell to cell. Water-conducting cells called HYDROIDS are elongated with thin walls. Mosses have no true roots. Their underground rootlike organs, called RHIZOIDS, are wispy stem extensions that anchor plants to a surface. Reproduction is by air-spread spores produced in capsules (sporophytes) that remain on the plants for about a year (fig. 31.5).

Mosses can be dioecious or monoecious, and they experience a two-phased life cycle referred to as the ALTERNATION OF GENERATIONS. The female plant (or part) is a FEMALE GAMETOPHYTE, and the male plant (or part) is a MALE GAMETOPHYTE.

The third type of plant (or part) is a SPOROPHYTE. It's the spore-producing capsule held by the female. Sporophytes form after fertilization by male sperm of female-borne egg cells. The spores will disperse and grow into male and female plants (or parts) to complete the life cycle.

The alternation of generations life cycle has two phases. The HAPLOID PHASE, with one set of chromosomes, is the gamete-producing (gametophyte) generation. The DIPLOID PHASE, with two sets of chromosomes, is the spore-producing (sporophyte) generation. Reproductive sex cells, or GAMETES, have half the genetic complement of parental cells. The diploid cell, or ZYGOTE, results from the fusion of male and female gametes. This cell grows into the embryo that is a young sporophyte. It's dependent on the larger, free-living parental gametophyte. Sporic-meiosis (division) occurs in the sporophyte. Spores are dispersed and give rise to new gametophytes.

An informal use of the name *moss* is tagged to some finely textured plants that have mosslike features but hold no kinship with true mosses. Several examples include Irish-moss, an alga; Spanish-moss, a bromeliad (flowering

FIG. 31.5 Capsules (sporophytes) are reproductive structures of mosses.

plant); and reindeer-moss, a lichen. Peat mosses belong to the class Sphagnidae, of which there is only one genus, *Sphagnum*, with many species distributed worldwide. It's one of the three classes of the phylum Bryophyta. The groups are distinct and vary in features. Another class is the Andreaeidae, granite mosses of mountainous or arctic regions. The vast majority of true moss species are in the class Bryidae.

LIVERWORTS (or hepatics) are a diverse group of small green plants similar to mosses, their close relatives. They are often found growing together in shaded, moist settings on soil, rocks and trees. It's thought that liverworts evolved from algal seaweed and modified themselves to life on land. Mosses are more advanced and more closely linked to vascular plants. Liverworts lack stomata, and their sporophyte capsules remain for only a short time. The leaves of mosses often have a midrib and tend to be equal in size and uniformly arranged around the stem. Leafy liverworts lack this structure, and leaves are usually less uniform and more lobed or segmented. Although the body (gametophyte) of some liverworts is leafy, others have a pad-form thallus with irregular flat patches of green tissue.

After sexual fertilization, the small sporophyte structure grows on or in the gametophyte. Asexual reproduction, common to many liverworts, is by fragmentation of GEMMA-CUPS, budlike masses of vegetative tissue. The medieval Anglo-Saxon word *wyrt* for wort means herb, as in plant medicine.

LYCOPODIUM (club moss) and *Selaginella* (spike moss) are seedless vascular plants. Unlike mosses, they're more closely related to ferns. With mosses, the gametophyte generation is dominant, whereas for these plants, it's the sporophyte generation. The club- and spike-shaped reproductive structures, the STROBILI, carry spores and were the precursors of gymnosperm seed and pollen cones.

Living members of the phylum Lycophyta represent an ancient plant line dating back to the Devonian period (417 to 354 million years ago). This period experienced much diversification of land plants and marked the beginning of modern vascular plants. The evolution of specialized vascular tissue to transport water, minerals and sugars allowed plants to grow taller. During the Carboniferous period of coal-swamp forests (354 to 290 million years ago), large lycophyte trees with secondary woody growth dominated other plants. They went extinct before the end of Paleozoic era (248 million years ago).

Club moss belongs to the family Lycopodiaceae. Most of the several hundred species in this family are tropical and often live as tree epiphytes. *Lycopodium* species that grow in temperate regions are low-profile members of the plant community. These herbaceous evergreens, also known as Ground-pine or Ground-cedar (fig. 31.6), live in moist areas with humus-rich soil and form ground cover mats on the forest floor.

Mycorrhizae are thought to be necessary for healthy growth. The plant body is a SPOROPHYTE. It's composed of a branching ground stem, or RHIZOME, with attached upright aerial stems, terminal strobili and roots. The protostelic vascular system is a solid cylinder of xylem and phloem tissue. The small, scale-like leaves, called MICROPHYLLS, have an epidermis, stomata, and a midvein.

Lycopodium have a two-phased ALTERNATION OF GENERATIONS life cycle. A sporophyte develops from a comparatively small, but independent, underground gametophyte. *Lycopodium* are homosporous, producing only one kind of spore. A germinating spore, released from spore-bearing structures in strobili, gives rise to a bisexual gametophyte with sperm- and egg-producing parts. A sporophyte embryo develops from a sperm-fertilized egg (zygote) in the gametophyte to become an independent entity.

SELAGINELLA, a lycophyte, is the only living genus of the family of Selaginellaceae. Most of the hundreds of species are tropical. These small plants have short, branched stems and a slow, creeping growth habit. The foliage of

FIG. 31.6 *Lycopodium obscurum* (Ground-pine).

some species appears fernlike. They generally live in moist places. A few species can lie dormant during dry periods. The herbaceous sporophyte bears microphylls with a spikelike strobilus, from which spores are formed in a way similar to *Lycopodium*. Roots and stems are protostelic, having a solid pithless core. Mature sporophytes have only adventitious roots, which grow from creeping surface stems.

Two subtle differences distinguish *Lycopodium* and *Selaginella*. Strobili of both are composed of a group of modified, nonphotosynthetic leaves, or SPO-ROPHYLLS, and spore-containing structures, or SPORANGIA. *Selaginella* have a minute outgrowth, or LIGULE, in the strobilus. They're also heterosporous with unisexual gametophytes. Two kinds of sporangia—micro and mega—are in the same strobilus. They produce two spore types—microform sperm and megaform eggs—that shed near one another for swimming sperm to reach an egg. The development of gametophytes (micro and mega) begins within spore walls. The fertilized zygote (sporophyte embryo) grows and is nurtured in the ARCHEGONIUM, the structure of the megagametophyte in which the egg is produced. There is no dormant period as with seed plants.

FERNS (phylum Pterophyta) are a large, diverse group of seedless vascular plants. Fossil records date them back to the Carboniferous period. Over ten thousand species currently exist. Most are tropical with many as tree epiphytes. Nearly all familiar ferns are members of the large order Filicales.

FIG. 31.7 Tightly coiled fronds (fiddleheads) push up through soil in spring.

Fern sporophytes are composed of underground stems, or RHIZOMES, with attached adventitious roots and leaf fronds. The fronds, called MEGA-PHYLLS, are the most noticeable and familiar part of ferns. Sporophytes have a well-developed xylem and phloem, but no secondary growth. Most ferns don't have above-ground stems. The rhizome is perennial and grows laterally from nodal tips. Roots and fronds sprout from nodes along the rhizome.

Young fronds, commonly known as *fiddleheads*, are tightly coiled to push up though the ground (fig. 31.7). Once fully opened, the large leaves are efficient for capturing light. Leaves are generally compound and divided into feather-shaped leaflets called PINNAE. The leaf stalk is a PETIOLE with a side extension, or RACHIS, to support the leaflet. Fronds tend to be annual on woodland ferns of temperate regions, and live for multiple years on species in milder climates.

Spore-containing reproductive organs, or SPORANGIA, are located along the margin or underside of fronds. They generally form off-color, dot- or patch-like clusters called SORI (fig. 31.8). The features of the sorus helps to classify fern species. Fern spores are extremely durable and produced in huge numbers.

The mature sporangium of many fern species physically propels spores when ripe. Carried by air or water, fern spores are seldom reliant on insect vectors. The defensive mechanism of ferns rarely involves spines or thorns; instead, secondary metabolites are synthesized to produce compounds poisonous to animals. Fiddleheads of the Ostrich Fern (*Matteuccia struthiopteris*) are edible for a brief period when young.

With few exceptions, ferns are homosporous. Most become sexually mature in one to ten years. The prominent adult sporophyte is the spore-producing, diploid phase of the fern's two-part alternation of generations life cycle. A germinating spore develops into a free-living bisexual gametophyte. This haploid phase bears both ARCHEGONIA (egg-producing structures) and ANTHERIDIA (sperm-producing structures).

A fern gametophyte is a prothallus structure. It generally forms quickly and has a flat heart shape. Short, rootlike, nonvascular organs, or RHIZOIDS, help anchor the structure. Moist conditions are required for a sperm to reach an egg cell. Ferns grow in dry situations, but fertilization is unlikely. A zygote (fertilized egg) develops into a sporophyte embryo. Nurtured by the gametophyte, the young sporophyte produces a short-lived true root. Sporophytes mature rapidly and become independent. The gametophyte decomposes.

THE EARLY EVOLUTION OF TREES IS CONTAINED IN THE HISTORY OF EPIPHYTES. The ancestral lineages resulted in seed-bearing plants and their progressive dominance of the plant realm. Reproduction by seeds afforded independence from water for fertilization. Distribution potential expanded, because the seed vessel protects the enclosed embryo and provides food for it at the time of germination.

FIG. 31.8 Sori, spore-containing reproductive structures on underside of fern frond (*right*).

Diversity of vascular plants, through seeds, exponentially increased demands on resources. It also offered greater opportunity for specialization, as illustrated by epiphytes in their relationship with trees. Environmental and ecological factors influenced the process. Climate changes to drier, cooler conditions, plus increases in the depth and makeup of soils, favored the expansion of seed plants. They were able to prosper in the less wet, elevated ground. Strategies for pollination, fertilization and distribution were advanced first by gymnosperms, then to a greater degree by the angiosperms. The complexity of nature over time to adapt, compete, and form associations is nowhere more evident and sustained than through the success of trees.

32   Tree Evolution

DNA, which carries hereditary information from succeeding generations, is altered through the processes of mutation, recombination and natural selection. Hereditary characteristics of species change over many generations based on those individuals that leave the most offspring from within a population. Environmental interactions allow some members of a species to reproduce more effectively than others. Species can multiply by dividing into separate populations, which may then either lose the ability to reproduce with each other or vanish by extinction.

The diversity of life includes millions of forms. Fossils suggest that, over the 3.5 to 3.8 billion years since the genesis of bacterial life on earth, a hundred times as many species have come and gone as exist today. Archean studies, through chemical analysis of rocks, suggest that Cyanobacteria (Blue-green Algae) were the first photosynthetic organisms. They increased oxygen levels in the atmosphere. The difficult move by plants from water to land took another 3 billion years. First appearing during the ORDOVICIAN PERIOD (495–443 million years ago), they presaged a steady increase in diversity.

Ancestral forms of seedless plants developed during the SILURIAN PERIOD (443–417 million years ago). The DEVONIAN PERIOD (417–354 million years ago) saw a rapid proliferation and diversification of plant species. Although leaves and roots were initially absent, the cortex of stems is thought to have been photosynthetic. Leaves evolved from small epidermal protrusions into large vascular structures.

The first tree, *Archaeopteris*, had fern-like foliage and evolved 370 million years ago. It had branches able to produce buds, a root system and a woody trunk. The life span was about fifty years. Fossils of this unique plant offer a botanical missing link between ferns and conifers. Primitive conifers (progymnosperms) were abundant in the tropical climate of the period. They gave rise to seed ferns, such as *Medullosa*, which combined fern leaves with seeds on branch ends. Cordaites were early gymnosperms and grew up to thirty meters tall, with strap-shaped leaves and seed cones.

The CARBONIFEROUS PERIOD (354–290 million years ago) was a time of lush swamp forests. Periodic changes in sea levels buried plants in silt as successions of new plants grew over older ones. The compressed organic remains produced coal deposits that formed the basis of fossil fuel.

Carboniferous forests were dominated by lycophyte trees. One, the *Lepidodendron,* was believed to have grown thirty-five meters tall with a trunk three meters in diameter. It had secondary growth, a large quantity of cortex, cork and fernlike fronds with spore structures. Large understory ferns (Pterophyta) with other club moss plants (Lycophyta) and giant horsetails (Sphenophyta) also occupied forest settings.

Seedless vascular plants dominated the PALAEOPHYTIC AGE (400 to 250 million years ago), the first of three great plant ages. Climates became cooler and drier during the PERMIAN PERIOD (290–248 million years ago). Massive plant and animal extinctions marked an end to the PALEOZOIC ERA (545–248 million years ago).

The MESOZOIC ERA (248–65 million years ago) included the MESOPHYTIC AGE of plants (250–100 million years ago). This, the age of gymnosperms, was also the time of dinosaurs and continental movement.

☙

PANGAEA, the equatorial super landmass, existed 280–193 million years ago. It began to break apart at the beginning of the TRIASSIC PERIOD (248–206 million years ago). North America, Europe and Africa split from LAURASIA, forming the Atlantic ocean. GONDWANALAND split and India became an island.

The distribution of many tree species indicates that their ancestors evolved during the time when the continents were joined. Gymnosperms adapted successfully to the changes and were the precursors of modern conifers. They included early cycads, as well as modern forms of *Araucaria* (fig. 32.1), *Taxus, Sequoia, Pinus, Cupressus* and *Juniperus.*

At the close of the era, as mountain building led to continental and climatic changes, distinct variations in regional weather conditions affected flora and fauna. Early in the CRETACEOUS PERIOD (142–65 million years ago), angiosperms appeared and evolved rapidly. Social insects and mammals also multiplied and diversified. The dinosaurs and seed ferns, along with many conifer trees and other plants, became extinct.

The two groups of seed plants — gymnosperms and angiosperms, — gave rise to modern trees (fig. 32.2 & plate 13). Reproductive biology indicates a close but distant relationship between the two. Changes from spore-based to a seed-based reproductive strategy took place during the TRIASSIC PERIOD (248–206 million years ago). Seeds provide increased reproductive success under diverse environmental conditions, because they protect the enclosed embryo and provide nutrition during germination.

Fossils show that *Ginkgo biloba* grew throughout the northern hemisphere

FIG. 32.1 *Araucaria arauncana* (Monkey-puzzle) is a member of a genus that was prominent in the Mesozoic forests. Ashland, Oregon.

FIG. 32.2 Seed plants, including gymnosperms, gave rise to modern trees. Conifers, Portland, Oregon.

FIG. 32.3 *Ginkgo biloba* has changed little in over 150 million years.

during the Mesozoic Era (fig. 32.3). *Metasequoia glyptostroboides*, once thought to be extinct, grew during the JURASSIC PERIOD (206–142 million years ago). Flowering trees evolved during the CRETACEOUS PERIOD (142–65 million years ago). Among the earliest were woody magnoliids, including *Archaeanthus*, which is thought to be closely related to living *Magnolia* and *Liriodendron* trees. The advancements of flowers and pollination are believed to first have occurred with insect pollination on small, herbaceous plants. Adaptations for dispersal by larger animals co-evolved with birds and mammals late in the period.

Angiosperms (Anthophyla) are the largest phylum of photosynthetic organisms. Appearing suddenly in the geologic record 130 million years ago, they experienced a substantial increase in diversity and numbers at the close of the Cretaceous period. The sustained increase continued throughout the CENOZOIC ERA (65 million years ago to the present). Early angiosperms left relatively few fossils, and questions persist about their origins.

The CENOPHYTIC AGE (100 million years ago to the present) is the third great age of plant life; the age of flowers. Flowering plants are estimated to account for over 80 percent of known living plant species, and new species continue to evolve. Conifers have become acclimated to regions with harsher growing conditions and climates.

Many trees of the TERTIARY PERIOD (65–1.8 million years ago) still grow today (fig. 32.4). The planet was warmer at that time, and forests covered virtually all land masses. The climate of Europe and North America was similar to that of present-day Southeast Asia. Broadleaf deciduous, tropical palms and conifer trees grew together.

For approximately the last two million years, the climate has cooled by a few degrees. Accumulated snow and its compressed ice layers formed glaciers covering large tracts of land in cool temperate regions. Sea levels have fallen and freshwater bodies increased. Four great ice ages, beginning 1.5 million years ago, caused trees at the further reaches of their range to die in high numbers. Those closer to the tropics survived and adapted, and recolonized previous ranges within the interglacial periods, which lasted up to sixty thousand years.

Mountain ranges influenced the spread of trees. In North America the mountains ran north to south, which allowed tree species to retreat from the ice. Isolated pockets between mountains led to the divergence of separate populations. In Europe, the Pyrenees and Alps stretched east to west, which blocked movement. Trapped trees perished and reduced plant diversity compared to that of North America or Asia. Since the last ice age, temperatures have gradually increased, and modern trees have again expanded their range (see chap. 2).

The intervention of humans has substantially altered tree and plant ecology over a short period of time. From the earliest nomadic hunting and gathering through the development of agriculture, tools and social cooperation has allowed man to occupy and alter the natural world. Exploration and settlement of new lands introduced competitive plants and diseases to formally closed ecological systems. The momentum of current population and technical surges may produce consequences that rival any other known extinction event throughout geological time.

FIG. 32.4 Stump of *Sequoia* (3.7 m diameter) preserved by a volcanic mudslide 34 million years ago. Florissant fossil beds, Colorado.

FIG. 32.5 Trees have shaped the diversity of life and our modern world for over 200 million years.

Tree evolution spans over three hundred million years. For two hundred million years, trees were arguably the most dominant and successful organisms on earth. Their ability to capture solar energy, store carbon, and produce oxygen has allowed a great diversity of life forms to exist (fig. 32.5 & plate 16).

PART IV

Projects

Winter Window

Pleasing is the view outside the winter window.
The movement of trees gives evidence of wind.
See life on the wing, passing through the branches.
See change from the clouds that cover yesterday's blue.
I hear water moving and the call of crows.
Buds tell of flowers to come.
Through eyes and ears thoughts are fixed.
Nature's near with her subtleties to discover.

33   Planting and Pruning

TREE PLANTING is about establishing and nurturing young trees in a way that offers them the best chance for a long, healthy life. In nature, long-term survival is more the exception than the rule.

The primary steps for planting are to match tree species to appropriate sites and to choose high-quality plant stock. Defective nursery stock, poorly planted in a mismatched site, ultimately yields low-quality trees with greater maintenance requirements. Specific circumstances should influence planting decisions and procedures. Sound ecological choices allow for compatible diversity, take wildlife into consideration, and avoid invasive or high-maintenance species. If enough space is available, trees grow well in groups. Regulatory efforts to standardize growing and planting methods don't guarantee favorable results.

Choosing and planting trees takes practice; mistakes will happen. Every tree is unique, as are the dynamics of each planting site. The long-term outcome will reflect the effectiveness of physical efforts and financial investments. Chances for success are increased when consumers and producers are well informed.

Trees are planted for shade, privacy, fruit, timber and many other reasons. Plant sizes vary greatly. A bundle of fifty bare-root whiplike seedlings can be held in one hand, whereas larger maturing trees must be moved with industrial equipment.

Trees from the wild can be successfully transplanted when young, but the results are unpredictable. Nature plants trees through the distribution of seeds, and more than 99 percent are unsuccessful. People generally cultivate trees in a starter setting and incrementally transfer them to either pots or burlapped root balls for transport.

The optimistic goal is for most trees to survive for decades; however, the actual survival average may be as little as seven years. Many factors cause failure: two common reasons are planting trees too deep, and planting trees with container-bound roots. Trees grown commercially by nurseries for the public are often five to eight years old when sold (fig. 33.1). The following are general suggestions for planting (fig. 33.2).

1. Prepare a planting site instead of simply digging a hole. Loosen soil well beyond the width of the root ball, but never deeper. Other

FIG. 33.1 Commercial nursery trees, 5 to 8 years old, balled and burlapped (B&B), heeled in mulch.

than integrating compost, it's usually unnecessary to change the soil or add amendments such as fertilizer.

2. Transporting and handling trees is hard on them. Exercise care to avoid damage, such as drying out the roots and foliage or disturbing the root ball. The trunk shouldn't be used as a lever.

3. Carefully remove the wire basket and burlap if feasible (fig. 33.3). If the soil ball is loose, cut away the top part of the burlap. Remove tie strings and plastic tags from around the trunk, roots or limbs.

4. Proper plant depth requires the trunk flare to be at or ten percent higher than grade, and may require the delicate removal of excess soil around the stem. Allow the tree to stand upright on its own, then backfill with three-quarters of the soil. Water to settle soil, but don't tamp it down. Wait for the water to drain, then complete the backfill and grading. Don't dig a surrounding moat or build a donut-like berm. Staking isn't necessary unless a tree is unstable, and then only passively for no more than a year or two.

FIG. 33.2 Tree planting (3" × 15' Sugar Maple). Excess soil on stem lowered to field grade. Watering to settle soil. Note coarse compost for mulch. *Photo Linda Bartlett.*

FIG. 33.3 Removing wire basket. *Photo Mary Pat Rowan.*

FIG. 33.4 Woody perennial
died (girdling roots) after
eight years in the ground.
Roots still retain shape of pot.

5. Mulch the soil area lightly with one or two inches of noncom-
   pacting material such as coarse leaf compost, aged wood chips or
   pine needles. Don't allow mulch or soil to build up against the
   trunk stem.
6. Avoid pruning, except for torn, crushed or dried-out roots and
   broken or larger-sized dead limbs. Don't use trunk wrap or paint
   (wound dressing).
7. Be cautious of bucket-grown trees, as root growth patterns and soil
   mixtures can lead to permanent problems (fig. 33.4). Methods for
   splaying bound roots on trees and shrubs are generally ineffective.
8. Water the tree root and soil areas, slowly and thoroughly, two to
   four times monthly (spring through fall) for the first season, and
   once or twice monthly for the second and third season.
9. Avoid planting flowers, bulbs or grass near trees. Don't edge out or
   build up soil around trees. Protect young trees from injuries.
10. Allocate resources for conservative but proper maintenance, such
    as light periodic aeration, mulching, pruning and weeding.

TREE PRUNING architecturally manipulates trees by selectively removing parts. It combines aspects of both art and science. The art involves the
acquired skill of altering by taking away unwanted parts to achieve a desired
purpose, such as an aesthetic form. The science involves working within the
parameters of understood facts. This means that pruning must take into
account tree health, safety, and long-term preservation. Proper pruning
achieves the desired goals without compromising the biological health or
structural stability of trees. Factors such as tree age, species and health status,
along with site limitations, influence pruning decisions. Pruning often involves
compromises.

FIG. 33.5 Live limb was pruned from Crape-myrtle. Tree contained resulting infection and continued to grow. Note woundwood around pruning cut (*above*) and branch protection zone behind cut (*below*).

Trees are injured, to some degree, through pruning live parts (fig. 33.5). Natural boundaries are breached and energy-containing sections are removed. The openings expose trees to pathogens and can be a starting point for disease and structural problems. Pruning cuts are basically controlled wounds, and wounds are permanent because trees don't have the ability to heal cuts or rid themselves of infection. The tree's defense response, triggered by pruning cuts, works to contain infections (see chap. 9). The defense process and the process of growing new wood over wounds demands energy.

The essence of fine pruning comes not from tools and techniques, but from familiarity with trees. It respects their natural design characteristics. The basic aspects of trees involved with pruning include anatomy for structure, phenology for timing, and species for type characteristics. Branch attachment anatomy is especially important, and encompasses a combination of the collar, the branch protection zone, the branch bark ridge, codominant stems, and included bark (see chap. 11). Recognition of different sprout types is also important (see chap. 12). Familiarity with common tree species and their phenological cycles and aging stages contributes to sound pruning judgement. Trees with biological or structural problems may require a special pruning strategy based on their specific situation.

The physical aspects of pruning require practice to gain skill. Proficiency usually improves with experience. Safety considerations always come first. Inductive training for the mechanical use of tools is helpful. Good equipment and techniques are important, but knowing what to prune, when and how much, is more important. Deductive reasoning is a critical part of good pruning. All trees and all situations vary. Decisions often have no clear right or wrong, and require broad knowledge mixed with a degree of common sense. Mistakes inevitably happen but can be limited by following the adage, "when in doubt, don't."

Before pruning, a visual safety inspection for cracks, rot and other tree defects is recommended. Sanitation and safety issues are two primary reasons for pruning. Start with the obvious: larger-sized dead wood and stubs, plus broken and diseased limbs. For mature trees, stop here (fig. 33.6). Except for safety reasons, pruning live foliage-bearing limbs should be kept to a minimum. Pruning limbs to clear physical property, such as buildings in urban areas, is sometimes necessary. Middle-aged and younger trees may need to have crossing or poorly formed limbs removed. Injurious pruning practices such as topping (removing portions of a tree's crown) or flush cutting (removing or wounding a collar) aren't recommended (see fig. 12.3). If a tree is unsafe and in a populated area, removal makes sense. People performing tree work need to recognize their limitations. A tree of any size is dangerous, especially those with defects or that are near utility wires.

Overpruning means taking off too much. It's a form of wounding and seldom in the best interest of a tree. The concept also applies to forest situations. Clearing too many trees over too short a period of time is often harmful to the remaining trees and to the forest environment.

The broad range of reasons for pruning fall under a handful of special-interest disciplines associated with forestry, orchards, nurseries, gardening and utilities. The common denominator is the tree itself, which evolved in group forest settings over millions of years. The genetic codes of the past are still carried and control the growth and development in the trees of this era. Understanding how forest trees grow, change with age, and die offers insights into the management of trees in any setting. The fundamental way in which pruning helps trees is by establishing good form, and by providing sanitation through the removal of diseased and dead wood.

Periodic pruning of young trees, when properly done, predisposes them for success. It takes relatively little time and minimizes future problems and maintenance needs as they mature. Pruning starts by eliminating codominant stems, branches with included bark, and crossing limbs. Well-executed cuts are close to a collar or nodal point (bud or stem junction). They avoid crushing or tearing trunk, branch or bark tissues.

FIG. 33.6 Conservative pruning of mature Oak focuses on safety and sanitation (dead and broken branches), and minimizes pruning parts that support foliage.

Certain strategies help to train young trees for a desired effect. For example, tip-prune lateral limbs to encourage a strong central leader, or do the opposite to promote a spreading canopy. When young trees are diseased or have serious defects, culling is more practical than pruning. A healthier replacement can be started sooner rather than later.

Pruning to control size and shape is possible, but there are limitations and practical considerations. The natural growth tendency of a species (or cultivar) affects its eventual size and shape. The physical environment also influences growth and development. The current age, size and health of a tree are factors

FIG. 33.7 Bonsai, pruning
art form, tests survival
limits of trees. Requires
patience and skill.

as well. Small, younger trees can be kept small, but large, older trees can't be
made small again in a healthy way.

Good pruning practices, especially when applied to younger trees, generally
yield positive results. Some of the most extreme pruning styles, such as pol-
larding, pleaching, espalier, topiary and bonsai, are only possible because they
start with young trees (fig. 33.7). These styles are respected cultural art forms.
They are a metaphor of man's relationship to nature and his desire to control
it. It's admirable that enthusiasts choose to carry on the traditions, for they
require a considerable amount of skill, time and resources.

The timing of pruning depends on the situation and purpose. After the initial training of young trees, prune only as needed. It may be three to five years
for young trees, and five to ten or more years for maturing trees. Schedules
aren't necessary, other than for specific ornamental pruning styles. Constant
pruning isn't good for trees. Except for safety and disease concerns, the time
between pruning sessions can be stretched out. This is especially true for dying
limbs. A distinction can be drawn between dying and being killed. As tree
parts die, biological processes related to the event occur. Trees alter chemical compounds and strengthen natural boundaries. With a dying branch, for
example, the associated collar swells and a protection zone develops at the
branch base (fig. 33.8).

When is the best time to prune? Providing cuts are made properly, it

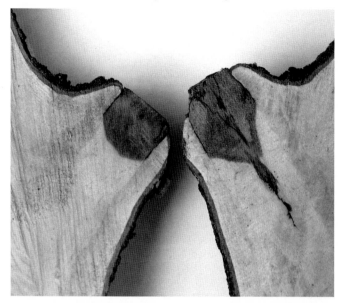

FIG. 33.8 Dogwood (*Cornus florida*) collar swelled and branch
protection zone formed as branch died. Note formation of
woundwood after branch death. Pruning cut made close to collar
without injuring live tissue.

doesn't matter. The opposite question, when not to prune, may be more relevant. The few weeks when leaves are forming or falling are active transition
periods. Energy demands are high and reserves are low. Pruning mistakes at
these times pose greater risks to trees. The active life cycle of many insect and
fungal pathogens evolved around seasonal periods of low energy. The primary
risk associated with pruning at times of transition isn't directly from insect
wounds or fungal infections, but from energy depletion. Healthy trees effectively defend themselves when wounded or infected. Defense, however, is an
energy-demanding process and can be compromised, as can the other biological processes, when energy reserves are low. A loss or interruption of energy
supplies, even briefly, predisposes trees to problems.

Proper pruning cuts to remove branches aim close to the collar on the trunk
stem or a parent limb. They avoid leaving stubs or making flush cuts. Stubs are
defenseless and allow easy access for rot-causing fungi. Flush cuts cause serious
trunk wounds through the injury or removal of collar tissue (fig. 33.9). Seal-
ants (wound dressings) such as paint to cover pruning cuts or other wounds is
never necessary. They inhibit the tree's defense process and create conditions
that benefit decay organisms and rot.

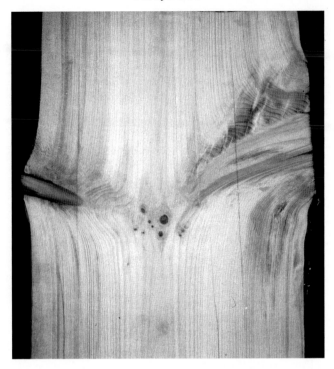

FIG. 33.9 Flush cut (*right*) injured trunk of White Pine (*Pinus strobus*). Note formation of discolored (resinous) wood. Small dead limb core (*left*) contained within trunk without infection.

Pruning cuts follow the angle of collars. After pruning, a donut-like ring of woundwood usually develops evenly around proper cuts (fig. 33.10). When woundwood grows only at the sides, it means the cut was too deep and injured the trunk by removing part or all of the collar. Mistakes can be reduced if the bulk of a limb is cut off first, followed by the final cut at the collar.

Codominant stems don't have collars, but most have a bark ridge at the stem junction. A pruning cut should aim for and angle off from this upper point. Included bark between codominant stems doesn't allow for a perfect cut because of the nature of the union.

Pruning dead branches and stems is determined by where live and dead tissues meet. The goal is to not leave a protruding stub or remove live tissue, no matter how far it extends outward (see fig. 11.7). Pruning woody shrubbery involves the same principle for branches and stems as with trees. A notable difference is their smaller size. For ornamental purposes, numerous nodal (tip-pruning) cuts are sometimes made to create a formal shape.

Published material about pruning isn't always current or written from a tree-health perspective. Confusion occurs when publications are obsolete, or when they combine pruning information for annual and herbaceous perennial plants with that of trees. For example, techniques to produce fruit on raspberries or flowers on geraniums don't apply to trees. Terminology can also create confusion by being misleading or having multiple meanings. The term *sucker* — excessive axillary leaf growth, such as nonfruit-bearing leaves on tomato plants — is an example. The word implies the drawing out of energy and water. It doesn't apply to trees and has become confused with an aerial tree sprout, which is a bud or epicormic growth appendage that develops into a foliage-bearing stem. Sprouts provide photosynthates, energy-containing substances (nutrients), to a localized region of a stem. Inaccurate reference material and terms, after continual repetition, tend to become accepted. They promote misconceptions and contribute to the mismanagement of trees.

Trees and forests develop slowly, and changes associated with the quality of their health aren't immediately evident. It's difficult to connect what we do

FIG. 33.10 Zelkova (*Z. serrata*). Uniform growth forming over accurate pruning cut. Note: bark ridge (*upper left*) marks upper position of branch/trunk junction.

now with the future outcome. Long-term insight to understand natural processes isn't necessarily intrinsic to human nature. Take the example of global warming. The rate of response to change, based on convincing evidence, is slow.

There are several ways to improve pruning results: adjust what, when and how much we do at any given time; use care with language to describe parts, processes and procedures; keep records to monitor results; critique work through observation, autopsies and discussion.

34

Autopsy, Dissection and Activities

AUTOPSY means to see for yourself. Necropsy is a postmortem (the study of the dead), but the word autopsy has become more associated with the medical procedure investigating dead bodies. Tree autopsies allow for a close examination of tree parts in order to become better acquainted with their anatomical characteristics and abnormalities. Trees keep an accurate record of events in their lives. To better understand these events, it's important to know how trees are put together. Autopsy studies, coupled with field trip observations and textbook references, enhance learning. Touching trees and handling their parts provide tangible connections.

DISSECTION means to take something apart. Tree dissections allow for detailed anatomical study, familiarizing us with the arrangement, texture, color and odor of the parts. We can compare features between tree species and between normal and defective parts. Dissection analysis to interpret events that occurred in trees can be difficult. Productive autopsies begin with background information about the subject tree, as well as thoughtfully chosen, carefully prepared samples (see fig. 12.6). Poorly prepared samples can yield artifacts and lead to inaccurate or misleading conclusions. Avoid drawing conclusions when information is incomplete.

Autopsies provide a method to read the life story of a tree. The skill of reading is to interpret the changes that took place during the formation of a tree's parts. Individual events such as a wound or a broken limb may be obvious, but the reaction of a tree to these events can be difficult to understand. The key for investigating trees is to learn what to look for, where to look, and the meaning of what is seen.

Peering inside a tree is to explore the past. A tree grows a new tree over itself every year, which allows a four-dimensional view; that is, the three-dimensional tree over time. Look for patterns and features that occurred over time. More than revealing the history of individual trees, dissections give insight into living trees (fig. 34.1).

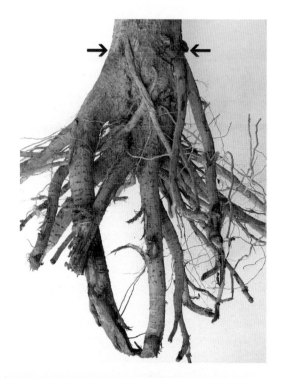

AUTOPSY OBSERVATIONS, whether made for general curiosity or for more detailed study, will show some combination of the anatomic features listed below. Many are visible in a natural state to the unaided eye. Those requiring preparation or enhancement involve only a hand lens or low-power microscope and basic hand tools. Many of the features listed below are shown in photos throughout the book.

WOOD TYPE: diffuse porous and ring porous, resinous and nonresinous

WOOD: cambial zone, growth increments (rings), age, growth patterns, sapwood, heartwood, rays, pith, pith plugs, callus or woundwood, false heartwood, discolored wood, discolored heartwood, wetwood, compression wood, burls, tracheids, resin ducts, fibers, vessels, tyloses, axial and radial parenchyma, meristematic points and traces

BARK: epidermis, cortex, lenticels, phloem, phloem rays, phellem, phellogen, fissures

EPIPHYTES: mosses, lichens, algae

TWIG: buds (terminal, lateral, flower), bud scales and scars, stipules, leaves, flowers, cones, thorns, nuts, fruit

SPROUTS: from preformed buds or epicormic growth (meristematic or adventitious, elite or suppressed)

BRANCHES: collars, branch bark ridge, branch core and protection zone, compacted xylem, branch rot patterns, codominant stems

ROOTS: woody, nonwoody, pioneer, tap, root hairs, mycorrhizae, growth patterns

COMPARTMENTALIZATION: CODIT patterns, reaction zone (wall 1-2-3), barrier zone (wall 4), column boundary layers

DEFECTS: wounds, rot cavities, cracks, included bark, cambial zone dieback, canker lesions, fungal wedges, zone lines, sporophores,

---

FIG. 34.1 *(Opposite page)* Autopsy of White Oak (*Quercus alba*) investigated factors associated with its death. (1) Tree transferred (replanted) too deep about 4 years ago, causing secondary root system to grow from meristematic points on stem (*arrows, left*). (2) Woody roots torn and crushed when dug at nursery. Most absorbing (nonwoody) roots were lost at this time. (3) Dissection of trunk stem (*below*) shows that the tree was seven years and about two weeks old. The first three growth increments are even. The fourth season shows stunted growth. Fifth, sixth and seventh seasons had rapid growth. Tree dug and injured in late winter. Stored starch, from previous season, allowed buds to open and earlywood vessels to form (*small arrows*) during first two weeks of the growth season (May 1 to 15 in central Maryland). A dysfunctional root system and depletion of stored starch contributed to the tree's death.

mycelium mats, insect galleries, galls, animal damage, pruning
injuries

Tree identification information is readily available. Good quality photos
often accompany published material. In this digital age, the floodgates are
open to information on practically everything. With easy access to information, the need to gather samples and perform dissections may be questioned.
It's a slow, dirty, and sometimes dangerous activity. The response is that a
hands-on approach to learning through field studies and dissections enhances
the understanding of trees by allowing us to see for ourselves. Through personal experience, we can accept, question or expound on published material
and conventional wisdom.

Working with trees on any level (scientific, professional or recreational)
requires some basic precautions and preparations. First is safety awareness.
Trees are large and, along with the work tools, can be dangerous. Good quality
samples are necessary for productive results. Preparing specimens starts with
fresh samples. Collecting more than are needed increases choices (fig. 34.2).
Extras allow for experiments and compensate for mistakes.

Observations of features and growth patterns can be discussed and noted.
Sketching aids the learning process as the hand-brain connection helps instill
the subject in memory. The use of a microscope opens up wonderful views into
the tree, and it illustrates that these large organisms are built of small cells in
orderly arrangements. A low-power microscope works well. The magnification
range of 7× to 30× is adequate, with 45× to 60× reaching the limit needed
for basic observations. Useful field tools include a saw, axe, knife, shovel, hand
lens, planer and eye protection. Lab tools include a notebook, colored pencils,
razor blade, petri dish, eye dropper and I_2KI (fig. 34.3).

IODINE IN POTASSIUM IODIDE (I_2KI) stains starch granules purple. It's
used as a diagnostic technique to detect energy potential in trees (fig. 34.4).
Only living cells contain starch, and color gradations indicate the concentration. Dark purple has the highest, light purple contains moderate levels, and
yellow has none. Stained core plugs from standing trees or slab samples from
fresh-cut trees show starch (energy) reserves in sapwood at specific times of
the year.

Iodine is a poison. It's important to avoid skin contact, ingestion and inha-
lation of fumes. A 2 percent solution of I_2KI consists of 0.3 grams of iodine
crystals and 1.5 grams of potassium iodide crystals in 100 milliliters of water.
The solution, after a long period of shaking, should be strained and stored in a
light-resistant bottle with an eyedropper dispenser.

FIG. 34.2 Samples
collected for
workshops.

FIG. 34.3 Study
setup with low-power
microscope.

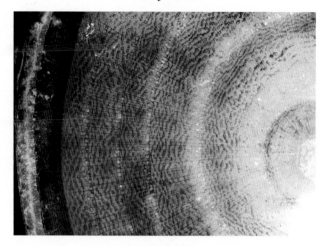

FIG. 34.4 Elm stained with I₂KI. Dark color indicates starch. Note higher concentration in younger wood. *Photo Alex Shigo. Courtesy Shigo & Trees, Associates.*

To obtain the best results, sample specimens should be fresh and free of debris before applying I₂KI. Should the test surface need to be cleaned or smoothed, a razor, straight-edge blade, or planer can be used. Common grade sandpaper can leave small particles (artifacts).

The cambial zone and vessels don't store starch and shouldn't turn purple. Newly formed wood cells don't begin to store starch until the latter part of the growth period. Buds don't contain starch, but the tissue behind them does. Starch is the primary energy-storage substance for trees. It fuels metabolic and growth activities. Reproduction and defense potential are also contingent on energy reserves.

Suggestions for tree dissection projects follow. See the index to locate reference information.

    1. Begin with ring-porous trees. Collect samples from common species (Oak, Locust, Elm). Avoid pieces with defects. Choose modest-sized samples (2.5 to 5 cm in diameter). Cut lengths of about 2.5 cm and discard the end pieces. Smooth the transverse (cross cut) surface with a razor or knife. Place under the microscope on lowest magnification. Draw the image, and list the parts and color features (epidermis, green cortex, phloem, cambial zone, growth increments, vessels, rays, pith, etc.). Split samples radially between two rays to the pith (wedge shape). Also split a few samples along the tangential surface by taking off the

FIG. 34.5 Orienta-
tions of wood
surfaces: Transverse
(*top*), Oak; Radial
(*center*), Locust, Oak;
Tangential (*bottom*),
Locust, Oak.

outer wood curve perpendicular to a ray (triangular shape; fig. 34.5).
Razor planing isn't necessary for either surface (radial/tangential). View
through the microscope on low and high power. Use a small ball of clay
to secure and level samples. Draw and list features (cellular arrangements, radial parenchyma sheets, vessel segments, etc.; see fig. 19.2).

2. With fresh samples, repeat dissections and apply I_2KI to viewing
surfaces. The purple color indicates starch and parenchyma cells. Note
the cellular arrangements and how axial and radial parenchyma inter-
mix (see fig. 18.4). Date how far back into the wood starch is found.
Repeat the process for different tree species. Contrast and note characteristic distinctions. Dissections seem to always reveal something previously unknown or unrecognized.

3. Next examine diffuse porous species (Sycamore, Maple, Cherry)
and resinous/nonresinous species (Pine, Hemlock, Spruce). Transverse
samples require the thinnest possible slivers of wood tissue in order to
see the vessel/tracheid arrangements (fig. 34.6). Prepare tangential and
radial samples as described above. Water can sometimes be seen moving
in the tracheids of conifers.

4. Collect root samples. Be careful not to damage fragile root samples
or mix them with other plants. Look at woody roots following the same
procedures. Contrast differences between roots and aerial stems (see fig.
16.2). Keep finer root sections in plastic with a little soil attached to prevent drying. Gently pull apart root sections and lightly shake off some
soil. Place in a petri dish and use an eyedropper with water to lightly
clean root samples and to keep them moist. Look though the microscope for clusters of ectomycorrhizae and nonwoody root hairs. Note
color variations (light to dark) that indicate gradations of living, dying
and dead roots (see fig. 8.2). Tiny insects or fungal hyphae will often be
present.

FIG. 34.6 Thin slivers can be examined under the microscope to view cellular arrangements: radial (*top*), transverse (*bottom*).

5. Dissect branch unions lengthwise (radially) and observe features (collar, branch protection zone, branch core, codominant stems, etc.). Radial dissections must follow the pith center (see fig. 11.4). Cut and planed samples show false heartwood, discolored wood, branch rot patterns, and defect columns. Closure growth, associated with pruned or shed branches, dates branch death. Axe-split wood shows the interlocking characteristics of branch and trunk tissues in collars, and compacted xylem in the crotches (see fig. 11.3).

6. Dissect samples with defects (wounds, discolored wood, cracks, included bark, etc.). Contrast them to samples without defects. Start with small stems (5 to 15 cm in diameter). Proceed to larger samples that don't require a microscope. Transverse surfaces and some of the radial surfaces should be planed. Look at the three surface orientations without I$_2$KI, then with it. Allow radial dissections to extend beyond columns of discolored wood. Identify barrier and reaction zones. Based on the barrier zone, date wounds. Look at cracks associated with wound-wood growth. Analyze defect patterns associated with escalating cracks and canker infections.

Not all learning comes from the proverbial book and pen. Just as the scientist learns through investigation, the artist through practice, and the traveler from exposure to new things, there are many opportunities to learn more about trees. Simple activities and projects can lead to an understanding of bigger concepts. Some suggestions follow.

Observe the branching patterns of trees in different settings. Examine the tips and buds in their seasonal stages, as well as other twig features, leaf arrangements, and collar attachments. Look at the shape of branch crotches. Compare strong unions to those with defects, such as included bark and cracks. Note the height level where codominant stems develop in forest versus city trees. Observe sprout growth patterns. Determine if they're a natural characteristic of a healthy tree or related to stress (see fig. 12.2). Old, declining trees often have epicormic trunk sprouts, and topped trees usually grow adventitious sprouts (see fig 12.3).

Several projects to illustrate tree features involve looking at small branches dislodged from stems. It shows how branches are attached by a series of collars (see fig. 11.1). Put small stem samples in a pot of boiling water for a few minutes. The bark will peel easily, revealing grain patterns and other wood features (see figs. 11.6 & 12.5). Count terminal bud scale scars on branch twigs to assess their growth rate and age. Count branch whorls on a white pine trunk to age the tree. Both counting activities illustrate how unrelated size and age are when comparing open-grown trees, forest trees, and trees in locations that suppress growth.

Profile city and forest trees. List physical features and collect samples of leaves, flowers, seeds and cones. Observe and record the timing of phenological events (growth, reproduction, shedding). Note preferred soil and site conditions. Look for associations with other trees, plants, insects and larger animals. Discuss changes related to aging. Try to identify growth patterns related to wounds, disease and climate. Contrast differences between city and forest, introduced versus native, and nursery versus nature-grown trees (fig. 34.7).

Instruments are available to help detect and measure defects and decay in the lower trunk and surface root areas of trees. Methods involve measuring either electrical or physical patterns of resistance between healthy and altered wood. X-ray techniques are also being tested. Interpretations are contingent on establishing species-specific baseline information. No method negates the necessity for a broad knowledge of trees. Data must be properly gathered and put into perspective with other relevant biological and environmental factors. The quality of tree care, research, education, and public policy relies on sound and current information to deal effectively with tree issues.

Tree biology workshops can be a useful educational resource (fig. 34.8). A productive experience has an organized teaching presentation geared to the level of those attending. They combine lecture, lab and field work, as well as a summary period for engaging participants in discussions.

Visiting the places where trees grow is fundamental to tree study. Forest

FIG. 34.7 Linden (*Tilia cordata*). Durable shade tree often planted in urban areas. Note decurrent growth pattern.

FIG. 34.8 Speaker utilizes samples to provide workshop participants an opportunity to connect with trees.

FIG. 34.9 Aged White Oak (*Quercus alba*) about three hundred years old. It survived transitions from forest through agriculture to urbanization. Although now struggling, it continues to offer inspiration.

areas are the starting point, in order to observe and experience trees in their natural state. City parks and residential properties offer a contrast in how trees adapt to environmental influences. Overgrown fields, cut-over woodlots, and nursery locations show how young trees develop and compete to succeed. Settings with old majestic trees are inspirational (fig. 34.9 & plate 15). The stature and longevity of an ancient tree tells of the tenacity and degree of luck necessary for survival. Small, humble lessons, on foot, with hands and through the mind, connect the opportunities for learning to yield a greater understanding of trees and their ecology.

APPENDIX A: *Keywords*

ECOLOGY: The study of living organisms in relationship to the environment.

ENVIRONMENT: The surroundings and conditions influencing life.

NATURE: The intrinsic characteristics and qualities of the physical world, including its forces, processes and phenomena.

FOREST: A system of trees in nature connected with each other and with diversified communities of other organisms in ways that insure mutual survival.

TREES: Woody, perennial, compartmented, shedding plants that generally have a single trunk and the ability to grow tall and live long.

PLANTS: Nonmotile, vegetative organisms that are cellulose based, contain chlorophyll, and make food through photosynthesis. They can be annuals or perennials, herbaceous or woody (containing lignin).

MODERN ARBORICULTURE: A holistic biological perspective of the living tree system and associated tree issues. It focuses on trees as a major part of the earth's ecological system.

BIOLOGY: The science of life.

CHEMISTRY: The science of the arrangements of atoms and their properties.

ORGANIC CHEMISTRY: The study of carbon and its capacity to form long chains of atoms. Life forms derive and manage energy through carbon-based molecules.

LIFE: a biological state with the capacity to maintain an energy-dependent system and the ability to compete and repeat over a limited period of time.

SYSTEM: An orderly collection or connection of parts and processes that produce a predetermined product or service.

MASS ENERGY RATIO: The ratio of dynamic (live) to static (dead) parts. The ratio for trees changes with age. No system will survive when growth (mass) exceeds the energy available to maintain order.

DYNAMIC EQUILIBRIUM: The constant motion of opposing forces in living systems.

SURVIVAL: An ability to stay alive under conditions that have the potential to stop a system. To compete effectively with other organisms for space and an energy source. To respond rapidly and effectively to injury. To live long enough to complete a life cycle and reproduce.

SURVIVAL FACTORS: Components that affect survival. These include energy, genetics, space, water, essential elements, temperature, time, and the percentages of these factors.

VIGOR: A genetic capacity to survive and reproduce. Capacity is what you have.

VITALITY: An ability to maintain orderly growth under an existing set of conditions. Ability is what you do with what you have.

HEALTH: The ability to resist stress and maintain order.

STRESS: A condition in which a system operates near its limits for survival.

PRIMARY STRESS: A loss or interruption in the continuous supply of energy needed to remain in an orderly state (healthy).

SECONDARY STRESS: Substances and conditions essential for life that are at extremes (too little, too much).

PREDISPOSITION: Events influencing susceptibility; to be inclined towards something in advance.

DISEASE: An abnormal physiological or anatomical process that causes injury or death to an organism.

DEFENSE: A dynamic survival action to preserve an organism from injuries, infections, and death by an outside agent.

APPENDIX B: *Chemistry Review*

CHEMISTRY: The science of the arrangements of atoms and their properties. Chemistry runs through all life processes on the molecular level.

ATOM: The smallest part of an element that exists as a stable entity.

ELEMENT: The basic building blocks of the universe. They can't be broken down into simpler substances by ordinary chemical means. There are about 92 naturally occurring elements (on earth), each with its own name and properties.

MOLECULE: Two or more atoms chemically bonded together into a geometric arrangement. In the molecular structure of an element all atoms are identical. In a compound different atoms are joined together.

COMPOUND: A chemical combination of atoms of different elements that form a substance (material).

CHEMICAL SYMBOLS: An abbreviation for an element's name and the number of atoms and/or molecules (H_2 = two molecules of hydrogen; $3O$ = three atoms of oxygen; $5H_2O$ = five molecules of water).

ELEMENTARY PARTICLES: The inner and outer components of an atom. The inner core of an atom, the NUCLEUS, is composed of PROTONS (particles with a positive charge) and NEUTRONS (neutrally charged particles).

ELECTRONS: Particles with a negative charge. They orbit the nucleus in an ELECTRON CLOUD (the negatively charged outer shell of an atom).

ATOMIC NUMBER: Refers to the number of protons in the nucleus. It also indicates the number of electrons.

MASS NUMBER: The number of protons and neutrons in the nucleus (electrons are considered to have zero mass). Subtracting the atomic number from the mass number yields the number of neutrons.

ISOTOPES: Atoms that have different mass numbers and the same atomic number (different amount of neutrons and a different atomic weight). Radioisotopes are isotopes that emit radiation.

ELECTRON ENERGY LEVEL: Electrons that makeup the electron cloud are subdivided into different levels. The first level is nearest the nucleus, followed by the second, ect. Each level holds a certain number of electrons. The maximum number per level can be determined by the formula $X = 2n^2$, where X is the number of electrons and n is the energy level. Energy levels must be filled before moving to the next level (1st = 2, 2nd = 8, 3rd = 18, etc.).

VALENCE SHELL: The outermost energy level of an atom. An element and most atoms reach their most stable (inert/unreactive) state with 8 electrons in their outer energy level.

ISOMER: Two or more compounds with the same molecular formula (number and type of atoms in a molecule) but each with a different structural formula. Examples are glucose/fructose.

FREE RADICAL: Unstable compounds that contain an unpaired electron. They often behave as an OXIDANT, taking electrons away from other compounds. Certain REDUCTANTS provide electrons and are referred to as ANTIOXIDANTS. They can transfer electrons to an oxidant, rendering it harmless.

OXIDATION: Refers to the loss of electrons by atoms or molecules. Oxygen is gained and hydrogen lost.

REDUCTION: Refers to the gain of electrons. Oxygen is lost and hydrogen gained.
    These two essential biological processes (oxidation and reduction) occur simultaneously. The coupled reaction of the electron transport chain, occurring during respiration in mitochondria, is an example.

ION: A charged particle. Atoms acquire an electrical charge by either gaining or losing an electron. Atoms with equal numbers of protons and electrons are electrically neutral and are not ions.

ANION: An ion with a negative charge that results from gaining electrons.

CATION: An ion with a positive charge that results from losing electrons.

ION SYMBOLS: A shorthand system for indicating the electrical charge of an ion. It is based on the gain or loss of electrons. Examples: sodium cation Na^+ (has lost one electron); nitrate anion NO_3^- (has gained one electron).

IONIC BOND: Ions held together by the attraction of their opposite charges. They are not energy bonds.

ACID: Substances yielding hydrogen ions (H^+) in solution.

BASE: Substances accepting hydrogen ions (protons) in solution. Hydroxide ions (OH^-) are a base and accept hydrogen ions (H^+) in solution to form water (H_2O).

SALT: Compounds yielding ions other than hydroxide ions (OH^-) or hydrogen ions (H^+) in solution.

ELECTROLYTE: Liquids with positive and negative ions conducting electricity by the flow of the charges. Acids, bases and salts are electrolytes. Nonelectrolytes don't produce ions and so cannot produce electricity.

SALT INDEX: The rate at which materials ionize in water. Sodium nitrate is used as a baseline and assigned the number 100. Materials ionizing faster have higher numbers, when slower they have lower numbers.

PLASMOLYSIS: The movement of water out of a cell. When water is pulled from a cell the protoplasm shrinks and breaks away from the cell wall causing cell death. Salt on a ham kills bacteria by plasmolysis.

OSMATIC PRESSURE: The force exerted (pressure required) to stop osmosis.

OSMOSIS: Movement of a solvent from a dilute solution to a more concentrated solution through a membrane.

DIFFUSION: To move away from an area of high concentration to a lower one.

pH: The concentration of hydrogen ions and hydroxide ions in solution ("p" for power, "H" for hydrogen ions).

pH SCALE: A scale of 1 to 14 that defines the acid or base strength (acidity or alkalinity) of a solution. The pH values represent logarithms (an exponent) and can't be averaged. A difference of 1 is a ten fold difference of a solution strength. A pH of 7 indicates the neutral point with an equal amount of H^+ and OH^- ions. The lower the number the stronger the acid, the higher the number the stronger the base.

BUFFER: A solution maintaining a consistent pH with the addition of either a weak acid or a weak base.

MIXTURES: Solutions containing a solute dissolved in a solvent. Salt dissolved in water yields a saltwater solution. Solutions are homogeneous and pass through a membrane.

COLLOIDS: Solutions containing small particles suspended in a liquid. The particles don't settle or pass through membranes.

SUSPENSIONS: Substances that are heterogeneous and don't dissolve in solution.

COVALENT BOND: Chemical bonds formed when atoms share electrons equally. The compound is a nonelectrolyte as no ions are produced. Atoms are most likely to share electrons and form covalent bonds when there are 4 or 5 electrons in their outer energy level. Molecules are combinations of atoms bound together by covalent bonds.

NONPOLAR COVALENT BONDS: A pair of electrons shared equally between two atoms with no difference in electronegativity. When the electrons are no closer to either atom, and the compound is symmetrical, it's referred to as a nonpolar compound.

POLAR COVALENT BONDS: Polar compounds have a difference in electronegativity. Electrons closer to the atom with greater electronegativity will have a partial negative charge. Those farther from the atom have lower electronegativity and a partial positive charge. This partial charge is not an ionic charge or bond.

SOLUBILITY: The ability to be dissolved. Polar compounds are dissolved by polar liquids and nonpolar compounds by nonpolar liquids. Salt is a polar compound and dissolves in water, a polar liquid. Oil is a nonpolar liquid.

ELECTRONEGATIVITY: Refers to the attraction of an atom for an electron.

HYDROGEN BOND: An intermolecular bond between polar molecules where hydrogen is bound to a stronger electronegative element. A hydrogen bond is weak bond that is easily broken; whereas, a covalent bond is usually strong and not readily broken.

FUNCTIONAL GROUPS: The chemically active parts of organic molecules. They impart a certain set of properties to compounds. Examples: ALCOHOLS, covalent compounds (aren't electrolytes) in which the oxygen atom has two bonds (frequently written as −OH). ORGANIC ACIDS, the carboxyl group −COOH, also called carboxylic acids. They yield H^+ ions.

CARBOHYDRATES: Compounds that contain carbon, hydrogen and oxygen. The ratio is usually two H to one O. Carbohydrates are biological fuel. The three types are: MONOSACCHARIDES (one sugar), DISACCHARIDES (two sugars) and POLYSACCHARIDES (many sugars). Mono- and disaccharides are water soluble; polysaccharides are not. Di- and polysaccharides must be hydrolyzed to monosaccharides to be utilized.

GLYCOSIDIC BOND: The bond (linkage) holding a disaccharide together and the multiple bonds holding polysaccharides together.

GLYCOLYSIS: The splitting of glucose molecules to pyruvate during respiration in cells.

HYDROLYSIS: The breaking apart of molecules by a reaction between water and a compound.

LIPIDS: Substances such as fats and oils that are insoluble in water. Consisting mostly of carbon, hydrogen and low levels of oxygen, they are nonpolar and soluble in nonpolar solvents.

PROTEINS: A large group of substances important in the structure and function of all living organisms. Containing CHON (sometimes SPFe), they are polypeptides made of amino acids joined by peptide links in simple proteins. Simple proteins are joined together into more complex proteins.

AMINO ACIDS: A general class of 20 organic molecules that are the building blocks of proteins. They contain the functional groups amines (NH_2) and organic acids.

PEPTIDE BOND: The link between amino acid molecules. The bond occurs between a carbon and a nitrogen atom of different amino acids. DIPEPTIDE is the product when two amino acids combine and a POLYPEPTIDE when many combine.

PROTEIN STRUCTURE: Refers to the sequence of amino acids with peptide bonds and the structural arrangement of amino acid chains held by hydrogen bonds.

DENATURATION: When the hydrogen bonds of a protein are broken, the shape of the protein changes. It can't react or perform its physiologic function.

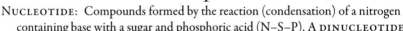

NUCLEOTIDE: Compounds formed by the reaction (condensation) of a nitrogen containing base with a sugar and phosphoric acid (N–S–P). A DINUCLEOTIDE is two linked nucleotides.

NUCLEIC ACIDS: Polynucleotides consisting of chains of many linked nucleotides. Nucleotides form polymers (compounds with large molecules made up of repeating monomers or molecular units).

DNA and RNA are nucleic acids. DNA (deoxyribonucleic acid) consists of a DOUBLE HELIX (coil) of polynucleotide chains (alternating sugar and phosphoric acid groups). The opposing sides are held together by hydrogen bonds. A (adenine) always bonds to T (thymine) with two hydrogen bonds and C (cytosine) bonds to G (guanine) with three hydrogen bonds. DNA is found in CHROMOSOMES and contains the hereditary information of organisms. The sequence of bases (genes) forms the GENETIC CODE. In RNA (ribonucleic acid), A (adenine) always bonds to U (uracil) with two hydrogen bonds and C to G with three hydrogen bonds. RNA is found mainly in the cytoplast and is involved with the transfer of information in protein synthesis.

AMP, ADP, and ATP: Nucleotides of adenosine with phosphate. AMP (adenosine monophosphate) contains no high energy bonds. ADP (adenosine diphosphate) contains one high energy bond (P–P). ATP (adenosine triphosphate) contains two high energy bonds (P–P–P). As ATP is converted to ADP and then to AMP energy is produced. ATP is derived from the metabolism of glucose and provides chemical energy in cells.

❧

CATALYST: A substance that alters (increases) the rate of a chemical reaction without itself being changed. In general enzymes are highly specific and catalysts are non-specific.

ENZYMES: Specific biologic catalysts formed from protein compounds. Acting in conjunction with a substrate, they increase the rate of chemical reactions without themselves being consumed. Certain enzymes are formed only from proteins while others have protein and nonprotein parts, both of which must be present to function. APOENZYME is the protein part of an enzyme. COENZYME is the nonprotein part. Some vitamins act as a coenzyme.

VITAMINS: Organic compounds essential in small quantities for metabolic function.

SUBSTRATE: Molecules that are acted on by a catalyst. An ACTIVE SITE is the part of the enzyme which combines with the substrate.

INHIBITOR: A substance that fits into part of the active site, preventing the substrate from reacting with the enzyme. A competitive inhibitor competes for a position in the active site while a noncompetitive inhibitor alters the shape of the active site by reacting with the enzyme at some point other than the active site. Enzymes can also be altered or destroyed by extremes in temperature and pH.

Bibliography

Atkins, P. W. *Molecules*. New York: W. H. Freeman, 1987.

Coder, Kim D. "Flood Damaged Trees." *Arborist News* (June 1997).

Coder, Kim D. "Nitrogen's Journey: From Soils into Trees." *Arborist News* (Fall 1997).

Coder, Kim D. "Lightning Damage in Trees." *Arborist News* (June 2004).

Coder, Kim D. "American Mistletoe." *Arborist News* (December 2004).

Cranshaw, Whitney. *Garden Insects of North America*. Princeton: Princeton University Press, 2004.

Ehrlich, Paul R. *Human Natures: Genes, Cultures, and the Human Prospect*. Washington, D.C.: Island Press/Shearwater Books, 2000.

Farrar, John Laird. *Trees of the Northern United States and Canada*. Iowa: Iowa State University Press, 1995.

Garber, Steven D. *Biology: A Self-Teaching Guide*. New York: John Wiley and Sons, 1989.

Gray, Harry B., et al. *Braving the Elements*. Sausalito, California: University Science Books, 1995.

Harlow, William M., and Ellwood S. Harrar. *Textbook of Dendrology*. New York: McGraw-Hill, 1937.

Hoadley, R. Bruce. *Understanding Wood*. Newtown, Connecticut: The Taunton Press, 1989.

Kenrick, Paul, and Paul Davis. *Fossil Plants*. London: Smithsonian Books, 2004.

Leopold, Donald, et al. *Trees of the Central Hardwood Forests of North America*. Oregon: Timber Press, 1998.

Little, Charles E. *The Dying of the Trees*. New York: Viking, 1995.

Lowenfels, Jeff, and Wayne Lewis. *Teaming with Microbes*. Portland, Oregon: Timber Press, 2006.

Marx, Donald H. "Mycorrhizal Fungi and Other Microorganisms." *Tree Care Industry* (August 2000).

Marx, Donald H. "Carbon and Tree Growth." *Tree Care Industry* (July 2001).

Mattheck, Claus, and Helge Breloer. *The Body Language of Trees*. London: Her Majesty's Stationery Office, 1994.

Mohr, Hans, and Peter Schopfer. *Plant Physiology*. Berlin: Springer, 1995.

Montgomery, Carla W., and David Dathe. *Earth Then and Now*. Dubuque, Iowa: William C. Brown, 1994.

Pielou, E. C. *The World of Northern Evergreens*. Ithaca, New York: Comstock Publishing Associates, 1988.

Raven, Peter H., et al. *Biology of Plants*, 6th ed. New York: W. H. Freeman, 1999.

Rost, Thomas L., et al. *Plant Biology*. Belmont, California: Wadsworth Publishing Company, 1998.

Russell, Tony, et al. *Trees: An Illustrated Identifier and Encyclopedia*. London: Hermes House, 2004.

Sackheim, George. *Introduction to Chemistry for Biology Students*. Redwood City, California: Benjamin/Cummings Publishing Company, 1991.

Schenk, George. *Moss Gardening*. Portland, Oregon: Timber Press, 1997.

Schwarze, F.W.M.R., et al. *Fungal Strategies of Wood Decay in Trees*. Berlin: Springer, 1999.

Shigo, Alex L. *A New Tree Biology*. Durham, New Hampshire: Shigo and Trees, Associates, 1986; reprint, 1989.

Shigo, Alex L. *Tree Pruning*. Durham, New Hampshire: Shigo and Trees, Associates, 1989.

Shigo, Alex L. *Modern Arboriculture*. Durham, New Hampshire: Shigo and Trees, Associates, 1991.

Shigo, Alex L. *Tree Anatomy*. Durham, New Hampshire: Shigo and Trees, Associates, 1994.

Shigo, Alex L. "Troubles in the Rhizosphere." *Tree Care Industry* (October 1996).

Shigo, Alex L., et al. "Patterns of Starch Reserves in Healthy and Diseased American Elms." *Canadian Journal of Forest Research* 16, no. 2 (1986).

Shigo, Alex L. "Compartmentalization: A Conceptual Framework for Understanding How Trees Grow and Defend Themselves." *Annual Review of Phytopathology* 22: 189–214 (1984).

Shigo, Alex L. "Tree Decay: An Expanded Concept," *Agricultural Information Bulletin* no. 419 (April 1979).

Shortle, Walter C. "Mechanisms of Compartmentalization of Decay in Living Trees." *Phytopathology* 69 (1979).

Sinclair, Wayne A., et al. *Diseases of Trees and Shrubs*. Ithaca, New York: Comstock Publishing Associates, 1987.

Sternberg, Guy, and Jim Wilson. *Landscaping with Native Trees*. Shelburne, Vermont: Chapters Publishing, 1995.

Smil, Vaclav. *Cycles of Life: Civilization and the Biosphere*. New York: Scientific American Library, 2001.

Smith, Kevin T. "Compartmentalization Today." *Arboricultural Journal* 29 (2006).

Smith, Kevin T. "Tree Biology and Problem Trees." *Arborist News* (2005).

Turnbull, Cass. "The Case Against Drop-Crotching." *Tree Care Industry* (November 2003).

Vaucher, Hugues. *Tree Bark: A Color Guide*. Portland, Oregon: Timber Press, 2003.

Wasowski, Andy, and Sally Wasowski. *The Landscape Revolution*. Chicago: Contemporary Books, 2000.

Zabel, Robert A., and Jeffrey J. Morrell. *Wood Microbiology: Decay and Its Prevention*. New York: Academic Press, 1992.

Index